Paths toward the Nation

Ohio University Research in International Studies

This series of publications on Africa, Latin America, Southeast Asia, and Global and Comparative Studies is designed to present significant research, translation, and opinion to area specialists and to a wide community of persons interested in world affairs. The editors seek manuscripts of quality on any subject and can usually make a decision regarding publication within three months of receipt of the original work. Production methods generally permit a work to appear within one year of acceptance. The editors work closely with authors to produce high-quality books. The series appears in a paperback format and is distributed worldwide. For more information, consult the Ohio University Press website, ohioswallow.com.

Books in the Ohio University Research in International Studies series are published by Ohio University Press in association with the Center for International Studies. The views expressed in individual volumes are those of the authors and should not be considered to represent the policies or beliefs of the Center for International Studies, Ohio University Press, or Ohio University.

Paths toward the Nation

ISLAM, COMMUNITY, AND EARLY NATIONALIST MOBILIZATION IN ERITREA, 1941–1961

Joseph L. Venosa

Ohio University Research in International Studies
Africa Series No. 92
Ohio University Press
Athens

Library of Congress Cataloging-in-Publication Data

Venosa, Joseph L., author.
 Paths toward the nation : Islam, community, and early nationalist mobilization in Eritrea,
1941–1961 / Joseph L. Venosa.
    pages cm. — (Ohio University research in international studies. Africa series ; no. 92)
 Includes bibliographical references and index.
 ISBN 978-0-89680-289-6 (pb : alk. paper) — ISBN 978-0-89680-487-6 (pdf)
 1. Eritrea—History—20th century. 2. Eritrea—History—Autonomy and independence
movements. 3. Eritrea—Politics and government—1941–1952. 4. Eritrea—Politics
and government—1952–1962. 5. Islam and politics—Eritrea. 6. Muslims—Political
activity—Eritrea. I. Title. II. Series: Research in international studies. Africa series ; no.
92.
 DT395.3.V46 2014
 963.506—dc23

                                      2014003339

To my parents, Louis Venosa and Francine Galati Venosa,
and to all Eritreans who have made
—and continue to make—the journey
across the Sinai and beyond . . . እዚ ውን ይሓልፍ . . .

Contents

Illustrations

Maps

Figures

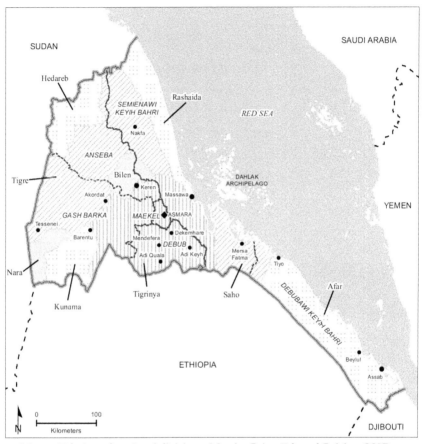

Map 1. Ethnic and regional divisions. Map by Brian Edward Balsley, GISP.

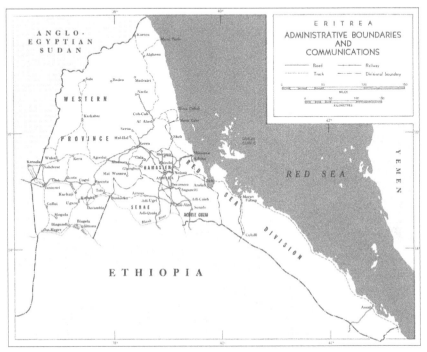

Map 2. Eritrean provinces (1950). Source: GAOR, 5th sess., Suppl. no. 8, A/1285, map no. 284. Map reproduced with permission from the United Nations Cartographic Section.

Acknowledgments

From this study's inception to its current form, I've incurred debts to many individuals for their intellectual and institutional support. Regardless of when our paths first crossed, all the friends and colleagues involved in this project have provided me with a level of camaraderie, support, and decency that I can only hope to reciprocate.

While completing my graduate studies at Ohio University, I benefited from being a part of both the African Studies Program and the Department of History. African Studies director W. Stephen Howard and associate director Ghirmai Negash have been important mentors who have provided me with generous support, especially with regard to my study of Tigrinya and Arabic. Knowledge of these regional languages, facilitated by several Title VI Foreign Language and Area Studies (FLAS) fellowships, was essential in conducting the research required for this study. In this respect, I am also grateful to all my friends in African Studies who served as guides in my language development, especially Abraham Gebrekidan, Selam Gerzher-Alemayo, Yosief Negussie, Muhammad Satti, and Selam Daniel. My former adviser and mentor in the Department of History, Nicholas M. Creary, provided constant encouragement and guidance throughout my graduate education. Under Professor Creary's advisement, I began the task of formulating many of the broader research questions in my doctoral dissertation and, eventually, this book.

I am also indebted to several members of Ohio University's history faculty, especially Professors John Brobst, Katherine Jellison, Bill Frederick, and Brian Schoen, for their guidance both in and outside the classroom. Likewise, I am especially grateful to Ohio University's Contemporary History Institute (CHI) and to its director, Steve Miner, for his endless assistance and encouragement. Kara Dunfee at CHI, Sherry Gillogy in the Department of History, and Acacia Nikoi in African Studies all made my life considerably easier due to their constant assistance and good humor through my endless queries. Field research was conducted in Eritrea, the United Kingdom, and across several locations in the United States and Canada. Funding for the project's multiple research trips was made possible by a generous Graduate Student Enhancement Award from Ohio University's Council for Research as well as by a CHI doctoral fellowship.

While composing this book, I received the assistance of several accomplished scholars whose critiques were absolutely critical in refining my study. In particular, I am grateful to Tricia Redeker Hepner for her insightful comments and suggestions on previous drafts and for her tremendous support in making this book a reality. Elizabeth Schmidt and Lindsay F. Braun both kindly provided me with timely, generous critiques of key chapters that have made this study a much more refined piece of scholarship. Likewise, Professors Sholeh Quinn and Robin Muhammad provided invaluable feedback and insight to make this study as comprehensive and intellectually relevant as possible. I owe a tremendous intellectual debt and thanks to Jonathan Miran. Since this project's origins, Professor Miran has been an enthusiastic supporter, mentor, and good friend who has always been willing to share his expertise on Islam and Eritrean history to enrich my study in numerous ways.

At Ohio University, I also benefited from the support and intellectual challenge of many within my graduate cohort, especially my friends Gerald F. Goodwin, Patrick Campbell, Kevin Grimm, and Meredith Hohe, who each provided invaluable comments and critiques of several draft chapters. Likewise, friends and colleagues Marlene De La Cruz-Guzmán, Christina Matzen, Jared Bibler, Maria Zoretic-Goodwin, Rob Barringer, and Sony Karsano were instrumental in helping me develop this project and in encouraging me to address difficult research questions for a broader audience. I am also thankful to Brian E. Balsley for his technical assistance as well to the members of the United Nations Cartographic Section for their help in procuring necessary research materials. Marion Lowman at the Bodleian Library at Oxford University also provided extensive help in procuring key archival documents. I also owe special thanks to Gill Berchowitz at Ohio University Press for her constant encouragement and help throughout the duration of this project. As an undergraduate student at Ramapo College of New Jersey, I benefited early on from the guidance and support of a talented group of historians who have all contributed to this project in their own way, including Alex Urbiel, Walter T. Brown, Charles Carreras, Sam Mustafa, and especially Walt F. Brown.

Several talented friends and scholars have assisted me in the sometimes difficult process of primary-source translation. In particular, Asmina Guta and Mariya Chakir were selfless in helping me clarify particular primary-source texts. I was also fortunate to have received assistance from many individuals both in Eritrea and across the wider diaspora. In particular, Nebil Ahmed, Saleh "Gadi" Johar, Mussie Tesfagiorgis, Ismael al-Mukhtar, Aberra Osman Aberra, Solomon G. Kelefa, Anwar Said, Merih Weldai, Umar Tesfai Muhammad, and Sium Tesfatsion contributed immensely to this project by sharing both materials and their insights on various aspects of contemporary Eritrean history. I am also grateful to the members of the Eritrean Muslim Council of North America for their research assistance. I owe special thanks to Günter Schröder for allowing me access to his extensive collection of primary source materials and interviews of former members of the Eritrean Liberation Movement (ELM) and Eritrean Liberation Front (ELF).

Throughout this project my family has been a constant source of strength and good humor. My sisters, Gina and Linda Venosa, as well as my relatives Nitshti Yemaneab and Amanuel Sahle, have all been major supporters during the past several years. My "brother" Ben Shaw has been nothing short of amazing in his friendship and support for me throughout the years, and I could not have finished this book without his encouragement. I am grateful to my parents, Louis and Francine Venosa. Their support for all my endeavors has been overshadowed only by the influence of their lifelong lessons about the need for compassion and understanding toward others. Such values have served as the foundation from which I have approached the study of African history. I owe the biggest thank you to my wife and partner, Sabrina Amanuel Sahle, for her love and endless *debinet*. This book and, much more important, the life outside of it would not have been possible without her.

This study appears at a time of tremendous change within Eritrea and across the global Eritrean diaspora. If there is any merit to the study herein, it is perhaps that this book will encourage greater debate and dialogue about how Eritrea's nationalist movement before the armed struggle still has great relevance to the country's contemporary political development. This book thus attempts both to articulate often neglected inquiries about Eritrea's past and to introduce new questions.

Abbreviations

BMA	British Military Administration
BA	British Administration
CAE	Comitato Assistenza Eritrei
EDF	Eritrean Democratic Front
ELM	Eritrean Liberation Movement
ELF	Eritrean Liberation Front
EPLF	Eritrean People's Liberation Front
IML	Independent Muslim League
LPP	Liberal Progressive Party
MFH	Mahber Fikri Hager (Party for the Love of Country)
MLWP	Muslim League of the Western Province
NEPIP	New Eritrea Pro-Italia Party
NPM	National Party of Massawa
PFDJ	People's Front for Democracy and Justice
SCAO	senior civil affairs officer
UP	Unionist Party

Note on Language, Terminology, and Translation

In general, transliterated Arabic terms have followed a simplified version of the most recent guidelines set forth by the *International Journal of Middle East Studies* (IJMES), while Tigrinya terms have adhered to the most common versions found within the previous English-language literature. While I have translated newspaper and periodical titles into English, the respective names of the various Arabic- and Tigrinya-language newspapers and periodicals remain in simplified transliteration. Additionally, traditional Eritrean honorific titles cited within the book have followed their most common English form. Standardization for the nisba form for transliterated Arabic terms has been rendered with "-iyya" spelling and where appropriate, single quotation marks represent symbols for the 'ayn and hamza marks. Likewise, individual names, places, and technical terms originating among Eritrea's Tigre-speaking regions have been rendered in the standardized form most familiar to English speakers. In the context of this book, I use the lowercase term *tigre* as the traditional marker for those Tigre-speaking peoples of vassal or "serf" origins across western Eritrea, rather than as a broad ethnolinguistic designation.

It is not my intention to disregard or disrespect the realities of linguistic diversity found across modern-day Eritrea or to infer the supremacy of the common English spelling of these indigenous terms. Rather, my goal has been to achieve a basic continuity that allows for a more inclusive representation of these often complex terms for a wider, nonspecialist audience.

Introduction

Islam, Community, and the
Cultural Politics of Eritrean Nationalism

On June 10, 1947, the various branches of the Eritrean Muslim League organized demonstrations in almost every major city and town across the country. Unprecedented in scale, the protests represented one of the high points of nationalist activism in then-British-occupied Eritrea. One of the largest demonstrations, held in the capital city of Asmara, saw members from the local league office lead a march through the city. In a widely circulated speech that the organization later published, Shaykh Abdelkadir Kebire, the president of the league's Asmara branch, elaborated on the significance of the demonstrations taking place across the country:

> Freedom is a natural right for all nations and something of value even for animals, let alone for human beings, who pursue it, make every effort to achieve it, and are willing to pay a high price to defend it. Therefore, it is no wonder that today this crowd and this nation are calling for freedom and want to destroy their chains. They raise their voices calling for it [freedom] and, walking toward it, they are guided by the light of this noble torch with which Allah has blessed Eritrea's heart. This torch is independence.[1]

Kebire's speech represented one of the earliest attempts among Eritrea's nationalist leaders to frame the case for self-determination as both a moral imperative and an issue of particular urgency within the broader Muslim community.

In February 2010, more than six decades after the league's initial protests, a group consisting of many of the descendants of the Muslim League membership issued a public call for rejuvenation in the political discourse within Eritrea and throughout the global Eritrean

1

diaspora. Harking back to the "long tradition of Eritrean Muslims in resisting oppression and domination," the group, referring to itself as Mejlis Ibrahim Mukhtar,[2] issued a manifesto for its new political program. Entitled "The Eritrean Covenant: Toward Sustainable Justice and Peace," the document addresses both the current human rights crisis in Eritrea and the often overlooked role of Islamic authorities and community leaders in leading past movements for political reform and social justice. More than sixty years since the Muslim League leadership first spoke out publicly on issues of political freedom and human rights, many contemporary opposition organizations across the diaspora continue to draw ideological inspiration from this early group of activists. Yet the precise reasons for the league's contemporary relevance as a political opposition organization and as a conduit for reframing human rights discourse in Eritrea can be understood only by first examining its role during the country's first two decades of nationalist mobilization.

This book presents three broad and critical arguments in regard to the early period of Eritrean nationalism between 1941 and 1961. First, that the Eritrean Muslim League's experience, among both its principal organizers and general membership, was tied to several larger social and political transformations across the region during the postwar period. Thus, the league's dominance of the broader pro-independence discourse, coupled with the influence of those in the organization's hierarchy who absorbed much of the anticolonial sentiment in the aftermath of World War II, gave rise to a nationalist ideology that looked to the broader Islamic world for inspiration and relied on Eritreans with links to that world as a means of furthering the cause of independence. Indeed, the intersection of Islam and nationalist politics throughout the 1940s and 1950s revealed a far broader range of ideological influences on Eritrea's Muslim nationalist actors than previous scholars have acknowledged. This study provides an important new framework to better understand how activists helped formulate notions of an emerging Eritrean nation-state within a truly "frontier" region between the contemporary Horn of Africa and the wider Middle East. Second, I argue that as a result of these wider changes and through the league's mobilization of the region's various Muslim communities, the organization represented one of the most significant vehicles for developing national consciousness by contributing to the public's understanding about what it meant to be "Eritrean." Third, I conclude that the Eritrean Muslim League, beyond simply developing into the largest and most influential nation-alist organization of the era, embodied an integral base of intellectual thought from which Eritrea's early pro-independence movement, including the beginnings of the early armed struggle against neigh-boring Ethiopia, emerged.

By illustrating how intellectuals utilized the Islamic religion and helped foment Muslim community activism within the context of Eritrea's independence movement, this book also explores the often overlooked relationship between religious identity and nationalism in one particular area in the Horn of Africa. If the Muslim League's ex-perience in Eritrea speaks to a unique example of how one region re-sponded to external threats of domination from a neighboring power such as Ethiopia, it also echoes broader trends across the region in which activist groups relied on their own interpretations of Islam and community identity to assert their territorial and cultural integrity. While several issues germane to Eritrea's current political crises help explain some of the reasons for the league's continuing popularity, a greater explanation lies in the broader ideological significance that such early nationalist groups across Africa, the Middle East, and South Asia had—and continue to have—on the public discussions about the role of Islam and its institutions in addressing broader social and po-litical challenges.

Emerging Trends in the Post–World War II Islamic World

From the resurgence of the political wing of Egypt's Muslim Brother-hood to the growing relevance of Islamic religious and aid organiza-tions across North Africa in the wake of the supposed Arab Spring, such changes remind us of the significance of religious dynamics in shaping and informing broad-based movements for reform. This book proceeds from the understanding that the trends that emerged within Eritrea's Muslim communities between 1941 and 1961 were both part of several global developments taking place across the Is-lamic world as well as a reflection of the complex cultural interactions unique to the Horn region. *Paths toward the Nation* thus engages Mus-lim community and political activism on a global and regional level while demonstrating that Eritrea's experience enriches our broader understanding about how religion and religious-affiliated organiza-tions contributed to what historian Elizabeth Schmidt has termed the "inclusive nationalism" that emerged across the African and Asian continents after the war.[3]

While such movements are not inherently new in contemporary history, they emerged with particular vigor across the Islamic world among peoples living under colonial rule during and immediately after World War II. The growth of anticolonial sentiment and the subsequent rise of nationalism represented the culmination of a particular era in which political mobilization emerged simultaneously with a growing reliance on a broad communal religious identity to achieve societal and political objectives. The intersection of populism, nationalism, and religious-based community activism in particular echoes sociologist Martin Riesebrodt's discussion of how societies in the midst of rapid social change throughout the twentieth century have developed either "fundamentalist" or "utopian" perspectives for using religion in overcoming a particular "experience of crisis."[4] That is, challenges within highly transformative societies often produce new understandings about how religion and religious teachings can be used to overcome political, social, and even economic difficulties. As a result, religious teachings may often receive a reassessment by those who either embrace reactionary, fundamentalist-leaning interpretations of their given theology or enunciate more expansive and inclusive ideas about how religious revival can achieve a harmonious, near utopian state of existence.[5] The dramatic postwar expansion of Egypt's Muslim Brotherhood, the steady campaign for a separate Muslim nation under the All-India Muslim League, and the swift turn toward militarism within Indonesia's largest Islamist organization, Nahdlatul Ulama (NU), during the colony's war for independence represented just some of the many ways that Islamic-influenced nationalist ideologies took on greater political significance during the period. Viewed in this context, the experience of Eritrea's first and largest nationalist group, the Eritrean Muslim League, represented just one of many such movements that fused the quest for political independence with a genuine interest in how Islamic institutions and religious thought could more broadly serve the public. Even the leadership's decision to name their organization the Eritrean Muslim League, a tribute to the All-India Muslim League, reflected activists' global awareness and sensitivity toward broader nationalist struggles occurring across the Islamic world.

However, the actions of Eritrea's Islamic leaders and their associates within the Muslim League also complicate this fundamentalist/

utopian dynamic by representing a new line of thought regarding how religious activism informed political mobilization. While the Muslim League in general displayed many broad-minded, inclusive qualities that would discount their activities from falling into a categorization of what Riesebrodt has referred to as the reactionary-minded "fundamentalist literalism" of some societies, Eritrean Muslim activism also lacked a reliance on an exclusively Islamic doctrine that qualified the movement as a strictly utopian Islamic phenomenon. The triumph of a fluid and largely inclusive Muslim-dominated nationalist discourse over more dogmatic interpretations of Islam thus demonstrates how activists within the league often fluctuated between such ideological extremes and developed a broad ideology that merged certain aspects of both "fundamentalist" and "utopian" thought.

While the post–World War II nationalist impulse occurred throughout the Islamic and non-Islamic worlds, what often defined the cause of many movements across the Middle East and Islamic Africa in particular was the growing influence of Muslim indigenous intellectuals in shaping and articulating formal political action. Developed by former civil servants in the colonial governments, religious officials, and the small group of university-educated elites, much of the emerging discourse that developed reflected the critical role of such intellectuals in facilitating early nationalist activity. From Muhammad Ali Jinnah and Huseyn Shaheed Suhrawardy's influence in British India to Messali Hadj's activities in postwar French Algeria, intellectual activism emerged as one of the major pillars within the early independence movements.

Viewed in this context, the impetus across the Islamic world represented a more proactive strain of nationalist thought than compared to most non-Muslim intellectual activists south of the Sahara. Kwame Anthony Appiah has argued that the dominance of "Europhone" intellectuals across sub-Saharan African colonies during this period largely kept in place colonial-inspired ideas of nationalism, language use, and nation-building even amid the push to decolonize.[6] Yet, as with many intellectual elites elsewhere in societies living under colonial rule, those in the Islamic world often sought to establish a "permanent relationship with the former occupying power" even after achieving independence.[7] Nevertheless, there remained an underlying resistance several years before the rise of postwar nationalism to the idea of simply replacing colonial rule with a European-defined nation-state.

Falling within this categorization, the Eritrean Muslim League essentially promoted their own version of Islamic modernism in which there evolved a broad tendency to understand nationalism as a vehicle for advancing both society and individuals toward a more progressive, "enlightened" condition. Activists thus used the idiom of an Islamic worldview to embrace political goals that promoted certain aspects of modernity, such as the practicality of the nation-state and the importance of functioning democratic institutions, though not necessarily an interpretation that mimicked prefabricated Western models. Proclaiming generalized ideas about the importance of revitalizing their faith, embracing the legacy of past Islamic civilization, doing away with particular social "ills," and adhering to the centrality of religious institutions, activists helped establish such ideas as the major tenets of intellectual nationalist thought across the broader Islamic world. In this sense, the nationalists of the 1940s and 1950s represented a continuation of many of the ideas of earlier proponents of Islamic modernism, including figures such as Jamal al-Din al-Afghani, Sayyid Ahmad Khan, Muhammad Iqbal, and others.

Equally significant to the rise of postwar nationalism across the Islamic world and of intellectual activism was the often complex relationship between the leadership of early political organizations and the broader grass roots. Across the Middle East, South and Southeast Asia, and sub-Saharan Africa there emerged a trend of pro-independence organizations that often treaded a challenging path of working toward long-term political and social change while also trying to address the immediate concerns of their political bases. Indeed, peasants, urban workers, lower-level religious officials, women, and youth organizations often represented essential components in formulating and executing nationalist activities. Important interactions between nationalist elites and grassroots supporters also developed, particularly with regard to the discussions between such groups about how to frame and to disseminate the nationalist program. Expanding popular mobilization often depended on how well intellectual elites navigated the tremendous social pressures emerging from those outside the nationalist hierarchy. The push for greater grassroots participation, ongoing concerns among the "masses" that nationalist leaders could become too accommodating with colonial officials, and the movement for more decentralized power within nationalist organizations all emerged as major issues confronting the leadership within these various groups. Thus, while many pro-independence parties represented a composite of elite intellectual influence, they also developed and formulated their strategies because of the actions of "popular groups already engaged in struggle against the colonial state."[8]

The process of navigating Islamic-influenced notions of community alongside such "modern" concepts of nationalism also reveals some of the ways that Islam as both a faith and a value system has been richly suited for helping ease the transition from colonial rule to complex nationalist movements. According to Victoria Bernal, the Islamic faith—particularly in the context of the Horn of Africa—has been historically significant to these transformations because, as a religion that is both "local and universal," it provides a "ready medium for crafting solutions to the contradictions between the local and global contexts that people must increasingly inhabit simultaneously."[9] Eritrea's experience during this period of postwar nationalism thus reflected many of the challenges inherent in these political and intellectual trends. In part, these changes were a result of Eritrea's unique geographic position. Indeed, the region now known as Eritrea has, historically, played a major role in the cultural, political, and economic exchanges across Africa and the Middle East in what many observers now refer to as the Red Sea world. Eritrea's centrality to the geographic and cultural exchanges unique to this region provided the country with an ideal setting where residents experienced a literal (as well as littoral) front-row seat in which broad strands of African and Arab nationalism emerged to inform local understandings about the nature and ultimate goals of independence.

The Human Setting and Colonial Context

Modern-day Eritrea lies in the Horn of Africa, sharing its borders with three countries: Sudan to the west and northwest, Ethiopia to the south, and Djibouti to the extreme southeast. The country's northern border rests along the Red Sea coast, and Eritrea's location has made the region an ideal trading location from ancient times to the present day. Eritrea's past linkages with such ancient trading powers as Damot and the Axumite Empire also allowed the region to develop as an important springboard for the spread of different spiritual traditions and religions across the region, including Orthodox Tewahedo Christianity and Sunni Islam.[10] An important zone of interaction between Africa and the Middle East, Eritrea is an integral setting in which indigenous appropriations of Christianity and Islam have developed side by side for centuries.

Eritrea's remarkably complex cultural and religious composition reflects its particular contemporary history. The country's nine officially recognized indigenous ethnic groups live scattered throughout diverse geographic zones; the majority of the country's Christian inhabitants reside in the temperate highland region (*kebesa*) and engage in agriculture, while most of the country's Muslim ethnicities reside in the more arid lowlands and practice pastoralism.[11] Eritrea's largest ethnic group, the Tigrinya, comprises roughly 50 percent of the population and has historically practiced Orthodox Tewahedo Christianity. Historically, Eritrea's Tigrinya people also embrace long-standing connections to the Tigrinya-dominated areas across the southern border in Ethiopia's Tigray region, which fostered ongoing kinship and community-based networks before colonial rule. The other half of Eritrea's population consists of smaller ethnic groups, including the Tigre, Saho, Afar, Nara, Hedarab (Beja), and Rashaida, who are all overwhelmingly Muslim. Other smaller ethnic groups, such as the Bilen and Kunama, have either retained their indigenous religions or adopted either Christianity or Islam to varying degrees. Each of the country's ethnic groups also speaks its own language. The ethnic groups fall into three categories: those who speak Semitic languages (Tigrinya, Tigre, Rashaida), Cushitic languages (Afar, Bilen, Beja, Saho), and Nilo-Saharan languages (Kunama, Nara).[12] Since the early twentieth century the country's religious heterogeneity has led to an almost even split between the number of Muslim and Christian inhabitants.

Modern-day Eritrea's physical boundaries are very much the product of Europe's Scramble for Africa during the late nineteenth century. The arbitrary nature of the country's borders stemmed from the political rivalries between the region's three major powers during that period: Ethiopia, Great Britain, and Italy. Italian colonial authorities claimed and secured Eritrea in 1890 and it became, along with Somalia, the principal colonial possessions from which Italian authorities hoped to establish their own East African Empire amid the wider scramble. Nearly two decades of Italian economic and military infiltration into the Red Sea coast (1869–89) and more than fifty years of colonial rule (1890–1941) forged the territory into a cohesive administrative unit. While Eritrea's coastal region had

long existed as a peripheral zone for other regional powers in previous centuries, the late nineteenth century witnessed the growth of
concentrated Italian authority over the various pastoralist peoples
across the coastal lowlands, as officials secured sections of the Sem-
har and Sahel regions in the late 1880s before acquiring part of the
interior highlands extending to the Mareb River, which Ethiopian
authorities ceded to Italy through the Treaty of Wichale in May
1889.[13] Italy's failed attempts to extend its influence further into the
Ethiopian highlands, best illustrated by the Italian army's resound-
ing loss to Ethiopian forces at the Battle of Adowa, in March 1896,
relegated Italian authority to the official colonial boundaries demarcated in 1889 and 1890. After its 1896 defeat, the Italian government renewed its investment in Eritrea under the administration of
colonial governor Fernando Martini (1897–1907) who, according to
historian Tekeste Negash, "succeeded admirably well in laying down
the foundations of a colonial government more or less along the lines
used by Britain and France."[14]

   With the growth of Italian economic influence along the Eritrean
coast, during the late 1860s and the establishment of formal colonial
rule in 1890, Italian officials adopted an "initial favorable tendency
towards Islam" that reflected Italy's geopolitical concerns across the
Horn of Africa during the late nineteenth century. These concerns
included the Italian government's quest to secure colonial possessions overseas as a means of building its own imperial standing, to
safeguard against both British and French influence in the region,
and to encourage Italian agricultural migration to the predominately
Christian Eritrean highlands.[15] Because privileging some communities over others developed as official colonial policy "aimed at winning Muslim support by counter balancing and undermining the
legitimacy and authority of the traditionally dominant Christian
Highlanders" in Eritrea and northern Ethiopia, Islamic religious authorities represented a key component in helping facilitate the Italian
colonial project.[16]

   Consequently, Muslim authorities—especially Sufi Islamic groups
such as the Khatmiyya and the 'Ad Shaykh orders—became the focal
point of Italian campaigns in the late nineteenth century to win the
support of regional power structures across the predominately Muslim
lowlands and to limit the threat of other external threats, especially
the growing Mahdist movement taking place in nearby Sudan.[17] The
gradual privileging of Islam, and Muslim institutions more broadly,

continued throughout the 1890s and well into the twentieth century, as the Italian colonial government worked to legitimize its rule further by co-opting regional Sufi authorities in order to help solidify colonial control. Beginning in the 1920s, Italy's Fascist-led colonial administration increased Italian support for Muslim religious and educational institutions as a means of augmenting colonial authority.[18]

Serving as a source of manpower for conscripted soldiers used in Italy's war to secure Libya (1911–12) and as a foundation for trading relations with Ethiopia, Eritrea nevertheless remained an understaffed and largely marginal colony during its first four decades. Only during the early 1930s did investment within the colony substantially increase as authorities promoted full-scale industrialization in preparation for Italy's later invasion of Ethiopia. Capital investment, industrialization, and rapid urbanization throughout the mid-1930s also increased the Italian settler population in a short time to more than fifty thousand by the end of 1935. Italy's East African empire finally crumbled under the weight of a British-led Sudanese invasion force in April 1941. Questions emerged, however, about the future of the Italian colonies even before Britain had secured complete control over most of the territory. As with other regions across Africa immediately after the end of armed conflict related to World War II, the challenge posed by Eritrea's political future was fundamentally connected to the legacy of Italian colonialism. When the temporary "caretaker" British Military Administration (BMA) finally solidified its authority in May 1941, the colony's Italian population had grown to approximately seventy thousand, with most of those residents living in or around the capital city of Asmara.[19] The colony's ability to remain a cohesive entity faced several challenges during this period that all related in one way or another to the sudden end of Italian colonial rule; the threat of social fragmentation among the indigenous population, the rapid swelling of the small but influential settler population, and the push among indigenous Eritrean elites to exercise political and economic agency all emerged simultaneously as major areas of concern by the middle of 1941.

An Overview of Early Eritrean Political Activism

Following the sudden end to Fascist Italian rule in early 1941, the mainly urban Italian population and the still well-entrenched colonial administration remained in charge of running the colony's day-to-day operations and economic activities under the oversight of the BMA. British officials did not consider, nor necessarily care, that indigenous community leaders would be inclined to participate in the discussions about local political and economic affairs. Yet following the establishment of British authority, a small group of Tigrinya, Tigre, and Saho activists based mainly in Asmara began to discuss Eritrea's fate in the post-Italian period. In May 1941 these activists founded Mahber Fikri Hager (Party for the Love of Country; MFH), the first sizeable association to emerge from Eritrea's small intellectual class.[20] From its inception, the organization featured a diverse membership that included both those who called for political union between Eritrea and Ethiopia and members who argued that Eritrea's distinct ethnocultural makeup and its recent history entitled it to complete independence.

Although many of the earliest studies on Eritrean nationalist politics have argued that the organization espoused an inherently unionist stance, the more complicated reality suggests otherwise.[21] Although some activists argued for complete union between Eritrea and Ethiopia, other members of the MFH believed that Eritrea should be "reunited" with the mainly Tigrinya-speaking peoples across the border in the Tigray region of northern Ethiopia to form their own country.[22] Most of the organization's highland-based Tigrinya members supported such a push for a "greater Tigray," while a minority expressed wholehearted support for Eritrea's complete political union with the Ethiopian state. Initially, the small group of mainly Muslim Tigre and Saho activists within the MFH failed to articulate a cohesive message regarding their own views on the need instead for legitimate Eritrean independence.[23] Well before the end of World War II, as political differences between unionist and nationalist members intensified, the Ethiopian government also pressed its claims on Eritrea to the international community. The political fracturing unfolded as administrators within the occupying BMA struggled to maintain day-to-day control over the region. Meanwhile, the newly created UN General Assembly had yet to take up the independence debate, having only formed in October 1945.

Not until nearly a year after the formation of the United Nations did the nationalist impetus, in the form of the Eritrean Muslim League, finally materialize as a political entity, in late 1946. Made up of a diverse constituency of clan chiefs, traders, Islamic clerics, disaffected peasants, and urban-based colonial civil servants, the league espoused a broad nationalist platform that initially meant different things to each respective group. For some, particularly disaffected peasants living across Eritrea's Western Province, independence represented a dramatic reworking of the traditional landlord-client relationship that characterized much of rural society among the Tigre-speaking peoples in the region. Others, including urban intellectuals, former civil servants, and many Muslim merchants, expected that an independent Eritrea would provide the political mechanisms needed to build up the former colony's institutions and to revitalize the region's lagging postwar economy. Later in the decade the league's leadership, consisting largely of these former colonial civil servants and Islamic clerics, began making the case for independence in a more forceful manner. The league's program also veered increasingly toward a populist agenda that linked the nationalist movement with the need for broader social and cultural reforms. Their agenda included support for religious and educational reform across Muslim communities, attention to the concerns of the largely peasant population in western Eritrea, and efforts aimed at building camaraderie with non-Muslims in the independence movement.

Through the league's publications, political reports, sponsored lectures, and public events, the language of nationalism within the organization involved a complex discourse that addressed many of the cultural, religious, and economic concerns that different segments of the Muslim population raised throughout the late 1940s and 1950s. The sometimes contradictory and complicated nature of the league's communications illustrates historian James McDougall's point that at the heart of such nationalist dialogue, the very concept of the nation *"exists in the contests over meaning* engaged in by specifiable social actors," and within a particular historical context where those actors include the "specific symbolic, linguistic, and material sources present in the social world at a given moment in time."[24] The league's various factions thus often interpreted independence specifically as it related to each respective social and regional group. As a result, coastal merchants articulated that independence would bring greater commercial opportunities, Tigre-speaking peasants in the Western Province argued that independence would abolish their subservient position from the region's landowning class, and Eritrea's urban-based intellectuals viewed independence as a key mechanism needed to develop new institutions to educate the public. Such ideas represented just some of the many interpretations that possible independence embodied, especially as the organization began solidifying as a truly national party.

Modernity and the Nationalist Elite

The period between 1941 and 1961 represented an era of coalescence between long-standing ideas about the need to ensure collective security for traditional Islamic institutions and new notions about how exactly an independent Eritrean nation could deliver such refuge for Muslim residents. As a result, the Muslim League made great efforts to develop notions of a unified Eritrean Islamic community with a shared history and cultural orientation. In trying to understand how league activists worked to further indigenous understandings of this shared history, we must first address the seemingly contradictory notion that the league's leadership promoted the idea of a shared "traditional" regional Islamic cultural history while embracing and striving for the creation of a modern nation-state. Activists' simultaneous embrace of a national identity within a broader Islamic cultural continuity represents, according to McDougall, only one outgrowth of subjugated societies' confrontations with colonial modernity.[25] As a result of exposure to such discourse, "the development of nationalism and contemporary forms of Islam cannot be understood as integrally oppositional resistance to the imposition of 'modern, western civilization.' On the contrary, contemporary cultures of nationalism and Islam are themselves the products of the profound, global transformations effected in the imperial interrelationships of societies and cultures throughout the modern world."[26] Consequently, within Muslim societies under colonial rule, varying forms of "vernacular modernism" have developed within localized power structures that articulated new and meaningful historical imaginations by channeling the "interrelated fields of culture, religion, and history."[27]

The wider process of involving various Islamic-influenced interpretations of modernity offers a useful framework to consider historian Uoldelul Chelati Dirar's point about the need to examine the role of modernity in the "Eritrean colonial context." In doing so, attention must be given to the ways in which Eritrean nationalism involved an assimilation of colonial discourse mainly through the small but influential class of indigenous elites.[28] According to both Dirar and historian Alemseged Tesfai, these elites emerged principally from the Italian colonial civil service, particularly during the mid- to late 1930s. The generation of Eritreans working at "the lower levels of the civil service as interpreters, telegraph and telephone operators, and clerks" as well as the "urban *petit* [*sic*] *bourgeoisie* linked to trade and land concessions" helped fill a vital social space between colonial authorities and the broader indigenous population.[29] Because such a substantial portion of these elites came from Islamic backgrounds and often served as intermediaries between the colonial administration and religious officials within mosques, Islamic schools, charity organizations, and other community entities, they developed important ideas about how Islamic institutions could and should function within an Eritrean state. Many of the more prominent nationalist leaders within the Muslim League had either direct connections to the regional Islamic clergy or even functioned as members of the religious leadership themselves. Specifically, nationalist leaders' attitudes about how to reconcile the institutional and cultural legacy of Islam with newfound political realities informed much of the intellectual dialogue on how to develop an independent state compatible with such long-standing religious and cultural traditions. The experience of this first generation of Muslim nationalist leaders paralleled many of the wider transformations among activists across the African continent who concerned themselves with the need to modernize the former colonies and employed the very rhetoric "on which colonial rulers depended for their legitimacy and self-image."[30]

Reengaging the Nationalist Narrative

Within a broader African nationalist context, the league's tactics embodied what Louis Brenner termed a process of "rationalization," in which Muslim leaders and political organizations often use Islamic institutions and engage in politicized struggles against perceived oppression and injustice.[31] Consequently, the league relied on the centrality of Muslim community leaders and Islamic institutions, including the authority of Mosques, shari'a courts, and Qur'anic schools to strengthen the broader nationalist cause. Thus, the league's framing of autonomy as a moral struggle that united all Eritreans helped create room for a national identity to emerge while embracing a societal "awakening of Islam."[32]

In looking at recent Eritrean history with an emphasis on how activists used religion to mobilize both political interest and social activism, there is a general silence among scholars and the public in addressing how indigenous articulations about a discernible Muslim identity influenced the emergence of Eritrean nationalism. Despite the significance of Islam within Eritrea and the importance of many nationalist figures from Muslim backgrounds, scholars have devoted much less attention to this portion of the Eritrean population. With few exceptions, the research focus has remained centered on the political and cultural contributions of Eritrea's predominately Christian populations in the highlands. This trend has been largely a result of the politicization of religion that first emerged during the early 1970s and has remained relevant to much of Eritrea's contemporary political discourse. Yet as both the Muslim League's 1947 protests and the release of "The Eritrean Covenant" illustrate, ideas about an Islamic communal identity have had major ramifications on past and contemporary debates across the global diaspora.[33] Indeed, the ongoing fight for control of the national narrative between the current government and the various opposition parties across the Eritrean diaspora has fostered a growing preoccupation with the importance of religion—and Islam in particular—to the earliest generation of nationalist actors. The debate has only increased in recent years, as Muslim Eritreans have become some of the most vocal opponents of Eritrea's current one-party state led by the People's Front for Democracy and Justice (PFDJ). Thus, the creation of Mejlis Ibrahim Mukhtar and its public embrace of Eritrea's political past now appear as testimonies to the current relevance that the early period continues to have on the country's ongoing political developments.

This book reflects the ever-increasing "diasporization" of African historical studies by bringing together materials and testimonies from locations across North and sub-Saharan Africa, Europe, and North America. It contributes to our current understanding of nationalism by shedding new light on how regional interpretations of Muslim communal consciousness progressed in the twenty years before Eritreans took up arms against Ethiopia. It does not presume that Eritrea's diverse and multifaceted movement toward independence was inherently Islamic or exclusively the domain of regional Muslim intellectual leaders. Furthermore, as the following chapters illustrate, the Muslim League recognized that they could not achieve an independent Eritrea without the participation of a broad range of social and religious segments of society. Thus, while the book argues that the league served as the primary political engine driving nationalist dialogue and the related cultural activism among pro-independence Muslims, it recognizes that a deeper process of social transformation took place, even beyond the confines of Eritrea's Muslim communities,

that helped nourish a truly national consciousness. My emphasis on
the Muslim League's overriding ideological contributions to the nationalist cause represents a major divergence from the general trend
in Eritreanist scholarship. This study thus fundamentally challenges
many of the previous narratives that have dominated both the framing and overall discussion of Eritrean nationalism during the past
three decades.

The outbreak of Eritrea's war of independence against Ethiopia
(1961–91) led to a fixation among scholars to inquire about various
aspects of the armed struggle, resulting in the emergence of several
narratives that each reflected the political trends taking place within
the armed revolution and, later, within Eritrea's postwar government.[34] At the heart of the discourse is the tendency to promote a
collective experience of the simultaneous liberation war alongside the
nationalist revolution that has prevented the emergence of alternate
narratives seeking to understand the growth of Eritrean national
consciousness away from the battlefield.[35] In the years immediately
before and after Eritrea's victory over Ethiopia, a flood of publications
appeared that provided either an elementary overview of nationalism in relation to the military struggle or only journalistic coverage
of actions of the revolution's dominant political entity, the Eritrean
People's Liberation Front (EPLF).[36]

Within much of the scholarship, the practice of latching onto the
statist narrative of Eritrea's "revolutionary nationalist project" complicated the discourse in two major ways.[37] First, the privileging of
the period of the armed struggle subsumed and neglected much of
the record on the pre-1961 independence movement. Second, the
EPLF's armed victory over the rival nationalist organization, the
Eritrean Liberation Front (ELF), in 1982, succeeded in framing the
nationalist struggle largely along class and ethnic lines and simultaneously deemphasized religious activism as a factor in the movement. Although much of the EPLF-sanctioned narrative alluded
to the development of political activism during the 1940s, scholars
have rarely mentioned the issue of religion, and especially Islamic
community mobilization. Part of this aversion to discussing the
relevance of religion occurred because the EPLF and its supporters
established a basic discourse that painted the group's emergence as a
reaction against Islamist (socially conservative, exclusionary, and
anti-Christian) tendencies within the ELF, the previous vanguard
organization of the armed revolution. Framing the ELF's ideological

base as an uneasy mixture of Islamic zealotry and calculative pan-Arabism led by "peasant chieftains and reactionary petty bourgeois intellectuals," the EPLF's campaign against ELF activists succeeded in omitting any mention of the legacy of Islam or Muslim community activism as legitimate sources of national consciousness.[38] With the publication of several studies during the second half of the 1980s concerning the armed struggle, a broader consensus began to take hold that eventually crystallized as the EPLF-sanctioned "nation-history." According to Tricia Redeker Hepner, the "dissemination of nation-history" served as a key aspect of the "political aims and social transformations the revolution sought to bring about," as well as a key reason for supporting the continuation of the fighting and the need for all Eritreans to share the burdens of the war.[39] The EPLF-sanctioned national narrative solidified further following Eritrea's achieving independence from Ethiopia, in 1993. The EPLF's transformation from a military organization into the postwar political entity, the PDFJ signaled another phase in the state's push to standardize its own national narrative.[40]

The general trend within the scholarship and the wider nonacademic literature has been to downplay the significance of the pre-armed struggle period and to overlook the intellectual contributions of Muslim activists in developing much of the early nationalist discourse. With the exception of a handful of recent contributions, most of the scholarship has largely continued to echo these trends. The few alternate approaches that have emerged in recent years have been works that both speak to the dominance of the PFDJ-sanctioned narrative and have begun to reconfigure the scope and ideological nature of Eritrean nationalism, particularly in regard to the significance of diaspora communities and the nature of political violence in Eritrea's recent history. Redeker Hepner's innovative 2009 study *Soldiers, Martyrs, Traitors, and Exiles* posits that Eritrea emerged as a "transnational" nation-state amid the broad international networks that developed during armed struggle, revealing how ideas about Eritrean identity and nationalism occurred within a diaspora-based political discourse.[41] Indeed, one cannot overstate the influence of such diasporic networks in facilitating and enriching the contours of Eritrean nationalism. The present study presents the argument that such trends toward transnationalism were quite pronounced as early as the mid-1940s, far earlier than previously thought. In his 2011 monograph *Frontiers of Violence in North-East Africa*, Richard J. Reid also observes

that Eritrea's historical experience needs to be reassessed as part of
several broader regional trends. The tendency toward such intense
political and cultural mobilization across Eritrea has occurred largely
because the region itself exists as a "mosaic of fault lines and frontier
zones" and "shifting borderlands" that often lead to competition over
tangible resources and ideas.[42] The growth of new ideologies, activism, and even politically motivated violence across Eritrea's Muslim
communities during the 1940s and 1950s revealed, as Reid suggests,
the full extent to which these frontier societies existed as true "zones
of interaction" often as "constructive, creative, and fertile as they are
destructive and violent."[43] By examining an otherwise neglected era
of Eritrean history as part of such a frontier society, this book revises
current understandings about the intellectual origins and content of
the early nationalist movement.

The Nationalist Contact Zone

Within a specific intellectual arena, what I term the "nationalist contact zone," Muslim leaders and activists sought to reframe the debate
about the existence of an independent Eritrean culture and historical
experience. While the concept of nationhood among the majority of
Eritreans may have developed only after decades of armed struggle,
important factions within Muslim communities began generating
their own particular sense of "national" history and peoplehood based
largely on their shared cultural legacy and their relationship to the
wider Islamic world. In effect, they established their own "nation
language" by the late 1940s in which written Arabic commentaries,
as well as broader discussions in the various vernacular languages,
solidified an ongoing public dialogue that stressed ideas of political
independence, argued for an embrace of Islamic values and institutions, and promoted a positive vision of Eritrean society based on its
ethnic and cultural heterogeneity.[44] In the context of the growing politicization of religion, Eritrea's Muslim nationalist leaders emerged
and refined their arguments in what became a nationalist contact
zone of political discourse.

   While the outlines of an "Eritrean consciousness" emerged only
gradually from the shared experience of Italian rule between 1890 and
1941, this growing self-awareness fully materialized under BMA rule
and forced the presiding colonial authorities to cope with increasingly

proactive intellectual and community leaders.[45] Combined with the increased rate of urbanization throughout Eritrea that began during the mid-1930s and continued through the end of Fascist rule, political activism developed as BMA authorities continually recruited Eritreans into the new fold as "clerks, accountants, medical orderlies, telephone operators and assistants in the public works and railway departments."[46] Within the confines of Eritrea's diverse multiethnic, multilingual population, Muslim community leaders facilitated early notions of civil society that correlated to continued urbanization. These transformations included several local initiatives to instill greater continuity within the Muslim population and the broader "associational life."[47] Leaders achieved these changes mainly by facilitating increased Arabic language education along with supporting the construction of new schools for Muslim students. Such institutional changes were part of the "spectacular organization, reform and centralization of Eritrean Islamic institutions" during the 1940s and, coupled with the growing political debates, helped forge a vague, but increasingly relevant, Islamic communal awareness.[48] In particular, activists' use and promotion of Arabic to influence perceptions of "shared religio-cultural, social-political and intellectual experiences" among Eritrean Muslims helped established the discursive anchor for many of the emerging debates.[49]

Concurrent with the cultural coalescence of different groups, the Eritrean Muslim League's experience in nationalist politics illustrated how a diverse group of indigenous intellectuals waged a broad African nationalist struggle to build what Frantz Fanon termed a tenable political party as a "tool in the hands of the people."[50] Activism within the league also revealed how Eritrea's unique geographic position within the Red Sea world made it an ideal convergence zone for nationalist ideologies from both sub-Saharan Africa and the Middle East. Muslim leaders looked to movements across the Islamic world to formulate their nationalist agenda and often discussed the broader international developments as a way to address their own immediate concerns.[51]

The Islamic intelligentsia's attempts at resisting threats of external domination during the 1940s echoed some of the earlier encounters that the previous generation of Eritreans confronted during the early 1920s and 1930s. Within the limits of a rigid Italian colonialism that had installed a de facto apartheid system and limited indigenous Eritreans' education to the fourth-grade level, activists' measures to negotiate and secure a degree of cultural and intellectual space proved difficult.[52] Nevertheless, the development of a comprehensive cultural contact zone, which Mary Louise Pratt defines as a social space where "cultures meet, clash, and grapple with each other, often in contexts of highly asymmetrical relations of power," characterized most of the debates and activities among indigenous intellectuals.[53] As Ghirmai Negash hinted at when he expanded on Pratt's concept in an Eritrean context, the awakening of anticolonial consciousness developed through the early use of indigenous languages in print as a way of critiquing the mechanisms of Italian rule. Over time, these efforts helped establish the early intellectual parameters that, by the 1940s, provided a significant degree of "political and cultural space" against both Ethiopian and European hegemony.[54]

Yet unlike these earlier discussions during the Italian era, the nationalist contact zone that developed during the early 1940s did not pertain exclusively to a colonizer-subject dichotomy. Instead, this contact zone denoted a more multifaceted space of political interaction and dialogue within the region's diverse indigenous communities. Moreover, the intellectual and political discussions often expanded far beyond the realm of the written word of local newspapers and commentaries. If anything, according to Alemseged Tesfai, most of the organizations that emerged during the mid- and late 1940s fell short of articulating a cohesive vision of independence because their leaders too often "acted out" their history rather than engaging in creating their own historical narratives for wider consumption.[55] In this sense, the nationalist contact zone's rapid growth during the 1940s reflected the broader intellectual trends of frontier zones across the Horn, as places where "political and cultural creativity" flourished in the public sphere in spite of rising social tensions and the looming threat of violence.[56] This intellectual nationalist mobilization within the Muslim League expanded as part of the larger public discussions that took place in mosques, private homes, and in the daily routines of urban and rural life among activists.

The nationalist contact zone also grew out of the sudden and, at times, haphazard social dilemmas that materialized in BMA-occupied Eritrea. If, as Astier M. Almedom argues, many of Eritrea's intellectual activists clearly viewed the British authorities as being "worse than the Italians" for their deceptiveness, Eritrean leaders nevertheless took advantage of the BMA's liberalization of political and media activity for the indigenous population.[57] Having arisen during the previous Italian era, many members of the indigenous elite easily "integrated" into the BMA in similar colonial-defined positions, albeit with much greater leverage than under Italian rule.[58] Thus, while British authorities certainly did not dictate the boundaries of the intellectual and cultural dialogue within this zone of interaction, the BMA's policies, initially, provided the setting for Eritreans of all political and ideological stripes to articulate their respective ideas.[59]

In contrast to many of the other rival organizations with broad Muslim-majority constituencies, the league not only had the backing of the majority of the country's Muslim residents, but also received backing from the country's leading Islamic clerics, giving the organization added credibility through the support of its affiliated intellectuals and community leaders. Because one of this study's primary aims is to contextualize these social and political transformations that spawned such intellectually driven discourse within the nationalist contact zone, a fresh analysis and interpretation is necessary of many key documents and primary sources that have been overlooked from this early period in Eritrea's nationalist history.

Source Material and Organization

This book builds on three general categories of sources. First, it relies heavily on a comprehensive analysis of the Arabic- and, to a lesser extent, Tigrinya-language newspapers, reports, and commentaries that activists produced across Eritrea within the confines of the nationalist contact zone from the mid-1940s to the beginning of the armed revolution, in 1961. With few exceptions, the Muslim League's publications and related literature have remained almost completely neglected in much of the scholarship. This neglect has obscured the organization's ideological and political relevance during the period in question. *Paths toward the Nation* thus engages materials written in local languages to gain greater understanding about how activists themselves formulated and articulated their own respective ideas on the nature of Eritrean independence.[60] Second, as a means of putting the league and Muslim political dynamics in a broader historical context, I also use documents produced mainly by officials within the BMA (1941–52) and by American observers stationed in Eritrea during the later period of the Eritrea-Ethiopia Federation. Utilizing the extensive intelligence reports, memoranda, and private correspondence taken from the British Foreign Office, the U.S. National Archives and Records Administration, Eritrea's Research and Documentation Centre, United Nations archives, and elsewhere, this research provides needed perspective on how activists shaped Muslim community mobilization as well as how colonial authorities often interpreted such developments on a broader level. Finally, this study relies on the oral testimonies of former activists and many of their descendants as a means of analyzing not only the various ways in which Muslim political activism crystallized, but also as a way to access previously silenced narratives that have either been ignored or minimized through the PFDJ-dominated discourse. In building on this wide array of sources, each of the chapters herein addresses a particular component of the wider process of early Eritrean nationalism.

Chapter 1 examines the major social and political transformations that took place during the first five and a half years of BMA rule to illustrate the origins and social context of the Muslim League's establishment. The chapter demonstrates the ways in which the movement for tigre emancipation in western Eritrea, the growth of greater Islamic institutional cohesion, and the actions of the small, urban-based Muslim intelligentsia all contributed to the league's ideological underpinning and its initial strengths as both a political and a social movement. Chapter 2 investigates specifically how the league and its leadership worked to build a political and intellectual base during its crucial first year of existence, from December 1946 to December 1947. The chapter addresses the various ways in which the organization contributed to the concerns within Eritrea's nationalist contact zone and how the leaders worked to build the organization as a truly national party, irrespective of religion. I argue that one of the major strengths of the league was the success of Muslim intellectuals and writers in presenting their organization to colonial authorities as an entity that supported the creation of a "modern" nation-state in opposition to the "uncivilized" feudal kingdom in Ethiopia.

Chapter 3 examines how the league and its allies in the nationalist movement responded to the political pressures surrounding the issue of Eritrean sovereignty as well as the crisis brought on by Ethiopian intervention and the rise of armed aggression against supporters of independence (1948–49). Building on these developments, Chapter 4 investigates how the league responded to the rise of rival Muslim political organizations that challenged its primacy in the independence movement through 1950. Examining the transitional period between the UN General Assembly's decision to federate Eritrea with Ethiopia from December 1950 to the federation's actual implementation, in September 1952, chapter 5 looks at how the league's intellectual base negotiated its political agenda and nationalist discourse while the new regional government took shape. Chapter 6 discusses how political action and nationalist discourse became even more intertwined as the perceived oppression against Muslims by Ethiopian authorities increased from the federation's inauguration, in late 1952, through the rise of mass civil discontent throughout 1957. Consequently, the protection and autonomy of Islamic institutions became one of the major rallying points for activists as the decade progressed. The chapter also explores the relationship between a broad Islamic identity within Eritrea and the larger political forces of pan-Arabism and Nasserism. Finally, Chapter 7 focuses on the crucial three-year period immediately before the outbreak of the armed revolution (1958–61) as way of examining the various competing ideologies that emerged among Muslim activists. This section also illustrates how the period in question witnessed a final break from the previous two decades of Muslim activism and the influence of the Muslim League. The chapter also demonstrates some of the ways in which the league and its leadership, despite the new circumstances and the wider ideological changes taking place within Eritrea and across the diaspora, managed to maintain influence among the first generation of activists in the ELF. The epilogue draws several broad conclusions about the significance of Muslim cultural and political action in relation to this early period of Eritrean nationalist mobilization.

Ultimately, explaining how the league and its offshoots contributed to the development of a separate Eritrean national identity also provides new essential information about the social, religious, and ethnic complexities that defined nationalist movements within many "frontier" societies throughout the 1940s and 1950s. Illuminating our understanding of this early period has direct relevance to the ongoing debates taking place across the global Eritrean diaspora, and consequently this study speaks to broader issues about how nationalism, intellectual activism, and religious affiliation continue to influence political and social change in both sub-Saharan Africa and across the wider Islamic world.

1

Early Rumblings

Muslim Activism in British-Occupied Eritrea,
April 1941–November 1946

With the coming of British-Sudanese forces, in April 1941, Eritreans found themselves living within the confines of a new colonial authority. For the next five and a half years, people across Eritrea adapted to the new realities, and opportunities, as a mandated territory under the British Military Administration. For communities across the region, especially in Eritrea's Western Province, the transition from Italian to British rule, in April 1941, presented an opportunity to rework the traditional social and economic constraints under which most residents had lived for roughly three centuries. Although Eritreans as a whole found themselves under a new colonial authority, those on the lower rungs of Tigre-speaking society—known pejoratively at the time as *tigre*—adapted to the new realities and opportunities that materialized during the BMA's "caretaker" rule, between 1941 and 1952.

During this period, three crucial social processes took place within Muslim communities across the Tigre-speaking region of western Eritrea as well as in the colony's major cities. Each of these transformations among Eritrea's various social groups had tremendous consequences for the formation of a broad Islamic consciousness across the country. First, tigre discontent toward local landlords (known both as *shumagulle* and also Tigre-speakers) surfaced with increased intensity. Refusing to comply with the traditional payment of customary dues and taxes to their respective shumagulle, disenfranchised tigre "serfs" pressed their claims for their own economic independence from the traditional system. This broad movement among tigre communities during the early and mid-1940s represented the first major thrust in Eritrea's movement toward decolonization, as activists simultaneously challenged both the "traditional" landlord-serf dynamic as well as the long-standing colonial acquiescence of the exploitative, quasi-feudal economic system. Ultimately, many of the leaders in the tigre emancipation movement helped articulate new understandings about tigre identity that stressed the righteousness of their cause as a Muslim people and the necessity of breaking away from the supposed primitive feudalism of the shumagulle. Second, the movement for tigre emancipation dovetailed with another critical movement in which increased efforts for religious standardization—meaning the creation of uniformity of Islamic practices and institutions across Eritrea—and the spread of more uniform Islamic education allowed scholars to help influence notions of a singular Muslim community across Eritrea. While these efforts aimed at establishing religious standardization gained momentum, the period also witnessed the emergence of a third significant movement; the rise of an engaged, politically active intelligentsia from among the mainly Asmara- and Keren-based professionals who began advocating for Muslim interests. Because so much of the Eritrean Muslim League's eventual activism challenged central tenets of Islamic life and social organization throughout the Western Province, the relationship between Islamic practices, institutions, and tigre identity more broadly requires further elaboration.

Islam in Eritrea

Taking stock of the inherent cultural and linguistic pluralism across Eritrea, Jonathan Miran has observed that the country's heterogeneous Muslim communities historically reflected a truly "kaleidoscopic historical configuration" of peoples from multiple ethnicities, speaking a variety of Semitic, Cushitic, and Nilo-Saharan languages, and living in diverse social and political organizations.[1] Traditionally, Eritrea's Tigre-speaking communities, which accounted for roughly forty percent of Eritrea's total population by the early 1940s, were divided "into a number of tribes and tribal confederations" and included groups such as the Beni-Amer of the western lowlands, the Marya, Bet Juk, and a large part of the communities in the area around the city of Keren, including groups such as the Habab, ʿAd Takles, ʿAd Temaryam, ʿAd Muʿallim, and other smaller groups inhabiting the interior region beyond the Red Sea port city of Massawa.[2]

The region comprising the heart of Tigre-speaking Eritrea also experienced several waves of Islamic diffusion since the first half of the eighth century CE. The majority of residents of the western lowlands and the affiliated coastal communities embraced Islam during the thirteenth century. The growth of regional sea-based trade routes and the accompanying "circulation of holy men" from across the Arabian Peninsula fueled this conversion.[3] However, not until the nineteenth century, with the emergence of multiple Islamic "revivalist movements" that spread across the greater Red Sea region, did several traveling Muslim preachers arrive in the area and begin establishing various Sufi orders. Across the region, "the energetic turuq and holy families fostered widespread spatial networks, or webs of connections, straddling the area between the Red Sea coasts and the inland regions in the eastern Sudan."[4]

Aiming both to deepen Islamic practices among Muslims and to gain new converts, two regional Islamic entities powered much of the revivalist momentum: the 'Ad Shaykh holy family and the Khatmiyya.[5] Originally of Meccan origin, the members of the 'Ad Shaykh family established operations in Eritrea during the early nineteenth century and successfully won over large segments of the Tigre-speaking population within a few years. With their Na'ib allies along the Red Sea coast, they helped bring locals into their ranks as members of the Qadiriyya Sufi order.[6] While the 'Ad Shaykh's success continued throughout much of the coastal region, western Eritrea experienced an equally significant degree of revivalism based on the growing influence of the Khatmiyya order under the leadership of the al-Mirghani family. Founded by Muhammad 'Uthman al-Mirghani (1793–1852), the Khatmiyya's success in expanding their membership and allegiance within local communities developed largely out of the order's ability to incorporate the "preexisting religious formations (notables and holy lineages) into a supra-community network" that had far reaching social consequences.[7] Ultimately, these developments solidified Islam among the majority of the population to the point where virtually all Tigre-speaking groups had adopted Islam by the nineteenth century.[8] The intensification of proselytization activity among the Sufi groups and holy families within the various segments of Tigre-speaking society effectively created an "Islamic space" throughout much of western, northern, and eastern Eritrea, one that became increasingly political over time.[9] These developments later had a profound influence on the course of Eritrean nationalism, as shifting ideas about Islam, social organization, and authority all contributed to the wider political changes during the 1940s and 1950s. The concretization of this Islamic space and its later political ramifications echo Richard J. Reid's argument about the wider historical trends unique to borderlands and "frontier societies" across the Horn of Africa. Reid observes that periods of economic and environmental upheaval often "rendered these frontiers highly volatile and competitive zones, where human suffering but also economic opportunity and political creativity coexisted."[10] Indeed, the later rise of political activism among Tigre-speaking Islamic communities and those affiliated with the Khatmiyya in particular demonstrate the extent to which the very creation and expansion of the Eritrean Muslim League owed to these broader regional trends within the frontier of western and northern Eritrea.

Social and Political Unrest among the Tigre

> The serfs, or tigre, as they were commonly known, were as much the property of their masters, the shumagulle, as their camels or goats. Each tigre was bound to an individual shumagulle; he and his sons passed in inheritance to the descendants of his shumagulle; and at the will of his shumagulle the tigre could be sold, given away, punished by flogging, or put to death.[11]

The subservient relationship between the tigre and their shumagulle "masters" stood at the heart of economic life in Tigre-speaking society.[12] Although the relationship between tigre and shumagulle depended on the latter's position as the proprietor of the land and its resources, relations between the two groups also varied according to clan, community size, and the particular nature of the local subsistence economy. Nevertheless, a basic continuity throughout the Tigre-speaking region had solidified well before the advent of European colonialism. Although the major clans (*qebelaat*) identified both the shumagulle and tigre as belonging to the same group, tigre residents generally viewed themselves as belonging to a series of smaller subclans or "races" that lived in proximity to one another and under larger clan markers such as the Bet Asghede, 'Ad Takles, and Bet Jut.[13]

Local variables notwithstanding, certain aspects of the relationship between tigre and shumagulle were universal. The tigre who worked the land paid customary dues in the form of locally harvested foodstuffs to the shumagulle landholder, yet he could not engage in debate or argue with his shumagulle, negotiate the terms of the traditional land "contract," or terminate the relationship of his own accord. Shumagulle could also expect their tigre vassals to provide unpaid supplemental labor when needed. Usually this included supplemental agricultural work like the milking of animals and the fetching of firewood and other supplies. Shumagulle also reserved the right to use tigre livestock for cultivation as well as other animals, such as camels and mules, for their own transportation needs.[14] Early in the BMA's rule, Keren's senior civil affairs officer (SCAO), Kennedy Trevaskis, took note of the peculiarities of the relationship, remarking during his tenure in the region that "even where the relationship between *tigre* and *shumagulle* was reasonably cordial, the two classes remained castes immutably divided from each other."[15] The divide between tigre and shumagulle also involved a complex system of political authority within the communities. While historically many of the tigre groups lived under the authority of a council of elders, or *mahaber*, that tied many of the kinship groups together, the shumagulle-led positions of *shum* (chief) and the subordinate ranks of subchiefs also developed into markers of respect, although the real legislative and judicial authority "lay with the 'mahaber' and not with the Shum personally, although he would act as its spokesman and leader."[16] Nevertheless, shumagulle economic power intertwined with political influence as the landlords solidified their authority as the main authorities within the clans over time.

Although uprisings against the landowners occurred throughout Italian colonial rule and surfaced with particular intensity during the 1920s and 1930s, the situation for most tigre had worsened by 1941. This deterioration owed partially to the increased economic burden placed on rural Eritreans during Italy's military involvement in Ethiopia and then by the wider instability brought about by fighting between Italian and allied forces in nearby Sudan in 1940, which only exacerbated the challenges of the landlord-serf arrangement that the majority of Tigre-speaking communities had lived under since the seventeenth century.[17] Set against the stresses of the wartime economy and the power vacuum brought on by the end of formal Italian rule in early 1941, many tigre again began refusing to pay customary dues to their respective shumagulle across the Western Province.

BMA Responses to Tigre Resistance

Initially, tigre mainly from the Bet Asghede clan in the Keren Division petitioned BMA authorities in the spring of 1941 for their support in the enforcement of "their rights" and protection against both the physical and financial abuse of the landowners, whom they viewed as attempting to extract unreasonable amounts of tribute and customary dues.[18] For their part, shumagulle representatives also approached the BMA, claiming that the refusals to pay tribute had prevented them from executing their own traditional duties as clan chiefs. Many shumagulle also claimed that their very livelihood depended on receiving the customary tribute.[19] At first, officials attempted to maneuver carefully between both groups so as to not risk any major social disruption. By December 1941, however, the situation worsened as tigre representatives from across the Western Province announced they would refuse to give the traditional payment (*magasa*) of one-fourth of the coming harvest to the shumagulle.[20] In February 1942, BMA officials met with shumagulle and tigre representatives and informed the interested parties that because British administrators believed that the land "was vested in the Government," the administration would not legally recognize or enforce the collection of traditional dues by the shumagulle. In response, shumagulle from the Bet Asghede threatened to evict all tigre from their land if they refused to make their payments.[21]

Refusals to pay the customary dues presented administrators with a serious dilemma. While British officials recognized their own reliance on the shumagulle as instruments of revenue collection and authority, the prospect of mass civil disobedience by tigre groups encouraged BMA authorities to seek a compromise. Rejecting tigre activists' suggestions that the traditional land dues be declared illegal and that all "tribal land" instead be considered government land, Kennedy Trevaskis developed a more moderate policy by mid-1942 of allowing the customary payments of one-fourth of their harvest and that additional payments continue if "rendered voluntarily by a *tigre* to his Shamagulle." Trevaskis also argued that the BMA should "sanction no change of individual ownership" of traditional shumagulle lands and added that no tigre could be evicted from the residence unless approved by the presiding civil affairs officer.[22] In trying to contain tigre discontent by promising greater oversight for the payment of customary dues, Trevaskis's plan won the support of the colony's then chief administrator, Brigadier Stephen Longrigg. Having considered the range of possible actions on the tigre land issue, Longrigg summarized the need for a cautious policy: "The abolition by a 'stroke of the pen' of all feudal dues, much as we may recommend it on general grounds, cannot be upheld. Such a change, which would have far reaching repercussions, must go hand in hand with a general re-organization of tribal society—its tributary system, political representation etc. The present time is hardly suitable for such far-reaching schemes."[23]

Although by June 1943 the BMA had fully articulated a policy that recognized shumagulle authority while promising to increase oversight to guarantee the tigre's "protection and security of tenure" against possible abuse, British attempts to sever the traditional subservience proved inadequate. Rather than petitioning to simply redress the terms of the traditional payments, tigre activists sought nothing short of guaranteeing their complete independence from conditions many tigre viewed as nothing short of slavery.[24]

Despite the BMA's apparent success in holding a joint public assembly for shumagulle and tigre representatives in Keren in late June 1943 to address the situation, the possibility that some activists would ultimately be unwilling to compromise only stoked administrators' fears. In particular, BMA officers worried about the actions of Keren resident Mohamed Hamid Tahgé and his group of tigre supporters from the 'Ad Takles clan. While British reports alleged that Tahgé himself did not cultivate land because he worked as a merchant, he gained a loyal following among the 'Ad Takles for his bold public declarations that he would "rather die than allow a single rubaiya of dura [*sic*] to be paid over to the Bet Asghede (Shamagulle)."[25] Tahgé's early activism as a spokesmen for the 'Ad Takles set a precedent within the larger tigre movement; while coming from the ranks of the local tigre communities, most of the representatives who gained prominence as leaders often did not work the land themselves but instead were members of the colonial-educated intelligentsia in the nearby cities.[26]

Beyond the inability of administrators to come to terms with the complexities of levying appropriate customary dues, many British officials believed that a substantial portion of the shumagulle themselves lived in conditions of abject poverty and therefore could not survive without the payment of tribute. A December 1941 report surmised that "the trouble in the Asgade tribes is that the Sciumagalle are mostly so miserably poor in animals that their customary dues are their livelihood."[27] Nearly four years later, officials in Keren echoed this claim and argued that the shumagulle's apparent domination was largely inflated because many of the landowners worked the lands "side by side with the Tigre" and many were so poor that they were forced to sell some of their surplus land.[28] Political scientist John Markakis also supports this claim, stating that the shumagulle's vulnerable position developed partially as a result of the nature of the local agricultural economy. For several years the growth in the tigre population resulted in a large increase in livestock and overall agricultural capabilities that helped transform many of the supposedly subservient tigre into a group "often wealthier than the nobles."[29]

Nevertheless, "emancipatory" activism progressed throughout the region with increased vigor. One of the more dramatic episodes occurred in early 1943 when a tigre from the Rugbat clan, Humid Shentub, purportedly killed a shumagulle during a confrontation after the landowners told Shentub to vacate his plot in the village of Tselim Dengel for refusing to pay tribute.[30] If some activists believed that openly refusing payment could end tigre subservience and a few were even moved to violence, others proposed that the best way to solve the crisis involved complete social reorganization of the clans. In January 1944 the SCAO in Keren reported that authorities had imprisoned five tigre from the 'Ad Takles on the grounds that they had illegally collected goats, durra, and money from serf families while "inciting people to disobey the Administration by breaking away from their tribes and forming a tribe of their own under the name of Asghede."[31] Commenting on the apparent widespread support for the activists, the report noted that all the residents of the local tigre clans "have taken an oath that they will not give evidence in court against the five above-named accused."[32] The concretization of this highly charged antifeudal movement, set against the backdrop of elite-supported Islamic institutions and colonial-approved social hierarchies, had tremendous ramifications on the overall ideology of tigre peasant activists in seeking to overturn what they viewed as the legacy of economic injustice against their respective communities. Their rapid mobilization supports Reid's argument that such communities, living within the confines of a frontier zone of "conflict and competition" within the Horn often produce militant movements of social upheaval, thereby reflecting the "deeper political tectonics" inherent to the region.[33]

Concerned that the tigre from the 'Ad Takles and other clans could realistically break away from the "Shumagelle-ruled tribes" and form their own "autonomous section," the BMA looked to local religious authorities to try and end the turmoil. Thus the Khatmiyya order's precise role in the tigre emancipation movement needs to be explored, particularly in light of its previous role as a useful tool of Italian interests in the period before BMA rule.

The al-Mirghani Family's Response to Tigre Resistance

With the advent of Italian rule, in the late nineteenth century, colonial authorities adopted an "initial favorable tendency towards Islam" that reflected Italy's geopolitical concerns in the region.[34] Accordingly, early Italian attitudes were shaped largely "by the need to maintain stability among the 'tribes,' and inseparably, by the need to respond to the divided Mahdist and anti-Mahdist loyalties of the Khatmiyya and the 'Ad Shaykh."[35] In this context, the gradual privileging of the Khatmiyya over the 'Ad Shaykh had major ramifications that ultimately weakened the latter's influence and allowed Khatmiyya authorities to continue their order's expansion.

Thus the coming of British authority, in 1941, presented a dilemma for the Khatmiyya, as its previous, privileged position as a co-opted authority under Italian administration came to an end. Nevertheless, within Eritrea's Islamic communities in general, the BMA's arrival represented an opportunity for engaged Muslim leaders to capitalize on what they had benefited from during the previous decades. Italian policies and attitudes toward Islamic institutions, in addition to solidifying the "shared experiences of Eritrean Muslims under colonial rule," also contributed to a more discernible Muslim consciousness, particularly among the ranks of the country's urban elite.[36] However, if the coming of British authority signaled an adverse change for some previously privileged groups such as the al-Mirghani family, the BMA's arrival also unleashed new possibilities for the majority of the communities living in the "Tigre frontier" of northern and western Eritrea.[37]

Echoing their earlier role in serving as an intermediary between residents and Italian administrators, the Khatmiyya order became an important source of indirect authority for BMA officials in 1941. Their influence reflected the significance of Sufi authorities, centered on the lodges (*zawayaat*) and Qur'anic schools as "crystallizing spaces and circuits of religious and social confluence among Muslims" throughout the Tigre-speaking territories.[38] Ever mindful of the region's religious dynamics, Trevaskis noted their influence early on during his tenure in Keren: "Today the whole of this bloc of Moslem, and Tigre-speaking, communities are culturally united not only by the fact that they are almost all Moslem, but also by the fact that (together with many communities in the Sudan) they adhere to the Tariga al-Khatmia, the religious 'path' or sect founded by Said Mohammad Osman El Mirghani, a descent [*sic*] of the Prophet, who died in the Northern Sudan in 1853."[39]

Khatmiyya leaders nevertheless faced a major dilemma as calls for tigre emancipation grew. Because the order's adherents stretched across the tigre-shumagulle divide, they provided a valued but fragile religious continuity across Tigre-speaking society that meant that the Khatmiyya order's position on the issue could adversely affect its support among both segments of society.[40] Both the BMA and many proactive shumagulle made a point of reaching out early to the al-Mirghani family in resolving the matter, especially in dissuading activists from creating new independent clan structures. According to BMA officers, the Assab-based exiles associated with Tahgé, who were responsible for promoting the idea of forming new tigre clans, also "went around collecting money from poor credulous people promising they won't have to pay and squandered the money collected on food and drink."[41]

Following the death of Eritrea's leading Khatmiyya authority, Sayyid Ja'far b. Bakri b. Ja'far b. Muhammad 'Uthman al-Mirghani, in 1943, the BMA turned to Ja'far's nephew and heir apparent, Sayyid Muhammad Abu Bakr al-Mirghani, for help. In February 1944, Sayyid Abu Bakr made an eight-day tour of the 'Ad Takles communities, after being asked by officials in Keren to convince some of the rebellious tigre *hisset* (subchiefs) into paying their customary payments and to withdraw support for creating the new clans.[42] Although al-Mirghani reported to British officials that most of the agitators had fled to the nearby mountains "rather than stay behind and be disrespectful" of his suggestions, he managed to procure a list of the names of the thirty activists allegedly responsible for inciting the local people to create new groups.[43]

If the BMA and shumagulle leaders had reasoned that the al-Mirghani family's involvement would help bring most of the tigre activists to heel, they were only partially correct. While al-Mirghani successfully dissuaded most 'Ad Takles residents from establishing new clan structures, his visit also served to legitimize the basic aims of the emancipation movement. In a petition sent to Eritrea's chief administrator, Darcy McCarthy, in late March 1945, some tigre representatives recalled al-Mirghani's earlier visit and its significance to their growing cause:

> He noticed in person the condition of those virgin lands, covered with woods and stones, and the hard work that was taking place to make the ground tillable. As a result of such ascertainment, he stated to the BET ASGHEDE that his conscience did not allow him to bid the TIGRE to pay them [the shumagulle] a share of the crops, as it is unjust to sweat peoples, in opposition to Sciaria [shari'a] as well as to any human law.[44]

Consequently, much of the justification for tigre emancipation stressed the dual violation of shari'a law and basic human rights. Although Sayyid Muhammad Abu Bakr served as an intermediary between the shumagulle and the tigre, his apparent sympathy for their cause gave some activists cause for celebration. When al-Mirghani himself later assumed the largely symbolic position of president of the Eritrean Muslim League, in 1946, the official connection between the Khatmiyya leadership and the tigre cause furthered solidified. Nevertheless, because a majority of shumagulle also served in positions of leadership within the order, Khatmiyya authorities as a whole neither sanctioned the tigre movement nor provided its leaders with significant material support during the early and mid-1940s.

Thus the movement's main actors, while acknowledging the significance and role of the Khatmiyya as the main regional Islamic authority, viewed their own identity as Muslims on different terms. In general, much of the justification for tigre emancipation included references to the fact that in the past the majority of the shumagulle within the clans had actually practiced Christianity until the Islamic revivals of the early nineteenth century.[45] This late "turn to Islam" by the dominant class provided activists with additional validation that their status as a true Muslim people justified the "moral" struggle for emancipation, arguing "we could call it an evolution in the opposite sense, as not we, the dependents, have adopted religion, language and customs of the dominating people, but they, the dominating class have adopted our religion, language and customs."[46]

This perspective regarding the shumagulle's supposed "inauthentic" religious and moral standing helps explain why many tigre representatives rejected the legitimacy of the elites as true Muslims. When discussing the origins and early activities of another influential Sufi authority, the 'Ad Shaykh holy family, tigre representatives noted that although the local shumagulle were descended from the venerated Sufi saint Shaykh al-Amin b. Hamid b. Nafutay, they eventually subjected the tigre population to the "same system and treatment" that other local Asghede (shumagulle) had practiced, despite the fact that "the Islamic religion does not impose such barbarous and abusive forms," they nonetheless "carried out the system in [a] false way."[47]

Accordingly, activists also made a point of appealing to British sympathies about how the legacy of both "divine and human laws" illustrated that the "residue of slavery" that was imposed on them could be wiped away only by the British applying the appropriate "principles of Civilization and Liberty."[48] Tigre representatives carefully argued that their emancipation did not necessitate a broad rejection of all local (i.e., BMA) authority, but specifically freedom from the customary tributes and "illegal taxes" unknown to British authorities.[49] Moreover, tigre leaders used their moralistic language and ideals to play on European sympathies as a means of garnering support. In describing their historical oppression, they made a point of mentioning that their condition represented a condition worse than even slavery, "a form that not even the Nazis have given the world, while shumagulle are being accused of the ill treatment of humanity, humanity created partially by God, with all the organs of the body and the senses of man."[50]

The strategic language employed by activists also demonstrated that although the discontent among much of the population materialized as mass protest and refusal to pay customary dues, the responsibility for directing and articulating tigre appeals to colonial authorities fell to a small group of politically savvy merchants that had originally come up through the ranks of the previous Italian administration. According to Trevaskis, the greatest irony regarding the surge in tigre activism was the fact that rather than being established exclusively by the discontented peasants themselves, it primarily "was led and organised by the commercial class—composed of merchants in the towns and petty traders in the country."[51] Tigre representatives themselves alluded to this phenomenon, boasting that while the shumagulle's ranks had fallen into a process of lethargy and "retrogression," the descendants of many tigre "progressed enormously, passing from shepherds and cultivators to the arts, the free professions, commerce and employment both in government and commercial institutions."[52] Markakis also echoed this professional imbalance between the two groups, stating that the tigre had "availed themselves of new employment opportunities in the colonial armies and police, raising their income, while also reducing the labour power available for herding their own and their masters' animals."[53] Among the tigre activists who emerged from the "free professions," Ibrahim Sultan became the most influential and politically astute leader to articulate tigre concerns and the need to initiate dramatic reform across western and northern Eritrea.

Ibrahim Sultan: Advocate of Tigre Emancipation

Born to a tigre family from the Rugbat clan of the Beni-Amer and raised in Keren, Ibrahim Sultan embodied the ascension of Eritrea's small Muslim professional class during Italian rule. Having received his initial Islamic education at a *khalwa* under the instruction of Ja'far al-Mirghani, he later began his primary Arabic-language education as a student of Shaykh Osman Hasebela, himself a former graduate of Al-Azhar University in Cairo.[54] As a youth Sultan worked at a train depot in Agordat from 1922 to 1926. After being fired for allegedly engaging in an altercation with his Italian supervisor, he eventually returned to Keren. Using his extensive knowledge of Arabic, he procured a job in the colonial civil service as a translator and for the next several years traveled throughout Eritrea as part of the Italian colonial government's Native Affairs Department; his duties took him to many of the major towns and cities in western Eritrea such as Agordat, Tessenai, and Adi Ugri (Mendefera), where he came into contact with other members of Eritrea's small class of Muslim civil servants.[55]

Sultan claimed that from an early age he developed a hatred for the injustices of the shumagulle. He recalled that as a child he and his friends were taunted and called "tiny worms" by their peers because of their serf origins. He also made a point of describing the most debasing treatment that shumagulle inflicted on the tigre:

> When a Nabtab [shumagulle] child is born, before the umbilical cord is cut, one of the Tigres will be called and the cord is cut in front of him. The Tigre who was being called will thus be the slave of the child. The 'bad-hair' [newborn's body hair] of the child is never shaven without a Tigre being summoned; and the same thing for circumcision. The Tigres presented between the shaving and the circumcision would become the slaves of the child.[56]

Like earlier figures such as Mohamed Hamid Tahgé, Sultan took a particularly passionate stand against the landowning aristocracy, denouncing their policies against the tigre as being both "un-Islamic" and a violation of basic human dignity.[57] Moreover, his efforts at building a political constituency from among the disgruntled peasant groups followed the earlier efforts of the 'Ad Takles activists, who had tried to create new clan structures.

Although Trevaskis correctly observed the origins and economic strength of many of the movement's leaders, Sultan and his closest supporters had not only benefited from their financial standing but also from their experiences as low-level members of the "native" colonial administration, coming of age with a clear sense of how the colonial system had exacerbated the tigre-shumagulle divide. According to Sultan, Italian administrators long understood that "this kind of local traditional system would make the society highly fragmented and weak, and so the Italians encouraged the existing master-serf relationship among tigre society."[58] Idris Shubek, a tigre activist and an apparent relative of Tahgé, echoed this belief when he argued that the colonial appropriation and perversion of the traditional land system effectively created "double slavery" for tigre living in servitude under both "native" and "colonial" authorities that lasted until the BMA period.[59] Representatives thus made an effort to place Italian colonialism in the wider historical context of tigre society by illustrating how officials both "approved and confirmed" the shumagulle's status.[60]

With Sultan's growing influence as a community organizer, and with discontent among the tigre communities reaching a boiling point by the summer of 1946, peasant representatives finally coalesced as a more cohesive political force. In August 1946, Ibrahim Sultan, along with Hamid Humed (one of Tahgé's confidents and a former fellow exile in Assab) and colleague Imam Musa, chaired a meeting of more than seven hundred tigre representatives in the village of Sheddem. The 1946 gathering, which excluded shumagulle representatives, explicitly laid out the basic objectives of the movement. Members passed a resolution nullifying their previous status as vassals and prohibited their brethren from milking animals or farming the land of the shumagulle. In addition, representatives also agreed to carry out their program into the rural areas to continue building support for the cause.[61]

What began initially as a series of localized opposition movements to the traditional land tenure system developed into a widespread movement for political power in the Tigre-speaking areas of western and northern Eritrea. Under the leadership of urban-based activists such as Ibrahim Sultan, Mohamed Hamid Tahgé, Idris Fa'id, and other activists of "serf origins," tigre peasants across the region resisted in various ways against both the shumagulle and the largely compromised BMA administration. Rejecting the above-mentioned parties' calls for more moderate solutions to their grievances, tigre leaders saw themselves engaged in nothing short of a struggle to end the "continuous state of slavery" within their society.[62] In this respect, the tigre movement against the shumagulle illustrated how localized peasant conscious developed not simply "by the properties and attributes of his own social being but by diminution, if not negation, of those of his superiors."[63] Indeed, as the later political ramifications of their movement demonstrate, tigre activists emerged with a profound belief in their own "negation" as a subject class whose existence under elite landowners remained the preferred system of governance for both Italian and British authorities.

Although it presaged the development of formal nationalist political parties by several years, the tigre emancipation movement demonstrated at least three key features that would later define the core intellectual preoccupations within Eritrea's nationalist contact zone. Broad ideas about the need for grassroots participation to address injustice, the use of Islamic teaching as a means of social and economic liberation, and the rise of a small, proactive Muslim intelligentsia within the leadership apparatus all signified how early tigre mobilization helped concretize ideas about religious identity, political representation, and the nature of community within an Eritrean context. Ironically, other key ideological elements also began to develop well beyond the traditional tigre heartland. In particular, Eritrea's urban centers displayed key qualities of institutional cohesion and civic mobilization that later enriched the intellectual foundations of the Muslim-dominated nationalist contact zone.

Developing Muslim Institutional Uniformity during BMA Rule

If social and political turmoil marked the early years of BMA rule in the tigre peasant communities, a different kind of activism took hold among Eritrea's small but influential class of Islamic scholars and clerics. Members of the *ulama* embraced a bold mission of promoting greater uniformity and centralization of Islamic legal and educational institutions. Although during Italian rule administrators had supported the construction of mosques and privileged regional Muslim authorities such as the Khatmiyya, the BMA period initiated an era of new possibilities for those Islamic scholars who wished to bring about greater uniformity across Eritrea. Grand mufti Ibrahim al-Mukhtar represented the most influential and proactive leader to address these broader community concerns. As the highest-ranking Muslim leader and judge in Eritrea, the mufti sought to regulate and standardize Islamic institutions throughout his tenure.

Born in 1909 near Mount Kended, in Akkele Guzay, Ibrahim al-Mukhtar came from a family with a legacy of involvement in Islamic religious affairs. Many of his family members within the Saho-speaking Harak Faqih subclan served as prominent Islamic scholars and jurists in the area. In January 1925 he traveled to Sudan to continue his religious education and eventually made his way to Omdurman, where he stayed for several months until finally arriving in Cairo, in 1926; he was only fifteen years old. However, beyond his academic abilities, Ibrahim al-Mukhtar also developed a keen political sense about the pitfalls of Italian colonialism. While still a student at Al-Azhar University, he became aware of Italy's military actions in neighboring Libya and noted how the Italian embassy in Cairo, which kept government officials informed about the activities of Eritrean students, often warned Cairo-based Eritreans about the "dangers" of getting involved in political activism.[64] Nevertheless, Ibrahim al-Mukhtar's political education developed during his time in Egypt and he began a close association with many of the resident Eritreans living in the city. As with many of the Eritrean students who trickled into Cairo during the 1920s and 1930s, he became increasingly apprehensive about how the colonial authorities had succeeded in co-opting Eritrea's traditional Islamic institutions.

Through Italy's "Muslim policy" in Eritrea—in which colonial officials subsidized and promoted Islamic religious activities and facilities to solidify government rule—Ibrahim al-Mukhtar eventually took up the position of mufti. When Italian authorities sought to appoint someone as the chair of the High Islamic Court, in Asmara, in 1939, a small group of Muslim community leaders approached al-Mukhtar.[65] Although he expressed hesitation about taking the position because of his own disapproval toward Italian rule, he apparently also recognized that Eritrea's Muslims needed greater religious guidance and more centralized leadership.[66] Through Degiat Hassan

'Ali and other leaders, and with the apparent pressure of the Italian embassy in Cairo, the mufti ultimately decided to return to Eritrea despite his own poor health. On December 4, 1939, Italian authorities appointed al-Mukhtar as Eritrea's grand mufti and by April 1940 he returned to Eritrea after more than fifteen years abroad to assume his new duties.[67]

Ibrahim al-Mukhtar's arrival signaled an important new transition within Eritrea's Muslim communities. In his brief tenure as mufti under Italian rule, he quickly established himself as the major Islamic authority in the colony. He served as the first ever head of Eritrea's Islamic court and, with the help of supporters, solidified his authority over what had previously existed as only a fragmented group of clerics. He also began demonstrating his own rejection of long-standing Italian attempts to co-opt and use Islam to support colonial objectives. For example, when Italian military officers approached him in November 1940 and asked that he declare a fatwa so that Muslim *askaris* in the Italian army could break their fast to fight in the military campaigns in East Africa, he refused.[68] More than his worry about how Italian authorities had helped pervert and control Eritrea's Islamic institutions, the mufti's concerns developed out of a belief that so much of the Muslim population lived in complete ignorance of their religion. He acknowledged that upon his return to Asmara he found the social and spiritual conditions of Muslims to be "pathetic" even though they enjoyed a relatively healthy financial situation because of the wartime economy. Because there were "no education, no schools and associations" that bound the community together, many of the residents lived under the influence of superstition and were divided by what he termed the forces of "tribalism."[69] From the mufti's perspective, these "forces" were especially potent with regard to Khatmiyya influence and specifically the role of the al-Mirghani family in everyday religious affairs.[70]

Although the mufti did not disapprove of Sufism in principle, "he was shocked by the excesses he saw by the people in their glorification of their Khatmiyya Sufi masters."[71] One of the mufti's major qualms about the Khatmiyya was the influence that many of its *khalifa*s exercised within the major cities and towns. This resentment stemmed from the fact that although many Khatmiyya representatives served in high-ranking positions in the Sufi order, they often had very limited knowledge about the Islamic sciences and the intricacies of the faith. The mufti also viewed them as an obstacle to change because he had witnessed how the few qualified Islamic leaders "who didn't toe their line" were often dismissed by the order's leadership.[72] Nevertheless, because of their considerable influence throughout Eritrea, the mufti dealt with the Khatmiyya authorities "very tactfully and discreetly" in his reform efforts. Part of that discretion also stemmed from the fact that many of Eritrea's influential merchants and Islamic leaders themselves served as khalifas for the al-Mirghani family, even as they supported the mufti's actions.[73]

In addition, as an adherent of the Hanafi *madhab* (school) of Islamic law, the mufti faced several challenges in trying to bridge the divisions of the various competing sects, who often vied for influence against one another.[74] The mufti's challenge against what he viewed as the widespread ignorance and promotion of vice by the fragmented Sufi leadership developed into a direct emphasis on the need for basic Islamic teaching. In 1944 the mufti issued a memorandum stipulating that only qualified Islamic teachers could give public sermons in mosques and that they had to have specific permission from the local *qadi*.[75] He also downplayed the importance of Sufi "innovation" and called for a return to the basic Islamic teachings of the Sunnah.

Part of this campaign also involved his public denunciations of such "un-Islamic" practices such as female circumcision, nose piercing, and other regional customs. He tried to "awaken observances of religious occasions," including traditional Islamic feasts and festivals and the commemoration of major holidays.[76] While he noted the dangers of following lax interpretations of Islam, he also had apprehensions about the rise of more hardline sects; he warned against the dangers of "extremism and militancy" that he saw in some of the communities that began to embrace Wahhabism. In March 1945 the mufti released a public proclamation that addressed the need to end the factionalism. Decrying the exclusion and hostilities against fellow Muslims in the mosques, he also warned against embracing the "harmful distinctions" between different Sufi and Wahhabi sects within Eritrea's Islamic community and called upon worshippers to embrace their community as one.[77]

When Italian authorities did lose their hold over Eritrea, in early 1941, the change in leadership from Italian to BMA rule presented the mufti with greater latitude to carry out his agenda. By June 1943, after completing a comprehensive tour of the more than seventeen separate Islamic courts within Eritrea, the mufti provided reports to each administrative unit with a list of recommendations for the courts. That same year, the mufti gained additional influence when BMA administrators transferred to him the authority to appoint members for Eritrea's waqf committees.[78] Specifically, the mufti issued a general rule "whereby each sharia qadi of the principal towns was vested with the power of establishing an awqaf committee and appointing its members in his administrative jurisdiction."[79] While the mufti's actions served as the driving force behind the process of standardizing and improving Muslim education across Eritrea, his efforts could not have materialized without the assistance of Muslim leaders who provided the much-needed funds to establish the new institutions. The mufti acknowledged as much, stating that despite the poor conditions of Islamic education upon his arrival, he felt encouraged initially because "the wealth concentrated in Muslim hands" could assist him in his efforts. His hopes increased after many of Eritrea's "rich Muslim merchants" answered his call.[80] Between 1943 and 1951, the Muslim community helped open several Islamic institutions in Asmara, Massawa, Keren, Agordat, and other major cities.[81]

In particular, Muslim businessmen made a point of contributing to the education of their respective communities through the institution of the waqf. One of the more opulent examples of this spirit came from Saleh Ahmed Kekiya, an influential merchant based in the village of Hirgigo, near Massawa. In 1944, Kekiya used the revenue he had received from property investments in Addis Ababa to fund the construction of an Islamic school in Hirgigo that enrolled more than five hundred students.[82] The facility, consisting of seven separate buildings, included a staff of several Al-Azhar graduates whose residence was arranged largely by the mufti and his supporters. At the grand opening of the school, in March, officials also announced that in addition to teaching the Arabic language and basic Qur'anic education, the founders planned to establish classes for formalized teaching in other local languages such as Tigre and Saho. Local writers expressed their jubilation at the school's opening and their appreciation for Kekiya's actions in a column printed in the weekly Tigrinya-language newspaper *Nay Ertra semunawi gazzetta* (Eritrean weekly gazette):

> Until today, we have never seen such work being done in our country. This deed must have had the help of the will of God, however, as we have never encountered such generosity and kindness in a human being. It is true that there are few wealthy people in our country, since most of our country's wealth is in the hands of foreigners, and we have never seen those people

do anything that helped the native people or the local government, only gather up whatever they find here and send it to
their country or expand their selfish practices and wealth.[83]

In addition to the merchant communities along the coast, one of the
most substantial sources of the support within the business community
came from the Jabarti leaders based in Asmara. Although members of
the Jabarti community were "instrumental in funding the construction
of mosques and other religious institutions" in Asmara and throughout
the Hamasien region during much of the early twentieth century, many
of the leading families proved especially supportive to the mufti's overall efforts at reform during the early and mid-1940s.[84]

Beyond providing the bulk of the finances for the Asmara waqf,
Jabarti merchants also promoted the mufti's wider efforts at encouraging Muslim youth to take advantage of the new push for educational
reform. Many of the leading merchant families in Asmara assisted in
opening new Qur'anic schools, organizing youth activities and subsi-
dizing private Arabic-language instruction.[85] The efforts of Shaykh
Adem Kusmallah and his brother, Shaykh Kusmallah Muhammad,
illustrate this kind of urban-based activism. As owners of a successful
clothing business in the city, they were involved in raising money
for local mosques and sponsoring meetings of different community
groups on their property. The Kusmallahs even made their storage
facilities in the Geza Berhanu section of the city available to local
Muslim youth groups to further their studies while being encouraged
by the brothers to maintain and "be attentive in their education."[86]

Other Jabarti leaders in Asmara, such as Berhanu Ahmedin, involved themselves not only in supporting institutional reform but
also used their substantial contacts with Jabarti community members
outside Eritrea to assist in attracting new teachers and Arabic instructors to the city.[87] Some leading community leaders and intellectuals, such as Shaykh Abdelkadir Kebire, made a point of regularly
visiting the new schools, observed the progress of students, and made
their own recommendations for further institutional improvement.[88]
Kebire's well-known zeal for supporting Muslim educational initiatives was also reflected in his contributions in organizing donation
drives among other Muslim leaders in Asmara and Massawa and
helping plan the construction of several trade and polytechnic schools
for Muslim youth. Largely because the mufti "was very well respected
and revered by the Asmara Jabarti," many leaders proved receptive to
the overall reform efforts that simultaneously contributed to a larger

mobilization of Islamic civil society.[89] The mufti's relationship with Asmara's Muslim leaders and those in other Eritrean cities revealed his considerable influence among the Muslim intellectual base: "the mufti had a strong relationship with the intellectuals of his time, particularly those who spoke Arabic. They naturally gravitated toward him, as he was a leading authority. The mufti was well versed not only in Islamic subjects but also classic Arabic literature, history, politics, etc., and that appealed to intellectuals of his time."[90]

While the mufti made it his personal mission to establish new schools and promote greater uniformity for the Muslim population, he also benefited from the small but active group of British administrators that also worked to improve basic education for the population. While their motives differed from those of local Muslim leaders, British administrators did contribute by expanding school attendance and establishing new educational institutions. BMA officials, working with the Muslim leadership, developed a growing network of local schools that ran parallel with Muslim reformers' agenda. According to Maj. H. F. Kynaston-Snell, eleven schools for indigenous students were established in January 1943 alone, with an additional fifty-four schools opened through April 1946.[91] BMA administrators also worked with Eritrea's Islamic clerics to import Arabic language texts from Cairo and Khartoum and even supported the employment of "native inspectors" to develop the Tigrinya- and Kunama-language materials. Kynaston-Snell also highlighted the fact that community elites played a major role in the affairs of schools: "each school has its committee of five or six notables whose duties are to seek the general welfare of the school."[92] Although in 1941 only sixteen elementary schools were in operation with a maximum of only 4,177 enrolled students throughout Eritrea (and the province of Tigray, in northern Ethiopia), Kennedy Trevaskis reported that by the end of 1947, fifty-nine elementary schools were established, employing 153 Eritrean-born teachers with emphasis on standardizing education through Arabic and Tigrinya as the primary languages of instruction.[93]

Concurrent with the growth of education and religious standardization, the Muslim leadership within the Eritrean capital also exhibited a greater degree of unity and self-awareness as representatives of regional interests. Part of this process included using the small but growing indigenous language print media in the city, especially the commentary sections of *Nay Ertra semunawi gazzetta*. In particular, leaders in Asmara made use of the growing media to develop greater community awareness and stress the need for moral guidance during the transitional BMA period. For Muslim-specific topics, written commentaries focused on stories from the Qur'an and the hadith to remind readers of their moral duties. One of the more colorful entries, published in February 1944, reminded readers that because God had the power to see all things, even "a black ant moving along on a black stone in complete darkness," the hearts of all people and their deeds would be seen and judged.[94] Other times, many of the commentaries appealed to the fundamental unity of Eritrean Muslims and Christians as "brothers." One of the most frequent ways that commentators expressed their hopes for equality and unity included the emphasis on education of the youth, particularly issues of language. Many editorials addressed the need to be adamant in using "native languages" in the schools, both as a means of preserving culture and of developing their country.[95]

Achievements in education and religious standardization represented one of the major accomplishments that the members of the Eritrean ulama achieved as the decade progressed, working in tandem with concerned merchants and community leaders. The proliferation of Islamic institutions added additional momentum to the growing activism among the Muslim urban intelligentsia. That activism became an important source of strength and cohesion for community leaders, particularly for those residing in Asmara, as the previously unknown forces of sectarianism emerged by the middle of the decade.

Muslim Intellectuals and Urban Life: The Case of Mahber Fikri Hager

Although its origins have remained largely obscured, the significance of the MFH has carried far beyond its initial creation, in May 1941, and its supposed pro-unionist transformation, in 1944. Initially, the group of community leaders that came together in the spring of 1941 to form the MFH expressed immediate concern over the fate of their respective communities and the future role of indigenous Eritreans in the new British-controlled administration. The heart of their concern, particularly for the group's principal founders, Abdelkadir Kebire and Gebremeskel Woldu, revolved around how the BMA continued employing Italian administrators in the day-to-day operations of government, which only increased residents' fears of possible Italian reprisals against the indigenous population.[96] Although established in secret, the organization made its presence known to BMA authorities by going against the ban on public gatherings, coordinating a demonstration of approximately three thousand people in Asmara on May 5, 1941.

The core group that founded the MFH represented the leading Eritrean intellectuals of their day. While some members came from Eritrea's previous generation of community elites, the thrust of the organization's program came from the group of former colonial civil servants that were born during the first decade of the twentieth century. Beyond sharing an "anti-Italian platform" and concerns about the overall objectives of BMA rule, this relatively young faction within the MFH represented the emerging streak of activism among Eritrea's Muslim intellectuals and community leaders; most of them had attained a modest education in the colonial system and worked in positions within the indigenous civil service.[97] Through their efforts, this small but influential group eventually established the basic parameters of the nationalist contact zone. Besides the MFH's official membership, the organization also had widespread support among the Jabarti community and other Muslim business elements. The organization itself developed supposedly as a result of an initial meeting held in the tea shop of the Red Sea Pearl Hotel, a popular establishment owned and operated by the Aberra family, one of Asmara's most prominent Jabarti families.[98] The MFH's formation represented the first solid instance in which Eritrea's urban intellectuals engaged each other as a formal, collective entity.

By seeking legitimate recognition by the presiding BMA administration and by working to improve conditions among the indigenous population more broadly, the MFH's members established an important precedent that later came to define the wider nationalist contact zone. Community leaders, be they prominent private citizens or well-respected religious figures, became increasingly proactive in articulating grassroots resentment about the lack of opportunity and agency on the part of nearly all indigenous Eritreans in the post-Italian period. And while the arrival of the BMA clearly represented an important paradigm shift, in that it allowed for a more tolerant political atmosphere than the previous era of Italian colonialism, the already burgeoning dialogue among local intellectuals signified that such mobilization did not develop simply as a response to BMA rule. In short, the nationalist contact zone that gave rise to the MFH emerged well before BMA authorities simply permitted indigenous civic and political groups to legally organize.

Despite their concern for Islamic religious interests, both the Muslim members within the MFH, much like the group's Christian associates, embraced broad political aims that allowed the organization to serve as a "common arena" where ideas of social reform, economic empowerment, and community awareness fused.[99] Nevertheless, because of the BMA-imposed ban on political organizations during the first five and a half years (until October 1946), the MFH's direct influence remained limited to that of a clandestine group whose activities consisted largely of secret meetings and discussions mainly in Asmara and other major cities. Both Jordan Gebre-Medhin's and Ruth Iyob's studies refute long-held claims that the MFH served from its inception as an irredentist organization with direct Ethiopian support. One of the more substantial points Gebre-Medhin raises is the fact that initially, many of the most ardent supporters of unionism, particularly those in the hierarchy of the Eritrean Tewahedo Church, rejected the MFH because its membership included Muslim, Protestant, and Catholic members of the urban intelligentsia rather than only the traditional elites from the Tewahedo community.[100] Thus, the linkages between Eritrea's Tewahedo Church and the broader support for political union between Eritrea and Ethiopia merit further discussion.

Intellectuals and Irredentism

The genuine movement among those who believed in the cultural and historical links between Ethiopia and Eritrea, particularly among the Tigrinya-speaking Christian residents in the Eritrean highlands, cannot be overlooked. Tekeste Negash's observation that "the Italians had failed to create loyal subjects of the Christian Eritreans" needs to be considered to understand how unionist political leaders within Eritrea helped mobilize the widespread irredentist movement fairly rapidly among many segments of the Christian community from 1941 onward.[101] Outside Eritrea, the Ethiopian state also succeeded during this period in embracing its historic connection with Eritrea's highland communities as the cradle of Orthodox Tewahedo Christianity. Having developed within the Axumite Empire in the early fourth century CE, the Tewahedo Church remained the major religious authority among the Tigrinya-majority communities both in the Eritrean highlands and throughout Ethiopia's northern province of Tigray. Despite the gradual decline of the Axumite Empire, the expansion of Islam across the region in later centuries, and even the eventual carving up of the traditional Tigrinya heartland between Eritrea and Tigray, Orthodox Tewahedo Christianity remained a central element throughout the region through the construction of churches, monasteries, and the preservation of the Old and New Testament in Ge'ez, the written language of ancient Axum. Based on this legacy, the modern Ethiopian state that emerged during the early twentieth century embraced this historical legacy in its attempt to gain support from Eritrea's mainly Tigrinya Christian inhabitants. Emperor Haile Selassie's government also embraced political union with Eritrea as part of its broader strategy to secure territorial and economic security. With concerns about possible European efforts to compromise Ethiopian sovereignty even after the country's liberation from Italy in 1941, officials within Haile Selassie's now reinstated monarchy viewed the acquisition of Eritrea as one of several major foreign policy priorities in the post–World War II period.

Thus, the links between the Eritrean Tewahedo Church and Ethiopian religious authorities, coupled with the Ethiopian government's support for the church's activities and the long history of mobility across the Eritrea-Ethiopia border, all contributed to the steady growth of a unionist political program throughout the early and mid-1940s. A significant and complex dialectic developed that witnessed the growing politicization of religion among the MFH membership, as each camp began articulating competing definitions of what it meant to be Eritrean. One faction, dominated mainly but not exclusively by Muslim intellectuals, argued in favor of Eritrea's unique status as a separate entity forged out of Italian colonialism, while the other emphasized the inherent historical connections to Ethiopia mainly through the legacy of the Tewahedo Church and the region's precolonial past.[102]

While the most hardline unionist elements within the organization eventually used the MFH to build support for unification with Ethiopia, the shift to unionism, or *hadinet*, among many within the intelligentsia did not occur overnight.[103] In fact, the trajectory of the MFH illustrates that the supposed political split between most Muslim and Christian Eritreans did not represent a major breakdown in interreligious cooperation, at least among the pro-independence intellectuals. When an explicitly pro-unionist faction finally emerged in 1944 with the establishment of the Ethiopian Liaison Office in Asmara and its puppet organization, the Society for the Unification of Ethiopia and Eritrea, most of the MFH's Muslim members and a small number of Protestant Christian representatives veered off in their own direction in an attempt to retain the earlier spirit of unity. MFH member Woldeab Woldemariam recalled how in 1944 Saleh Ahmed Kekiya organized a secret meeting of the pro-independence members at a residence in Asmara in which Muslim and Christian members shared a symbolic meal where the attendees ate meat slaughtered by both a Muslim and Christian and then swore to each other on both a Bible and a Qur'an that their group would remain united in their objectives.[104]

The Bet Giyorgis Conference and the "Muslim" Response

In theory, the political conference that took place on the outskirts of Asmara at Bet Giyorgis in late November 1946 should have illustrated the considerable strength of the Eritrean intelligentsia, both Muslim and Christian, in addressing the growing political fragmentation. With BMA chief administrator John Meredith Benoy having lifted the ban on formal political parties during the previous October, the intelligentsia, led by Woldeab Woldemariam and with the assistance of MFH president Gebremeskel Woldu, Muhammad Umar Kadi other more moderate representatives, planned to organize a general meeting to address the fragmentation. The official meeting on November 24 itself represented the culmination of several secret gatherings during the prior weeks, in which some members of the competing factions of the MFH attempted to stave off the division, forging a basic twelve-point agreement that sought to guarantee the local autonomy of most political and cultural institutions from Ethiopian control in the event of political union. According to Ruth Iyob, support for "conditional union" by some members encouraged most of the MFH's "radical unionists" to intensify their efforts at complete unification, especially those closest to Eritrea's Tewahedo Church hierarchy, under the leadership of Abune Markos.[105] Thus religion did not, at least prior to the November meeting, serve as a marker for political identity among the concerned intellectual class until hardline unionists under Markos and Tedla Bairu, the newly installed head of Eritrea's Unionist Party (UP), used it as one of the more prominent wedge issues during talks.[106]

Although often cited as a major participant at the Bet Giyorgis conference, Ibrahim Sultan came supposedly only as an observer and did not participate in the previous drafting committee for the first session of the conference.[107] Yet after observing the sudden turn of events, including Tedla Bairu's now infamous insulting of Woldeab Woldemariam and his lineage and the more general distain for Muslim concerns, Sultan (having been made to sit on the floor) stood up and attempted to leave the meeting. When some representatives noticed this and then asked Sultan to provide his opinion on the issues, a pro-unionist youth allegedly yelled out to Sultan that no matter what he said, the Muslim "herders" would *have* to obey what the Christian elders decided at Bet Giyorgis.[108] Sultan later claimed that one attendee told him that because "a thousand mules must follow one horse," he and every other Muslim leader, being mules themselves, had no right to instruct the Christian representatives on what needed to be done.[109] While Sultan retorted that he came to the meeting only as an observer and did not "represent all Muslims," he staged a walkout from the meeting with most of the attending Muslim representatives and immediately headed toward his office, at the Asmara Chamber of Commerce. Although some of the Asmara's more prominent pro-independence Muslim leaders remained at the meeting for the duration, Sultan began drafting the founding document for a new political organization that could represent pro-independence interests.

After later presenting the political program to associates Hajj Suleiman Ahmed Umar and Abdelkadir Kebire, Sultan and his supporters took the program to Degiat Hassan 'Ali and the mufti for their approval in the following days. Afterward the group made a point of going around to all of Asmara's mosques and Islamic centers to get signatures for Sultan's petition the BMA to form the new political organization.[110] On Friday, November 29, Sultan and his group organized a dinner in the Akriya section of Asmara and celebrated as they received approval for creating Eritrea's first official nationalist political organization. The leaders then set a date for December 4 to meet in Keren to elect the leadership for their new association, the Eritrean Muslim League.

Conclusions

Between the arrival of British authorities in April 1941 and the opening of the Bet Giyorgis Conference in 1946, an emerging generation of pro-independence Muslim leaders across Eritrea began articulating the concerns of their respective communities through social, religious, and political activism in several unprecedented ways. Whether concentrated among the Tigre-speaking clans of the Western Province, within the confines of religious and educational institutions or among the urban intelligentsia, the broad if somewhat crude formation of a distinctly Eritrean identity among the region's various Muslim peoples began to emerge. Although a singular, politically unified "Muslim" community did not materialize, the intelligentsia that made up the bulk of Muslim leadership took important steps in forging community cohesion like never before. This basic cohesion helped propel activists into establishing the Eritrean Muslim League by late 1946.

Those who established the organization and continued to build a program for Muslim interests illustrated the significance of the three major transformations that took place within "Islamic" Eritrea in the early and mid-1940s. The push among tigre communities for emancipation from the traditional land system built a highly mobilized movement that developed into a viable political force. Simultaneously, the concern that Islamic practices and education had fallen into despair led members of the ulama to establish stronger institutions on behalf of the Muslim community as a whole. Concurrent with these two phenomena, the small but active Muslim elements that emerged within the MFH in 1941 continued to push for safeguards for their communities against both European administrators, and later, against the perceived pressure of the unionists aligned with the Ethiopian government. With the establishment of the league, each of these interrelated transformations took on deeper social significance as the Muslim League's political program solidified. Although the politicization of religion that manifested during late 1946 demonstrated the "temporary fission between urban Eritrean Muslims and urban Christians," it did little to thwart those activists who committed themselves to establishing an independent Eritrea through new political means.[111]

2

Founding Success

*The Muslim League and the Early Nationalist Movement,
November 1946–December 1947*

> Just as the sky does not have a pillar, the Muslim does not have
> a nation.
>
> —Popular joke within Eritrea's Unionist Party[1]

In late November 1946, the various factions among Eritrea's indigenous political, social, and educated elites gathered in an indoor compound at Bet Giyorgis, on the outskirts of Asmara, in hopes of finding a workable solution to the growing fragmentation between the pro-independence and pro-union camps within Mahber Fikri Hager. Instead, perceived attacks by the predominantly Christian unionist supporters precipitated a walkout by a number of Muslim attendees. Citing opposition to the supposed disdain that unionists had displayed toward the Muslim delegations, Ibrahim Sultan decried the "Christian conspiracy" at Bet Giyorgis as a meeting designed to "sell Eritrea to the wolf."[2] Soon after, he and other leaders planned to form their own political organization, the Eritrean Muslim League, to help secure pro-independence interests.

During this period two main ideas emerged that both the league's leadership and the affiliated Muslim intellectuals used to further their agendas. First, the league refined its basic argument that Muslim identity and rights would be compromised if Ethiopian authorities annexed Eritrea. Second, the league presented the case to international observers that Eritreans wished to develop their own nation-state and played to Western sympathies that Eritrea be given an opportunity to establish a "civilized" government to guard against the "backward" feudal system inherent to Ethiopian rule.

Fig. 2.1. A crowd of Muslim League supporters gathers in Keren, November 1947. Photograph by Kennedy Trevaskis. MSS, Brit. Emp. s. 365, box 180, file 3, folio 39.

Establishing the Eritrean Muslim League

With the blessing of Asmara's leading Islamic clergy and the official approval of the British Military Administration, pro-independence leaders convened an initial meeting in Keren in early December 1946 at the invitation of Sayyid Muhammad Abu Bakr al-Mirghani. Held at the residence of the late Sayyid Ja'far al-Mirghani, the meeting reflected the considerable diversity within the initial nationalist constituency. Those in attendance included representatives from four influential and sometimes transposable factions: the urban intelligentsia, tigre emancipation leaders, Islamic officials, and the "local dignitaries" of Keren, including members of the powerful al-Mirghani family and their affiliated khalifas. The meeting also included a small number of pro-independence Tigrinya Christian activists who later formed their own nationalist organization, the Liberal Progressive Party (LPP). Attendees elected their colleagues to positions in the Muslim League's executive council.[3] Although league leaders later guarded against being labeled a purely "Islamic" organization, the founding conference illustrated that activists sought to build upon their basic strengths as a political outlet for all Eritrean Muslims. With Ibrahim Sultan elected to the position of secretary general and wielding much of the actual executive authority, officials elected Sayyid Muhammad Abu Bakr al-Mirghani as league president. Although al-Mirghani himself did not carry much official power within the organization, his symbolic position and informal influence illustrated how the new organization planned to build the broadest degree of support under the banner of Islam.[4] Besides Sayyid Muhammad Abu Bakr's position, other members of the al-Mirghani family in Eritrea played a pivotal role in the league's initial development and its introduction "to the outside world," particularly in major cities like Kassala and Khartoum, where their influence carried tremendous weight.[5] Several months after the league's formation, the organization's officials praised al-Mirghani publicly for his initial role in "bringing Muslims together" at Keren and helping representatives address their concerns "under one accord."[6]

Although the league's first meeting did not constitute a mass gathering of all of Eritrea's diverse Muslim constituencies, those in attendance established three main objectives, which they later presented to their respective communities across the country to help draw support. The basic points included the mission to preserve the "territorial unity of Eritrea" as demarcated by Italian officials before 1935, to support and pursue the unconditional independence of Eritrea (if not immediately, then after a period of European trusteeship), and to outright refuse Eritrea's union with or annexation by Ethiopia or any other country.[7] Because the executive council included many of Eritrea's most influential religious and community leaders, the inclusion of these "important personalities" only gave added credibility to the organization and allowed its overall membership to swell during its initial months.[8]

Building League Membership across Eritrea

Between the founding meeting, on December 3, 1946, and its first official conference, in late January 1947, the league relied on these Muslim community leaders and members of the intelligentsia to build support at all levels of society. While some held official positions within the organization as presidents, vice presidents, and secretaries of the various branches, many of the organization's older members served as advisers to the league's relatively young leadership. Some veteran political leaders from Asmara's Muslim community, including Degiat Hassan 'Ali and Imam Musa Abdu, served as key links between the executive council and clerics in the major cities while other religious officials gave their own tacit support to the organization.

In particular, mufti Ibrahim al-Mukhtar worked closely with the organization's leadership. Having been consulted by several pro-independence activists before the league's official establishment, the mufti gave considerable moral support to their agenda and served as a voice of counsel. Even before the meeting at Bet Giyorgis, the mufti became increasingly apprehensive about what he saw as Ethiopian-supported "unionist ploys" to gain influence in Eritrea's political affairs and he encouraged the formation of a new political organization as a way to protect Muslim interests. More than a month before the league's founding, in late November 1946, Sayyid Muhammad Abu Bakr al-Mirghani sent a letter to the mufti requesting his presence for a future conference in which all Muslims of "opinion and influence" could exchange their views about Eritrea's future.[9] Although, according to Ismael al-Mukhtar, the mufti "was a very passionate nationalist, who was probably among the most knowledgeable on the intricacies of Eritrean politics," his position as the highest-ranking Islamic authority placed him in a delicate situation where his official duties did not allow him to take a public stance on political issues; consequently, he did not attend the league conference in Keren in January 1947.[10] He did, however, send his representative, Shaykh Idris Hussein Suleiman to give the league his blessing and support. In addition, the mufti included a brief speech to be read aloud to delegates. In his communication he noted that the quest for independence reflected the pride of Eritreans everywhere who wished to breathe life into a homeland of "freedom and equality." In addition to agreeing with the league's three founding aims from the early December meeting, he implored all Muslims to maintain unity in their political objectives.[11]

Throughout the league's first few months, the mufti carefully followed the developments through his close association with many top officials, including his brother Hajj Suleiman Ahmed Umar, Qadi 'Ali Umar 'Uthman, and his former student and league official Shaykh Yasin Mahmud Ba Tuq.[12] Expressing to league leaders his worries of the "imminent danger facing the country" from continued Ethiopian and pro-unionist interference, Ibrahim al-Mukhtar remained well informed of the organization's intentions and remained in close contact with the league's leadership, especially Asmara-based leaders Degiat Hassan 'Ali and Abdelkadir Kebire.[13] Consequently, the mufti's allegiance as an unofficial supporter became an invaluable tool for the league in gaining further legitimacy as an organization capable of speaking on behalf of Eritrea's Muslim communities.

Rural Support for the League

In the weeks after the December meeting, members of the executive council traveled from Keren and Asmara across the country to inform their communities about the new developments. Accordingly, participating "district members" within the towns and villages had the task of convening their own meetings to elect representatives for the first general Muslim League conference, planned for late January 1947. Although news of the meeting spread quickly in the major cities, league leaders also made great efforts to get the support and participation of rural communities. Initially, officials sponsored meetings in the private homes of party supporters, held discussions within mosques, and, occasionally, instructed supporters through written correspondence.[14] Hajj Abdel Hadi Hajji Beshir Se'id, a tailor based in the village of Korboria, in Akkele Guzay, noted that community leaders first received a telegram from the executive council in Keren instructing them how to organize their own league branch.[15]

Other members also noted that the league, in addition to merchant communities, received considerable support from Muslims in the villages, although many of those who joined did so because they allegedly believed that, based on its name, the league represented a purely religious organization.[16] In spite of the supposed misinformation, religious leaders took up the task of educating their respective communities.[17] In this crucial period, before the initial printing of the league's political tracts and official newspaper, rural participation developed through public preaching and informal information sessions with leaders. For example, one of the strongest early voices to emerge came from Qadi 'Ali Umar 'Uthman, the president of the league's Akkele Guzay branch. A former judge on Asmara's shari'a court of appeals, Qadi 'Uthman served as a powerful orator for the league's cause by appearing in mosques to disseminate information on the league's pro-independence position.[18] This also included political speeches at other "public" events, including weddings, funerals, and religious gatherings.[19] In addition to preaching against union with Ethiopia, some leaders took harsher measures to garner support, including shunning community members who refused to join the league. 'Ali Se'id Bekhit

Umar, a resident of Dekemhare, described how even well-respected community members could be shunned if they came out against the league: "Religious leaders were pressuring their pious followers to come to the aid of the party. When Ahmed Telsem joined the Unionist Party, it was agreed that no one would come to his funeral or participate in any event related to his personal happiness. However, we later went to his funeral but we did not partake of the meal."[20]

Reports of apparent coercion from Muslim leaders also surfaced later in the year with the appearance of additional political parties, especially from another emerging group with a Muslim-majority membership: the New Eritrea Pro-Italia Party (NEPIP).[21] In their public testimony before the Four Power Commission of Inquiry in November 1947, NEPIP representatives testified that the Muslim League had "always tried, through the religious/religious heads (Islamic clerics and Sufi leaders), to intimidate anybody who spoke on the future of Eritrea, endeavoring to impede their work," and thus they had tried to monopolize the wider political activities taking place across the region's rural Muslim villages.[22] Other critics claimed that members of the al-Mirghani family directly approached those leaders who intended to voice their support for other organizations and threatened them with excommunication.[23]

The ability of the league to reach deep into the social fabric of both urban and rural areas speaks to the effectiveness of the executive council in merging the league's political program with community interests as a whole. This program included both the perceived material gains and ideological rationale for joining the league. For many urban residents in cities such as Asmara and especially Massawa and its surrounding areas, the promise of an independent and vibrant merchant-driven economy contributed to the popular sentiment that the league could deliver greater prosperity through its pro-Independence program than if Eritrea became a region under Ethiopian control. In the more rural areas and particularly among many of the Tigre-speaking clans of the Western Province, the league's antifeudal stance, combined with promises of meaningful political and social reform, also helped attract support for the league's argument that it alone could safeguard Eritrean Muslims' well-being.

The organization's self-professed status as a defender of Muslim social and economic justice was no doubt strengthened by the fact that the executive council went to great lengths to showcase how Islamic religious leaders and officials formed an integral part of the organization. Indeed, many influential shaykhs and qadis oversaw key aspects of the organization, including "ratifying budgets and expenditures, summoning meetings and selecting [the] time and place of meetings, ensuring the execution of laws and resolutions" as well as "coordinating the affairs of the party and determining its internal organization and operation."[24] Community leaders also made a point of gathering necessary funds from among villagers.[25] Donations to the league, usually made in the form of foodstuffs, cattle, and other payments in kind helped build the organization's resources, while urban residents usually provided direct cash donations and contributed raw materials and even office supplies.[26] These activities contributed to the rapid mobilization of the league's constituency that materialized when an estimated seven thousand representatives congregated in Keren on January 20 and 21, 1947, for the league's first general meeting.[27]

"National Participation" in the January Conference

Unlike the initial gathering the previous December, the January conference represented the first truly national meeting of Eritrea's Muslim communities. Because much of the league's program had yet to be drawn up, its vaguely nationalistic position drew a wide cross-section of representatives. Coordinated by the executive council, the two-day meeting heard testimonies from most of the major subfactions and ethnocultural groups across the country, including those from the major cities, "tribal leaders" from the villages, and representatives from various groups of tigre activists and shumagulle. Significantly, the meeting also included the presence of many of the leading pro-nationalist Christian figures from the Eritrean central highlands who had come to show their support for the league's cause. Their attendance marked the beginning of a long and cordial relationship between the league and progressive Christian nationalists. With the input and participation of these various groups, league elders set to work on finalizing their organization's statutes and the basic political program. In total, the league passed seven resolutions at the conclusion of the conference:

1. Eritrea should not be partitioned under any circumstances but stay as one united country.

2. The achievement of complete Eritrean Independence. However, if this is not possible because of a lack of basic education [political

readiness], the Eritrean people should have internal independence and remain under the trusteeship of Britain or the UN for a period of ten years. When these ten years have passed, immediate independence should be granted unconditionally.

3. The immediate aspirations of the Eritrean people are education and advancement. So until now, they have not wanted to place their property and circumstances with a government they do not know. Therefore, it is not the desire of the Eritrean people to be united with Ethiopia or any other country.

4. The Muslim League [Association of Muslims] of Eritrea calls on their brothers who reside outside Eritrea to be united and come back to their land and their country.

5. Any issue concerning full independence or trusteeship should be discussed and debated by those educated and wise people that are selected.

6. If it is not possible to achieve full independence, the country that administers Eritrea under trusteeship should be observed and monitored by the UN.

7. The People's Association of the Muslim League will present the drafted constitution to their Christian counterparts, hoping the two parties will discuss and be bound together by it.[28]

In each of the resolutions, league authorities demonstrated that their organization represented far more than an exclusively Islamic political association concerned solely with Eritrea's independence. At the core of its many official aims, the league sought to build on the growing sense of Eritreaness that had developed during the previous years of BMA rule. The league's founding statutes provide an important overview of how the leadership tried to integrate its program as a vehicle for wider social reform. While the executive council served as the guiding body on a national level, the provincial committees were a more direct reflection of grassroots political involvement. Twelve members were elected to each provincial council, and representatives had the right to choose their representatives by a majority public vote among its members and also to have meetings with the executive council upon request.

What is also striking about the league's initial statutes is the leadership's insistence that members of the provincial committees strive to "learn the views of personalities, chiefs and notables of the Moslem

League before taking any decision, merely to be conversant with their ideas."[29] In truth, such early edicts reflected the league's penchant for top-down organization that would prove problematic in subsequent years, when leaders faced growing resentment from among the grass roots about its overall direction. Yet the emphasis on building a more educated and critical membership at this early stage reflected the league's standing as an inherently intellectual organization whose leadership extended its activities from the political realm to broader cultural concerns among the public. The most effective means of facilitating public enthusiasm for defending Eritrean autonomy and addressing other community concerns came from the pages of the league's official newsletter, *Sawt al-rabita al-islamiyya* (Voice of the Muslim League).

Nationalist Discourse and *Sawt al-rabita*

Nearly a month after league representatives adjourned from the Keren conference, members of the executive council secured one of their major organizational aims by establishing their own Arabic-language publication, *Sawt al-rabita al-islamiyya,* in February 1947.[30] Originally managed by Bashir Osman Bashir and edited by Shaykh Yasin Ba Tuq and Shaykh Muhammad 'Uthman Hayuti, the Asmara-based writers established the weekly Arabic newsletter to serve as an outlet for the growing activism.[31] Although its publishers often faced financial difficulty and periodically ceased publication, the newsletter made an immediate impact on building the league as a national entity.[32] Beyond addressing immediate political concerns, the newsletter also represented the most significant outlet for the larger intellectual debates taking shape among the Arabic-literate public.

In a redaction that appeared in the newsletter's first edition on February 25, Muhammad 'Uthman Hayuti welcomed the participation of Eritreans of all faiths and viewpoints to contribute their opinions, even those who shared different positions from the league's. He remarked that the organization supported such contributions in part because the league's ideology and political decisions were not based "solely on considering the benefits to Muslims" and that the organization wished to take into account Christian citizens' concerns to help support a "common national interest." Eritrea's most prominent Muslim leaders lent their support to the new tract. Shaykh Hussein

Alamin, Degiat Hassan 'Ali, and Ibrahim al-Mukhtar each contributed pieces in the inaugural issue that addressed concerns within Eritrea's Muslim communities. Echoing Hayuti's spirit of solidarity with Eritreans of all faiths, 'Ali wrote that besides building solidarity with "Muslims around the world," the newsletter would be used for "strengthening the bilateral understanding between our Christian brothers, with whom we are connected in our national interest and economic and social responsibilities."[33]

Eritrea as a "Modern" Society

Many league officials used the newsletter in an attempt to demonstrate the tangible nature of their movement for Eritrean identity. The league's intelligentsia established the basic discourse on how to achieve sovereignty and the terms on which an independent Eritrean society should be based: "Eritrea can manage its affairs economically, but the essentials of ultimate independence have to be founded with the cultural, social and ethical requirements that without them cannot exist. It is essential that the children of this country are capable and possess the qualities that reflect the maturity of a political conscience so that they can take responsibility for administering the nation by themselves."[34]

Other contributors emphasized that Eritrean independence depended on the ability of all Muslims to strengthen their civic activism. Muhammad 'Uthman Hayuti warned that without establishing an autonomous government that included the "participation of all elements," Eritrea's leaders would not be able to manage the complex "matters of the age." He claimed that the league had assumed a major responsibility in trying to guarantee the rights, livelihood, and happiness of "every Muslim who is faithful to his homeland" and that the "momentum of national feeling" needed to be supported by a serious commitment among the Muslim leadership.[35]

In the commentary sections of *Sawt al-rabita*, contributors also equated Muslim education as a national priority on par with rejecting Ethiopian influence. Shaykh Muhammad Said Abu encouraged Muslim youth to explore their "interest in knowledge" because he believed in education as a foundation of progress that ultimately represented the "renaissance of all nations and peoples."[36] Yasin Ba Tuq argued that independence stood little chance of becoming a reality unless authorities made education readily available to "all categories of the public." He affirmed that taking an interest in the sciences and culture remained an essential goal if they wished to truly "reform the society" as a new country.[37] Several issues also featured commentaries addressed directly to Muslim youth, imploring them to attend the many newly built Islamic schools and work toward becoming functioning professionals for a new independent state. In other instances, students themselves published op-ed commentaries. One of the more notable pieces, by Abdel Nebi Muhammad Ibra Haqus, a student from Asmara's King Farouk Islamic Institute, expressed disappointment that "many parents do not send their children to the schools" and that unlike many Muslim schools, Christian schools had a far greater student enrollment and held an academic advantage that threatened the political future of all Muslims.[38]

As 1947 progressed, additional voices of concern emerged and argued that the league needed to guard against all possible threats to Muslim sovereignty. Shaykh Muhammad Nurhussein contended that, beyond the need to strengthen education, the league needed to protect Muslims both from the "dictatorship of the Ethiopian government" and the "silence of the international community." He argued that while Eritrea's Christian population had "never suffered from the repression" of Ethiopian rule, Muslims had long faced threats to their language and religious traditions.[39]

One of the most significant aspects of this growing activism within the pages of *Sawt al-rabita* included promoting the virtues of an independent nation-state to redress the perceived shortcomings within Eritrean society. Some of the most substantive calls for independence from Ethiopia relied on a defense of a "modern" Eritrean nation-state and the relationship between national progress and the fulfillment of Islamic ideals:

> Now we need to ask, what is the best way for reform or treatment? No doubt that sociologists in their search for treatment of social diseases have reached ways and theories that can protect societies from the dangers that surround them. They have also researched many of the theories that the Qur'an discusses. So if we want reform and morality, we have to take the responsibility put on our shoulders, and before everything, we have to start educating ourselves, because education is the best thing in this awakening. No nation can reach a more advanced stage of development if they do not have education and cultural knowledge.[40]

At a less abstract level, supporters argued that the Muslim League could serve as a tool for activists in establishing a functioning state that could succeed. In a commentary titled "Our Ministers Are Writing with Scissors," league member Mahmud Nurhussein Berhanu criticized many of Eritrea's unionist leaders for their "weak hearts" in taking many of the league's public statements out of context. He instead focused on justifying why Eritrean Muslims, as with cultural and religious groups in other societies, had the fundamental right to pursue social progress through an independent state. After defining a state as a group of people connected by common objectives, certain geographic ties, and a particular political tradition, Berhanu asked rhetorically of his critics, "What is the difference between the state [in other societies] that represents them and the league that represents us?"[41]

Echoing Berhanu's argument, 'Ali Muhammad Hassan, a league representative from the Tigre-speaking 'Ad Shaykh group, argued that a nation "was based on many things" and that, specifically for Muslims, their faith represented the cornerstone of national identity on which other aspects, including "language, rights, science, arts, traditions, history, shared pains of the past, and shared desires of the future" could be used to cement a national identity.[42] He went on to assert the guiding significance of Islam in the pursuit of national sovereignty: "It is apparent to the Muslim that the bigger nation is his Islam. In Islam is his happiness, pride, and glory. And he cannot be changed and he ought to protect his nation, because that is his duty to his ancestors, who fought and bore pain in order to protect it [the nation] for the Muslim individual and his fellow believers."[43]

Arguments in favor of establishing an Eritrean nation-state thus became increasingly intertwined with the rationale that only a new state could guarantee Muslim rights. Ahmed Abdelkarim, a league member from Massawa, proclaimed that "as long as there is respect for justice and humanity, a nation's self-determination is a right for everyone." He continued, "Our wishes and desires as Eritrean Muslims are that we live free and that we do not want to tie our destiny to a nation that we do not [already] have any ties with, such as Ethiopia."[44]

The nationalist language that league members employed changed little when representatives finally made their appeals directly to members of the international community charged with deciding Eritrea's fate. When representatives of the Four Power Commission of Inquiry

arrived in Eritrea, in November 1947, league members harked back
to the fundamental incompatibility between Eritrea's Muslim populations with a political system in which "the influence of the Church
over the Government of Ethiopia" by definition reduced Muslims to
second-class citizenship:

> A Muslem [*sic*] does not have the right to be equal to a
> Coptic Ethiopian or to fill an administrative vacancy of any
> nature. A government that goes ahead, under such religious
> influences to this extent cannot be allowed to rule over the
> lands of others, and if progressive civilization is being en-
> trusted to Civilized Countries, that have taken the obligation
> to protect the high principles of life and social justice, then it
> is their DUTY not to throw away the people of this country
> to the feet of Ethiopia.[45]

Indeed, fears about the conditions of Muslims within Ethiopia were
often a rallying point for arguing against any form of political union.
In private correspondence with his colleague Muhammad Nurhussein, the president of the league's Asmara branch, Abdelkadir Kebire,
confided that he and others had long worried about the situation of
the more than ten million Ethiopian Muslims who had become "mute
and powerless" under Ethiopian rule.[46]

Throughout 1947, league writers went to great lengths to illustrate
how the Ethiopian government historically refused to concern itself
with the welfare of its Muslim subjects. One league supporter argued
that Ethiopian indifference revealed itself immediately after the defeat
of the Italian army, in 1941, when "the Ethiopian government did
not include a single mosque when they gave money to rebuild many
of the churches in Ethiopia and Eritrea damaged in World War II."
According to league proponents, proof that the government did not
care about "Islamic issues" was also evident in Ethiopia's curtailing of
Arabic-language education, instead imposing Amharic instruction on
residents and reducing "the overall number of Muslims in their cen-
sus."[47] League writers also addressed the protection of Muslim rights
in different ways. One of the most effective campaigns included a push
by writers to place their struggle in a broader, international context.
Thus, many of the league's leading writers enriched the nature of the
nationalist contact zone by essentially internationalizing the movement. By framing Eritrean Muslims' struggle as simply part of the
broader quest for independence in the post–World War II period,

the league began a process in which its membership constructed new understandings about the role of Muslim "identity" that carried the political debate well beyond Eritrea's borders. As a result, these discussions took place within a nationalist contact zone that began to break out from its previous incarnation. While Eritrea's Muslim intellectuals had long promoted the idea of religious freedom and equal representation in politics for the country's various ethnic groups, the league's new emphasis on internationalism demonstrated a significant shift within the overall dialogue.

Sawt al-rabita and the Wider World

As international debate over Eritrea's political future increased throughout 1947, Muslim League officials increasingly framed their struggle as part of the wave of nationalism spreading across the world after World War II. Many articles provided reports on political uprisings in Syria, Somalia, and elsewhere across the Islamic world. The Somali independence movement received particular focus in the league's publications; writers often framed the struggle of their "Somali brothers" as a parallel development among the Muslim peoples of the two former Italian colonies. As one commentary asserted, "the political movements [within Eritrea and Somalia] express the alertness of the spirit of conscience among all Muslim nations spreading from the Indian Ocean to the Red Sea."[48] Yet of all the emerging international political developments, Muslim League writers showed particular interest in Pakistan's fortunes. Many league writers focused on how increased levels of formal education and Arabic-language training were helping promote Pakistani national unity across the new country.[49] In later years, as the league began addressing more direct threats to Muslim security from unionist supporters, developments in Pakistan received even greater coverage among commentators who tried to build momentum for the league's cause by highlighting Pakistan's successes.[50]

During deliberations on Eritrea's future at the UN General Assembly, the league began publishing a series of articles documenting the wide range of support that Eritrea's cause had received from other Muslim nations at the General Assembly, including Syria, Saudi Arabia and Pakistan. Some officials, including *Sawt al-rabita* editor Yasin Ba Tuq, traveled abroad during the UN debate and presented Eritrea's case, warning audiences throughout the Middle East and South Asia about the "crime of Ethiopian occupation."[51] Other leaders, particularly Abdelkadir Kebire, also used the newsletter to write about Eritrean independence in the context of regional political movements. According to Warka Solomon, Abdelkadir Kebire's political leanings were heavily influenced by many of the political figures he came in contact with while working as an Italian civil servant in Yemen (1930–34), including figures like Palestinian mufti Amin al-Husseini, Syrian writer Hashim al-Atassi, and others.[52]

Beyond emphasizing Muslim identity as a fundamental element needed in constructing an independent Eritrea, many league activists went on the offensive to use the nationalist cause to help break down the previous legacy of "tribalism" between different Muslim groups. The emphasis on a singular community became one of the major strategies that league writers employed to encourage Muslim unity. In other instances, the paper promoted the activities of other emerging Muslim organizations, such as the Society for Cultural Cooperation, an association that held fund-raisers and promoted events and lectures for Muslim residents in the major cities.[53] Through all these emerging initiatives, league activists developed a nationalist platform while articulating the need for drastic social reform to achieve independence. The proliferation of *Sawt al-rabita* had a tremendous influence on changing the political discourse of the emerging nationalist contact zone. Extending beyond calls for independence and emphasizing the inherent autonomy of Eritrean society, league authorities used the growing Arabic media to present Eritrean independence as a struggle similar to movements among other indigenous peoples. The Muslim League thus expanded the parameters of the nationalist contact zone by using emerging outlets of indigenous knowledge to articulate the shared interests of all Eritrea's Muslims, as well as to incorporate nationalist trends from the wider Islamic world.[54] Complementing these growing trends in the league's outreach efforts, a sizable number of students and Muslim youth also were drawn to the organization during its initial months.

Broad Participation in the League: Muslim Youth

As regional support for the league's cause increased, Muslim youth also began taking an interest in political mobilization. Tesfai notes that Muslim youth had a significant presence even at the outset of the league's creation, explaining that although many of them did not possess a "deep knowledge" about the organization and its inner workings, "they were all highly affected by the political environment." Several hundred youths from every province were also invited to observe the league's first national conference, in Keren. Afterward, support to create a separate wing specifically for Muslim youth gained momentum.[55]

Despite the early interest among the public to form a youth association, the branch's creation was largely due to Abdelkadir Kebire, who sought to engage the country's youth in the growing mobilization. Having witnessed the relative success of unionist supporters in tapping into the mainly urban Christian youth, Kebire sought to instill a greater sense of purpose for the Muslim students, who were now watching their elders within the independence struggle.[56] Eventually, Muslim League representatives established Shuban al-rabita (the Youth Association) in May 1947 after a meeting in Asmara's Red Sea Pearl Hotel.[57]

Responsibility for running the new organization fell mainly to Muhammad Se'id Aberra, Kebire's son-in-law. Besides serving as its first president, Aberra also used his family's commercial resources to help build the association into a viable organization that could serve and protect the interests of the league's elders.[58] With the assistance of other high-ranking youth leaders such as Se'id Sfaf and Mahmud Umar, the Youth Association quickly took on a major role in most of the league's affairs, and its members were charged with the responsibility to "organize demonstrations, mass mobilizations," and to ensure the "distribution of different pamphlets, booklets, leaflets etc. and dissemination of the party's objective through campaigns."[59] Following Shuban al-rabita's creation, many Jabarti families in Asmara stepped up their logistical support for the new wing. The Kusmallah brothers, as they had done previously for Muslim students, used their resources to assist the association and offered their storage compound in Geza Berhanu to allow local youth to gather for meetings and practice drilling exercises.[60] While Youth Association representatives also worked to expand membership, the most practical function involved serving as a security force to protect league members from supposed unionist aggression.[61]

As early as February 1947, BMA reports noted the steady rise in politically motivated attacks against Muslim residents, especially in Asmara. A particular cause for concern involved the fact that many of the "attacks" were actually instances where unionist Eritrean police constables had abused their power to physically harm or imprison those who identified themselves as league members.[62] Consequently, members of the Youth Association (or the Brotherhood, as they called themselves) became responsible for protecting league facilities, meetings, and those within the leadership most often targeted by unionists.[63] Thus, the Youth Association served as the principal security force, guarding meetings with sticks and swords. In particular, Muhammad Se'id Aberra put great effort into recording acts of aggression and other slights against league supporters. His major concerns included unionist influence within Asmara's police force and the financial support that unionist youth supporters in the city received from the Ethiopian Liaison Office. In keeping with the basic attitudes of the league's senior leadership, Aberra argued that unionist supporters represented "the worst enemies of the Moslems" and added that "the promises of equality made by the Ethiopian government certainly conceal their real plans—which aim at the suppression of the Islamic religion."[64] Often, the Youth Association's direct exposure to the urban unrest and abuses by the Eritrean police allowed its members to provide up-to-date information on events to the executive council.

In public, the Youth Association presented itself as a highly mobile and disciplined force. Most accounts also indicate that the organization actually served as one of the more open forums for participation in nationalist politics. In particular, the Youth Association seems to have provided a means for the wider involvement of Muslim youth in political activism, even, in some rare cases, for Muslim women.

Women's Participation in the Muslim League

Overall, the political role of Muslim women in early nationalist politics has been extremely difficult to assess. Almost universally, women's participation in the Muslim League has been dismissed as nonexistent. Ibrahim Sultan himself commented that women had no role whatsoever among the league or its supporters.[65] When questioned in public about women's involvement in the league, many former members simply stated that shari'a law did not allow their participation, in addition to the fact that most fathers had forbidden their daughters from taking part in any kind of public activity.[66] Owing to the general cultural climate and gender constraints in 1940s Eritrea, and among Muslim groups in particular, female political participation seems to have at best manifested itself as auxiliary support.

Most observers have noted that women were often responsible for sewing Youth Association members' uniforms, flags, and banners as well as preparing meals for meetings and other public gatherings. Beyond these basic contributions, the record of women's involvement leaves many unanswered questions. The Muslim League leadership's attitudes on the participation of women were perhaps best captured during an exchange between representatives from the Four Power Commission and league delegates in Asmara in late 1947. When the commission's Soviet representative asked the six league delegates in attendance about the duties and role of women in the league's political affairs, they responded curtly, "Women have no say in such matters, the men speak for them."[67] Nevertheless, some instances of more direct participation did occur. According to Hajj Ibrahim Otban Ahmed, an organizer for the Youth Association in Akkele Guzay Province during the late 1940s, many of the unmarried girls between the ages of fourteen and sixteen participated in Youth Association–sponsored marches in towns such as Adi Keyh and Ghinda. Accordingly, the girls joined in the chanting against Ethiopian rule with slogans such as "The flag of Habesha [Ethiopia] is burned" and "Long live the Eritrean Muslim League."[68] Thus, while Muslim women's official participation in the organization proved minimal, the few who did involve themselves appear to have supported the organization's basic aims.[69]

Ultimately, further research is needed to determine whether this initial nonparticipation indicated support, disapproval, or simply an acquiescence to their circumstances and cultural constraints.[70] Nevertheless, the Youth Association's attempts to branch off and attract the participation of such diverse groups illustrate how its supporters embraced the basic aims of the league's leadership in arguing that independence depended on unifying all segments of society, not simply the youth and elders, but also among Muslims and Christians.

League Support for Muslim-Christian Cooperation

In spite of Ibrahim Sultan's earlier contention that Christian unionist leaders betrayed Eritrea's Muslim groups at Bet Giyorgis, the league's establishment was, in large part, a compromise that addressed the need for political protection for Muslims and a guarantee of the continuation of the religious unity established years earlier within the MFH. Woldeab Woldemariam also addressed this dilemma in a commentary within *Nay Ertra semunawi gazzetta*, claiming that if there had only been a true "spirit of understanding with humility" among the delegates at Bet Giyorgis, the formation of separate organizations like the Muslim League and the LPP may not have even been necessary.[71] Yet even as Eritrea's political factions were increasingly politicized by religious differences during late 1946 and 1947, Ibrahim Sultan and other Muslim League leaders strove for a harmonious relationship with their Christian nationalist peers.[72]

Officials often implemented policy with the hope that observers would view the league as an association that embraced the cultural and religious pluralism within Eritrean society. Indeed, the league's resolution to adopt both Tigrinya and Arabic as its official languages represented a gesture to "demonstrate that it was a nationalist party," even though it was overwhelmingly composed of Muslims who did not speak Tigrinya as a first language.[73] Resisting unionist characterizations, the league's leadership argued that their organization already possessed a strong legacy of joint Muslim-Christian political cooperation, best illustrated by the partnership of Ibrahim Sultan and Woldeab Woldemariam, the Tigrinya Christian nationalist leader. British officials also took note during late 1946 and early 1947 that "the present state of affairs points to a merging of the Moslem League with those Coptic Christians who are unwilling to accept union with Ethiopia."[74]

Although many of the MFH's Christian members eventually joined with Eritrea's unionist camp after the regional Christian leadership's alliance with the Ethiopian government "changed the equilibrium in favor of pro-union sentiments," Woldeab and a small group from among the urban intelligentsia began pushing a nationalist platform.[75] After both the formation of the league and Woldeab's LPP, in February 1947, members who had formed the nucleus of the MFH continued to work together from within their new respective organizations. Following the league's first conference, in January 1947, Ibrahim Sultan affirmed that Muslim and Christians were "brothers and children of the same homeland" and independence could be achieved by coming together and embracing each other's "culture, religion, habits, and customs."[76] Interfaith cooperation also developed into one of the major criteria for entry into the league's membership. Beyond an individual's personal courage and efficiency, a representative's election to the party was based largely on his ability to build strong alliances with Christians, Italians, "half-castes," and other groups.[77] Under the banner of Islam, many league leaders used their credentials as Muslim scholars to remind followers that

their faith demanded "the liberty of all people without distinction between them by race or ethnicity" and that such freedom represented
"the founding principal of humanity by prohibiting the despotism of
the powerful against the oppressed."[78]

The league's executive council led by example to cultivate Christian
allegiance and supported the agenda of its sister organization, the LPP.
At the LPP's inaugural ceremony, in late February 1947, its president,
Ras Tessema Asberom, echoed the spirit of unity by proclaiming that
Eritrea had belonged to both religions "for thousands of years" and
that "we [Christians and Muslims] have lived in harmony with our
respective religions and helped each other."[79] The LPP's ideology of
an unconditionally independent Eritrea, although different from the
Muslim League's support for a period of European trusteeship, helped
cement mutual support between the organizations' respective leadership. Ibrahim Sultan, Abdelkadir Kebire, and other Muslim League
officials even made a point of attending the LPP's founding ceremony
as a sign of solidarity.[80] The executive council thus promoted religious
plurality as an integral component of its program by highlighting the
appeal of independence for *all* Eritreans.

Officials within the LPP were also proactive and "outspoken in their
demands" for independence, as well as in establishing their alliance
with the Muslim League. Ruth Iyob cited the testimony of Azmatch
Berhe Gebrekidan, vice president of the LPP's Serae Province branch,
who derided unionists for falsely proclaiming that all nationalist
Christians had "converted to Islam."[81] Even BMA officials could not
deny the strong message of religious unity between the league and
the LPP.[82] Concerns over maintaining religious camaraderie are also
evident in many of the private testimonies of Muslim League officials.
Writing to his colleague Muhammad Nurhussein, Abdelkadir Kebire
elaborated on the organization's rationale for Eritrean unity: "It is
not our purpose to dominate the Christians of our home country or
to expand the Muslim religion. The purpose is to reject, in all conditions, the supported statement of Ethiopian federation. Since Allah,
the Listener and the Knower, has given us the power of reasoning,
how do we stand united with the deceiver and colonizer Ethiopia?"[83]

Kebire's concerns help illustrate how leaders from within the league
made political overtures to Christian nationalists without reservation
that their gestures would be seen as detrimental to Muslim interests.
By and large, Islamic religious leaders, including both those within
the executive council and the general membership, recognized the

importance of this rich legacy of Muslim-Christian interaction and used it to their advantage as political activism developed throughout 1947. From the perspective of many within the organization's hierarchy, part of being a pious Muslim meant working with non-Muslims for the betterment of society.[84] Several league representatives even claimed, however incorrectly, that an overwhelming majority of "Hamasien Christians" belonged to the LPP and thus only a fraction of Christians didn't support the goal of independence.[85] While the league may have embellished the LPP's numbers, both organizations' leaders often viewed themselves as simply two branches of a wider nationalist consortium. Some league members even claimed that they heard Ras Tessema Asberom say on several occasions that he wished the Muslim League had never adopted its "Muslim" marker because it misconstrued its meaning and therefore could be used by unionists to encourage further division.[86] According to scholar Gaim Kibreab, the Muslim League label actually gave a false impression to the wider public by inferring that the organization represented only Muslim interests, when in fact "its sole intention was the establishment of a secular Eritrean state where Muslims and Christians would live harmoniously as they had always done in the past."[87] Yet while most within the league's leadership may have indeed believed in developing a state in which religious differences would not take precedence in the political process, the general mood among the organization's middle and lower ranks demonstrates that the "Muslim" emphasis within the organization's name represented far more than simply the adoption of a strategic label. The sheer level of support among both the Islamic clergy and disenfranchised Muslim groups across the country calls into question the accuracy of the claim that the organization truly stood for developing a "secular" state. While it may have had such sponsors in its upper echelons, grassroots concerns also influenced how the organization eventually adopted its position that Islamic practices and religious institutions needed to be at the very least protected and, ideally, even promoted in any future independent Eritrean government.

Regardless, social and political camaraderie between Muslims and pro-independence Christians was an integral part of the league's organizational philosophy. Aside from their rhetoric and public support for each other's endeavors, both organizations linked themselves in more concrete ways. Both adopted the same flag, which featured a half-green, half-red background against which a scale in equilibrium signals the equality of Islam and Christianity. The spirit of this religious accord was eloquently captured in the league's anthem, "Peace Be upon You, Flag of Eritrea":

> *Peace be upon you, flag of Eritrea*
> *Al-Rabita al-Islamiyya at the center of Asmara*
> *Consulting with her sister, the freedom seeker [LPP]*
> *Let her flag wave in the center of her country*
> *With her greenish hips and red lips*
> *Her strong mission like a bridge with a scale at her core*
> *Bringing both Christians and Muslims together*
> *At daybreak, she went down to Massawa*
> *She crossed through the Red Sea and came into sight of Assab*
> *Climbed up to Senafe*
> *Stopped by Adi-Keyh, saying, "hear me out"*
> *Toured Emni Hajer, Tessenei, and Barentu*
> *And she said she wouldn't leave behind Agordat, Keren, and Nakfa*
> *Whoever distances themselves from her or sees her as trivial*
> *Will not see our country developed.*[88]

Indeed, the idea that independence was a joint Muslim-Christian venture was a potent reality for league leaders, who came of age during the earlier part of the decade and had seen how unionist authorities used sectarian differences to weaken the nationalist movement.

Muslim League Protests

The six-month anniversary of the founding of the Muslim League, in June 1947, represented both the highpoint of the early nationalist movement and the most vivid illustration of the league's ability to arouse public enthusiasm. Planned in the wake of unionist demonstrations that took place the previous May, the league organized pro-independence activities in more than a dozen cities on Tuesday, June 10, 1947. Claiming to also be responding to the alleged harassment from Ethiopian-supported unionists, the executive council—through the Youth Association representatives—coordinated the protests to demonstrate that the league represented the "majority of the inhabitants who affirmed the claim of independence and rejected any incorporation or union with Ethiopia."[89] With the participation of Islamic clerics, council members, and energetic groups within the recently established the Youth Association, protesters filled city streets shouting slogans and carrying banners in support of independence. Demonstrations in Keren, Asmara, and Agordat each attracted more than five thousand people while other cities featured several thousand participants and an array of public proclamations from league officials.[90] In his own estimation, Abdelkadir Kebire believed that the protests across the country had "no resemblance in past history" and in his speech before an Asmara crowd, Kebire told supporters that the protests marked Eritrea's most "memorable day."[91] Elaborating on the protests' significance and the league's role in organizing them, he boasted that the demonstrations represented the day that the majority of Eritrean people "woke up and stood up to claim their existence and declare that they want one thing and nothing else, and they articulate that in two words; there is no third word: Freedom [and] Independence."[92]

Beyond the brazen and often idealistic arguments for independence, most of the official speakers at the demonstrations stressed the need to build unity between Eritrea's Muslim groups within the confines of a new nation by securing self-determination. Ahmed Abdelkarim, a league representative from Massawa, spoke about the independence struggle as a path toward achieving "natural rights" for all Muslims:

> We want independence and we call for freedom. We call for our natural right, a right that no force on Earth can keep from us. As long as there is respect for justice and humanity, a nation's self-determination is a right for everyone. Our wishes and desires as Eritrean Muslims are that we live free and that we do not want to tie our destiny with a nation with which we have nothing in common, like Ethiopia.[93]

While the league facilitated much of the activities for the occasion, the June 10 protests also featured substantial participation from the LPP. As a whole, the June protests illustrated on a grassroots level what its leadership had articulated since its founding. Although the league called for both political unity and the need to protect all Eritrean Muslims, its members did not present themselves as having an inherently religious cause. Even BMA officials recognized this strategy: "In the latest demonstrations of the M.L. the placards carried were purely political, denouncing union with Ethiopia and demanding independence of Eritrea. The flags which they carried were those of the four great powers as well as Moslem banners. The M.L.

knew its greatest strength & held its biggest demonstrations after it had declared its political policy."[94]

The significance of Muslim League and LPP cooperation during the protests should not be overlooked, particularly when noting that the LPP included not only many of Eritrea's most influential Tigrinya-speaking Christian intellectuals, but that it also commanded respectable numbers in the supposed unionist strongholds in the Eritrean highlands. Even the relatively conservative BMA estimates placed support for the LPP at 30 percent of the population in Akkele Guzay and Serae Provinces.[95] Public support also extended into politics in other meaningful ways. 'Ali Se'id Bekit Umar noted that some league members in the rural areas of Akkele Guzay and Hamasien publicly changed their affiliation to LPP to protect themselves from anti-Muslim unionist attacks. For their part, LPP leaders proved more than willing to protect their Muslim colleagues; Ras Tessema Asberom allegedly used his own automobile to safely transport members of the league's Youth Association to the various towns across Hamasien and Akkele Guzay.[96] This initial logistical cooperation between the LPP and the league continued in later months even as confrontations with unionist supporters intensified. As with its support for interreligious cooperation, the league's leadership continually branched out by tapping into wider movements for social reform during its first year of existence. While it secured its support base and furthered its partnership with the LPP, the league continued to make strides in addressing the issue dearest to many of its constituents: the push for permanent tigre emancipation.

Tigre Emancipation and Eritrean Sovereignty

The Muslim League's creation, in late 1946, developed, in part, as a result of Eritrean nationalists' investment in what Jordan Gebre-Medhin called the "new confidence of the serfs" as well as the growing political cohesion among Muslims as a whole.[97] The emphasis on empowering those most oppressed within the traditional social structures of western Eritrea was not lost on either league leaders or BMA authorities as the nationalist movement widened. In July 1947, Kennedy Trevaskis reflected on the surge of grassroots popularity of the league in connection with the tigre issue: "I made the mistake of expecting political leadership, if it came at all, to come from the chiefs.

In fact it came in the first instance from the huge mass of serf or subject classes which remain in a state of political & partial economic subjugation to the small aristocratic ruling groups of the Northern & Western Eritrean tribes."[98]

Indeed, the establishment of the Muslim League came at almost the exact time Ibrahim Sultan gained his broadest support for tigre emancipation and for British promises of intervention in the clan restructuring proposal.[99] According to Kibreab, Sultan and his supporters' later success in working with the BMA and the shumagulle by "resurrecting [the] social organizations" of traditional tigre society could not have been achieved without the legacy of the "deeply embedded social organization that was inherited from the past" and the subsequent contributions of many sympathetic members of the Muslim clergy in helping resolve the conflict.[100] This inheritance was linked to the considerable activism of Muslim leaders among the tigre, including Ibrahim Sultan's colleagues in cities such as Keren and Agordat, who used their religious authority, much as Muslim businessmen used their economic influence, to shape the negotiations with BMA officials and quell the uprising.[101] In the midst of these social transformations, wider forces were at work that soon helped dramatically shift the speed and aims of the nationalist movement.

Delegates from Britain, France, the United States, and the Soviet Union had first convened talks in London in September 1945 to discuss the future of Italy's former colonial territories. Only when representatives faced an impasse at the follow-up conference in Paris, in April 1946, did they agree to deploy a fact-finding commission to ascertain the political attitudes in the former colonies. In the case of Eritrea, the aptly named Four Power Commission finally arrived in early November 1947 and remained in country through the rest of the year. Having worked closely with the commission in planning the visit, many of the presiding BMA officers, including some officials who also served as commission members themselves, set up public hearings in approximately a dozen major cities and towns as a way to help facilitate the inquiries. Meanwhile, the Muslim League, LPP, UP, and the recently formed NEPIP prepared their representatives for the meetings.[102] With the arrival of the Four Power Commission, each major town and city where representatives convened their inquiries became flashpoints of political activism and civil unrest. Not surprisingly, the ongoing issue of tigre emancipation emerged with increased vigor before the international observers. Yet even well before the commission's arrival, the league had already done its part to keep the issue in the public consciousness.

The tone within *Sawt al-rabita* supports the idea that league members, even those from outside the Western Province, were genuinely sympathetic to the plight of the tigre. The newsletter's first edition mentioned the circumstances from which the need for the league came about, stating that the organization represented a "compromise" that resulted from discussions between dispossessed serfs, religious leaders, and merchants. Within the newsletter, writers and activists often brought up the tigre emancipation issue and sometimes even ridiculed those shumagulle who took exception to the league's agenda. For example, league members heavily criticized Diglal Gailani Hussien Pasha when he, as a shumagulle (*nabtab*) from the Beni-Amer renounced his allegiance to the league and joined the UP in late 1947.[103] Most commentators argued that his departure came about not because of any sincere political concerns, but rather his worry that he would eventually lose his lands and feudal dues in the event of independence. One writer, Ahmed Muhammad Ibrahim al-Tigrawi, argued that the existence of any of the shumagulle in an independent Eritrea was equivalent to a "plague" being cast upon the country's citizens.[104]

A group of designated tigre representatives later echoed this criticism before the commission. In a memorandum sent to the commission in early November 1947, activists from the Western Province claimed that with regard to the conditions under shumagulle rule, "a population of a half million souls is subjected to the will of 1,000 parasites."[105] Besides containing an identical political platform to the one that the league established at its initial meeting, in Keren, their memo included the signatures of representatives who served simultaneously as tigre spokesmen and league officials. Like most of the league's official memoranda, representatives rejected "categorically any system of annexation or union with Ethiopia or any other nation" and claimed they were willing to accept a period of British trusteeship before assuming full independence.[106] Moreover, representatives used their memorandum to craft a detailed history of the social and economic relations between their various clans and shumagulle rulers: "It is our duty to explain to your commission, with great displeasure, the very ugly situation in which we, the Tigré of Eritrea, find ourselves; a situation which has lasted for more than three centuries; a situation which could not even be applied to animals, seeing that there are laws that protect them from ill-treatment, and people who break these laws are liable to punishment."[107]

Although representatives went into detail to describe the ways in which the tigre were abused and forced to pay various forms of tribute to the shumagulle, their testimony also illustrates how abolishing serfdom and subjugation became, in the eyes of many, one of the central tenants in the Muslim League's push for social reform. BMA administrator Trevaskis took notice of the party's grassroots strength on the issue. He noted that although in the earliest stages many shumagulle chiefs "formed the party together with their subjects thinking that they would control its activities," they subsequently discovered that it was not "a Chief's party & that it is a party which stands (in their tribes) for serf emancipation."[108] Trevaskis also observed that the amalgamation of the league and the tigre emancipation issue took place as several "aristocratic ruling groups" from western Eritrea began joining the UP.[109]

Activism and Antifeudal Politics

When the Four Power Commission arrived in Eritrea, in early November 1947, shumagulle and tigre representatives alike articulated the indivisible nature of the league's nationalist aims and emancipation. In his testimony before the commission, Kantebay Osman Hedad Pasha of the Habab clan defended the tigre's previous social status, explaining that "all the Tigre had to do was to plough the land, give us one quarter of the crops and do the milking," but that the BMA and opportunistic tigre leaders had interfered and caused "much confusion" within the traditional system.[110] Echoing these concerns, Diglal Gailani Hussein Pasha discussed his continuing troubles with the tigre and the league's involvement. He noted "the people or organization who is telling the Arabs [tigre] not to pay tribute to us is the Moslem League." He went on to explain that because the organization encouraged "the Arabs and Tigre not to pay tribute to the Nabtab," he believed that the league's leaders could not have promoted their program unless they were being secretly supported by the BMA. When delegates questioned him about why he had recently changed his political affiliation from the Muslim League to the UP, the diglal again stressed that the organization harbored a tigre agenda: "First when we formed the Moslem League it was to decide its wishes regarding the future of Eritrea. Now the Moslem League has changed [turned its attention] from the future of Eritrea to the problem of the Tigre and the nabtab."[111]

In spite of the heated rhetoric from some shumagulle representatives, their resentment toward the league's pro-tigre stance did not surprise most observers who had watched since the league's founding the precarious situation between the clan chiefs and the rest of the largely populist organization. Ethiopian representatives had made a point of courting most of the clan chiefs in the Western Province and Kantebay Osman in particular. To him, they promised to permit "full powers over his tribe if he supported the Ethiopian cause," which included the resurrection of older "feudal dues" that the Ethiopian government would recognize if he supported union.[112] Observing the unionist strategy, British administrators noted that Ethiopian attempts to win the support of the "reactionary old chief" extinguished any possible support for their cause among the tigre, who flocked in mass to the Muslim League.[113] League representatives also used this practice as a means of discrediting those shumagulle who publicly endorsed union with Ethiopia both before and during the commission's visit. Resenting the chiefs' embrace of the apparent bribery and patronage, league representatives alleged in a memo to the commission that Ethiopian government representatives offered Kantebay Osman "a magnificent gift in pounds and a good monthly salary as compensation for his adherence to the 'annexionist' Party" after the league's creation.[114]

For others, particularly some of the clan heads and coastal merchants, the commission provided a forum to address their own unhappiness with the league's agenda now that it seemed to favor the tigre base from the Western Province. According to one former league member from Hirgigo, the league's priorities had changed:

> I joined the Moslem League on religious grounds and I was disappointed when I discovered that it did not include all Moslems and also that it should want Four Power Trusteeship and not British Trusteeship. The Program of the Moslem League was formed in two hours at Keren, where only the Keren and Agordat Divisions were represented, and I do not consider that two hours is a long enough time in which to decide the future of a country. When eventually I found that the Moslem League was run by the secret hands of the Italians, I left it for the National Party.[115]

For the league's executive council, the willingness of many shumagulle chiefs to support union represented only the most recent evidence of the nobles' own agenda that first emerged during the initial rebellions, in 1941. League leaders believed that shumagulle support for Ethiopia reflected the elites' own preoccupation with recovering their previous status and privileges. Testifying before the commission, representatives from the executive council alluded to the shumagulle's quest to reclaim their status: "These people have got federation systems, and the Ethiopian Government promised to help them, so they joined but only for their own benefit. They are deceiving their tribes and getting money from them without giving them any help. They are afraid of losing the federation system when the country receives its endependence [*sic*]."[116]

In their inquiry, commission members also noted that for some tigre representatives within the league, the concept of independence itself meant not so much Eritrea's future status but their own freedom from paying future tribute to the shumagulle. Some members went so far as to claim that "they would leave the Moslem League if it were to decide that tribute should be paid through the chiefs."[117]

In both their rhetoric and actions, league leaders viewed the tigre emancipation issue as a struggle to breakout of the previous feudal traditions that, coincidently, remained well-entrenched in Ethiopia. Consequently, support for the tigre also aided the organization in providing additional justification for Eritrea not being absorbed into Ethiopia. League representatives noted that their constituents, tigre and non-tigre alike "do not like any other system than that given under the Atlantic Charter, which gives freedom of religion, freedom of the press, etc."[118] Taking their rhetoric a step further before the commission, representatives again couched their goals as a movement to build a "modern" Eritrean nation rather than return to the archaic system in the Abyssinian tradition, noting that "it is certain that the Amharics [Amhara] are primitive. Their administration–which is based on ignoble dictatorship–is that of a very remote past, and can be compared to that of the Middle-Ages."[119] As the year progressed, the league's independence platform continually merged with its antiserfdom stance. By November 1947 the organization made it clear that both objectives were interrelated, stating that of the many reasons why the league rejected both union and annexation with Ethiopia, "the old worn out 'FEUDALE' system of government" represented another reason why the league did not think that even the Ethiopian

Fig. 2.2. Muslim League members carry Soviet, British, French, and American flags during the Four Power Commission's visit to Keren, November 1947. Photograph by Kennedy Trevaskis. MSS, Brit. Emp. s. 365, box 180, file 3, folio 38.

government itself possessed any particular "higher standard of administrative capacity" to warrant independence.[120]

League Activity and the Four Power Commission

Although much has been written about the problems related to the commission's visit, including the often-discussed conflicts between nationalist and unionist supporters and the rampant inflation of each party's membership estimates, it also represented the first instance where Muslim League leaders made their case directly to an international audience. Consequently, the league made a point of refining its nearly year-old program by again placing their movement in the context of wider global struggles for independence. Before the commission's arrival, Ibrahim Sultan sent a telegram to the delegates explaining the league's position: "The League invokes your assembly in the name of justice and humanity to safeguard the rights of all peoples in line with the Atlantic Charter and San Francisco Treaty" to guarantee complete independence.[121] Upon the commission's arrival, league representatives continued their petitions with a written appeal that included an extended description of its original resolutions, which they had passed the previous January. In emphasizing their independence aims, the league again crafted its appeal as a struggle against the perception of Ethiopian backwardness: "It is known and admitted by all reasonable men, that it is not right to place a nation which enjoys a standard of education and equality under an inferior nation."[122] Thus, the league framed independence as a right deserving of its strong intellectual composition: "Now the Eritrean People have achieved a certain intellectual evolution by its contact with the civilized nations, and for this it has to-day a level of education superior to that of the Ethiopian people. To this should be added that equity and equality amongst Moslems did not exist in Ethiopia where the traces of the Middle ages still exist to-day."[123]

On December 16, members of the executive council expanded their rationale to the commission. Besides providing extensive examples of the "bad behavior"[124] of unionists and Ethiopian agents during the commission's stay in the country, representatives again made the claim that unionist supporters wished to take Eritrea back into a period in which a "racial policy based on Feudalism" of the Amhara reigned supreme.[125]

In their attacks against unionists and "annexationists" working directly under Ethiopian authority, the league also derided the "ignorant class" of Eritreans that had recently chosen to support the NEPIP. Dismissing NEPIP supporters as a people who "did not know the word 'Honour,'" the league decried their alleged material-based reasons for joining the organization, which included receiving small financial payments and foodstuffs in exchange for official party membership.[126] These accusations were later confirmed by the commission. When delegates recorded findings from their second hearing in Keren, they noted the testimony of one NEPIP representative who admitted that many of his constituents had recently switched their allegiance from the league to the NEPIP because they had received "food, soap, flour, coffee and cloth" for their support.[127] This testimony thus supports the claims of some league representatives who argued that many from the NEPIP "were actually members of the league" who had simply joined the new organization to obtain uniforms for themselves and for their families had acquired "a little rice or flour with a piece of meat and a gift of a few shillings."[128] Hajj Ibrahim Otban Ahmed also recalled how representatives from the NEPIP came to Adi Keyh and "recruited people by handing out money, bread, and meat" on the eve of the commission's arrival.[129]

In addition, the league tried to discredit some members of Massawa's merchant community who had created a small counterorganization, the National Party of Massawa (NPM). Deriding the group's platform of supporting international trusteeship for an indefinite period as unrealistic, the league laid blame principally on Nazir Mohammad Nur, Osman Adam Bey, and a small group of elite merchants for attempting to create the party simply as a means to "deviate from the track followed by the mass[es]" in Massawa.[130] As they had argued against many of the shumagulle chiefs, league representatives countered that a handful of opportunistic individuals founded the NPM solely as means of preserving their power and privilege. That being said, the league also made distinctions when it came to discussing particular Muslim leaders who did not officially support the league's nationalist agenda. Saleh Ahmed Kekiya became the best example of how the league adapted to the new political realities. While Kekiya emerged previously as one of the strongest supporters for improved Muslim education and as a confidant to many of the independence-leaning members of the MFH, he came out publicly in favor of union in early 1947 and served as the vice president of the UP.

Despite his official support for union, Kekiya seems to have maintained close ties with independence supporters and apparently did not fall out of favor with most of the league leadership in Massawa and Asmara. Abdelkadir Kebire even praised Kekiya, calling him a "true friend" with whom he shared a strong friendship, in spite of unionist accusations to the contrary.[131] Even when the league heard that Kekiya was responsible for issuing unionist membership cards to residents in Hirgigo and Massawa, league leaders refused to condemn him in their public criticisms against the other shumagulle chiefs in the region.[132] The most common explanation for his stance seems to be that his choice to promote union reflected his own precarious economic position; his considerable business investments in Ethiopia had previously allowed him to use the revenue to support Muslim education, assist in the construction of mosques and other public buildings, and even to pay to send local students from the Hirgigo area abroad for advanced studies. His complex political position is also supported by later claims that Kekiya secretly supported the independence cause by advising youth in and around Hirgigo to support the league.[133] Moreover, Kekiya's extended stay in Ethiopia from much of the period between 1946 through 1949 suggests that his contribution to the UP was minimal at best and did not present any meaningful threat to the league's cause.

Fig. 2.3. Members from the Muslim League and the Liberal Progressive Party carry signs during the Four Power Commission's visit to Keren, November 1947. Photograph by Kennedy Trevaskis. MSS, Brit. Emp. s. 365, box 180, file 3, folio 40.

The League's Arguments to the Four Power Commission

Despite the aggressive language toward their political competitors, league leaders found themselves largely on the defensive when they finally appeared before the commission. Just under a year after the events at Bet Giyorgis, six members of the Muslim League's executive council appeared before British, French, American, and Soviet delegates on November 18, 1947, in Asmara.[134] Facing questions ranging from their inflated membership estimates, their relationship with the LPP, and their alleged connection to international organizations such as the Arab League, representatives attempted to legitimize their platform and to counter accusations about many Muslim League leaders' own supposed "unionist" pasts. For example, when one delegate asked Ibrahim Sultan about his past involvement in Eritrea's UP (still called by its old moniker, MFH) and inferred that he had once supported Ethiopian annexation, Sultan repudiated the accusation: "I was a member of the party called 'Love of Country' and not the Union Party. I changed my mind when Dr. Lorenzo and Dr. Zacharias came from the Ethiopian government with a donation of 3,000 pounds for support of the Union Party. People who left the 'Love of Country' Party formed the Moslem League Party."[135]

League officials also rejected unionist accusations that the league did not truly represent the majority of Muslim residents and that Eritrean sovereignty lacked any legitimate historical claims. In a report filed by the UP to the commission, unionist representatives had previously cited the membership of the leading nabtab, shumagulle, and "about 60,000 Tigré" from the Western Province in their organization as proof that the league did not truly represent Eritrea's Muslim communities.[136] In addition, they argued that the league's basic objectives served only the small urban elite. Arguing that "no ethnic, historical and economic reason" could be used to reject incorporation with Ethiopia, unionists claimed that league leaders were motivated more by the "financial considerations" involved with political independence.[137] Moreover, by arguing that the league relied on "religious sensitiveness" and a rabid promotion of "Arabian culture and language" to provoke Muslim fears of Ethiopian rule, the UP tried to paint the league as a reactionary force devoid of any historical justification for its platform. Representatives commented that "the Moslem League is certainly like somebody who has lost his case and tries to regain respect by talking with a big voice."[138]

Responding to these accusations, league representatives again testified that they instead sought self-determination from a country that had remained frozen in "ignorant" and ancient traditions. Because they believed that Ethiopia's leaders would continue to embrace their feudal system and maintain a standard of living "below that of the Eritreans," these differences justified independence. Representatives stated that if given the opportunity, they believed that Eritrea could be both economically and politically self-sufficient within a few years. Although they spoke out about their concerns for protecting Muslims' rights from Ethiopian influence, religion itself remained largely absent in their overall defense. None of the representatives claimed that the league and its agenda were guided by any particular religious zeal. Only when pressed by the commission about how the league planned to resolve Eritrea's "national and religious questions" if granted independence did they comment on the subject, with representatives answering, "There have never been any religious troubles. We are all brothers, the Muslims and the Christians."[139] While the delegation's appearance proved to be in some ways anticlimactic, it demonstrated that after nearly a full year of campaigning and expansion, the league maintained a remarkable continuity in articulating its original program among constituents and in its later appeals to the international community.

If the league and its supporters worried about how the commission would ultimately rule on Eritrea's political fate, their concerns took place in the backdrop of more immediate fears about the growing unrest throughout the country. In the midst of their contest to win the commission's favor, nationalist and unionist representatives were both accused of inflating their numbers at the hearings, and their rivalry often boiled over into violence. Across Eritrea's cities and major towns, Muslim League, LPP, and NEPIP supporters squared off against unionist supporters. Reports of assaults, stonings, and small-scale riots between the three nationalist parties and the UP became increasingly common during the commission's visit. For nationalists, concerns that unionist supporters were being supplied with arms and funds from the Ethiopian government began to alter the political climate in new, troubling ways.

By mid-November even BMA officials were alarmed at the increasing regularity of clashes between nationalists and unionists. In Massawa, unionists were accused of attacking congregations of Italian settlers and members of the NEPIP.[140] In Keren, Teramni, Agordat, Dekemhare, and other locations on the commission's itinerary, representatives from the league, the NEPIP, and the LPP all filed complaints against unionist supporters, claiming that UP members had threatened and in some cases physically beat them.[141] At an inquiry held at Geshnashim, in northern Hamasien Province, observers recorded that the "hostile demonstrations from the unionist-onlookers" forced Muslim League representatives to seek the commission's protection during its stay in the village.[142] In other instances, UP and league members repeatedly "came to blows" when representatives gathered outside the commission meetings before giving their respective testimonies.[143] For their part, league writers internalized the growing hostility and used the developments to build further support among Muslims to continue their "righteous struggle." By late December the league again connected its efforts with the wider aims of independence across the Islamic world. On December 23 the league published a speech given previously by Pakistani president Muhammad Ali Jinnah at Lahore University. The speech, cryptically titled "There Is Nothing More Preferable to the Muslim than Dying for the Truth," addressed many of the general themes related to Pakistan's independence movement. The speech's overall tenor and emphasis on the importance of its members being ready to sacrifice their lives and wealth to achieve the goal of political freedom echoed many of the ideas touted by league leaders throughout the previous year.[144] However, the timing of the article's publication amid the growing reports of hostilities signified that with the Four Power Commission's arrival, both the league's program and the wider nationalist movement had entered a new and more dangerous phase.

What began among the Muslim League and the other pro-independence parties as an opportunity to showcase their organizations' respective political strengths ended in a series of bitter public disturbances. However, the net effect of these clashes would not be realized until after the commission concluded its work in early January 1948, as a series of new challenges confronted the league and their nationalist allies. Unfortunately for the league and other nationalist groups, the rancor that revealed itself during the commission's visit only intensified as 1948 progressed. This shift in the political climate presented the league with a series of new problems that put its members in an increasingly difficult position. Nevertheless, the league's success in establishing itself as a significant political, social, and intellectual force during the previous year provided its leadership with important ammunition to guard against new challenges of anti-Muslim political violence, increased Ethiopian interference, and even against internal division within the league itself.

Conclusions

In its first year, the Eritrean Muslim League had much to celebrate: it formed, established its basic political program, and expanded its membership to at least half a million people in less than six months. Through the initial efforts of the executive council and later the energetic Youth Association, the league quickly established itself as Eritrea's first genuine nationalist organization and also made strides as an association committed to promoting Muslim interests across the country. One of the most significant contributions that league leaders made to Muslim civic engagement included establishing its own newspaper, *Sawt al-rabita al-islamiyya.*

Beyond simply discussing the basic objectives of the independence movement, the paper became a forum for addressing more complex ideas about Muslim identity, cultural concerns, and Eritrea's place in the wider movement for independence taking place across Africa and Asia. Through their efforts, Muslim League writers expressed a profound understanding of their own "ontological status as native intellectuals" charged with shaping a political movement in response to Ethiopian pressures and the larger skepticism among international observers.[145] By enriching the overall intellectual climate, the league established a stronger base from which its membership could engage the independence movement. This became evident in the instances where the league promoted its inclusive vision of an independent Eritrea by embracing Christian nationalists within what became the LPP. These early interactions between the league and the LPP hierarchy throughout 1947 helped set the stage for more widespread cooperation between nationalist groups in the coming years.

The international community's growing interest in resolving the question of Italy's former colonial possessions also placed Eritrean activists in a curious position by late 1947. While the former Allied powers entertained various positions about the future of Eritrea, Libya, and Somalia, a growing chorus of dissent from the Arab world began to also articulate the need to grant the former colonies independence. Indeed, the recent formation of the Arab League in 1945 led to a surge of interest across the region in the future of all European colonies. Pan-Arab promotion of the basic principles of the Atlantic Charter, coupled with the growing momentum of anticolonial activism across the Islamic world and sub-Saharan Africa placed Eritrean independence on the broader spectrum of postwar nationalism. As many of the commentaries within *Sawt al-rabita* suggest, league members were more than willing to seize on this fact and embrace these transnational connections.

With the coming of the Four Power Commission, the Muslim League intensified its assertions regarding Eritrea's fundamental incompatibility with Ethiopia. Fearing both the influence of the UP and the commission's own doubts about the legitimacy of Eritrean independence, the league wrapped itself in the language of Western modernity, appealing to the defenders of "civilization" to not let Eritrea come under Ethiopian authority. In their arguments, Muslim League representatives largely steered away from using overtly religious language. Although the league often appealed to the commission for the need to protect Muslims' rights and institutions from the influence of the Ethiopian-backed Tewahedo Orthodox Church, it rarely stressed that religion represented the main reason they rejected union with Ethiopia. And yet by looking outward at the wider Islamic world in their public commentaries, Muslim League writers also began engaging in new political and cultural discussions well outside the previous boundaries of Eritrea's nationalist contact zone. In doing so, the league distinguished itself from other contemporary nationalist groups by arguing that the country's right to independence was not based simply on political differences but instead on the fundamentally dissimilar cultural and religious makeup within Eritrea. In this way, the league's articulation of its separate, unconditionally nationalist platform foreshadowed the kind of concern and mistrust toward Ethiopian Christian influence that later came to define Eritrea's early armed struggle under the ELF. And because the league, unlike most of the other early political groups during the late 1940s, did not have any measurable sympathy for the idea of unionism, it allowed for a greater emphasis on the international dimensions of Eritrea's struggle as part of the broader Islamic world.

3

Navigating Rough Seas

The Muslim League's Internal Challenges,
January 1948–September 1949

Although 1947 represented a period of unprecedented grassroots expansion and optimism for the Muslim League, the next three years demonstrated that building upon its initial success would not be easy nor would even the league's most ardent supporters be able to guarantee the organization's survival. At the outset of 1948, the league faced several internal crises that tested both its leaders and broader membership as never before. With the Four Power Commission concluding its inquiry in early January, the league struggled to follow through with its agenda amid financial difficulties, increased tension with unionists, internal divisions, and ultimately the rise of armed banditry (*shiftanet*) against nationalist supporters.

This period also represented the most challenging era for activists who struggled to maintain a foothold in the wider nationalist movement, as multiple crises transformed both the strategies of the league's leading intellectuals and the prospects for the nationalist movement more broadly. At the heart of this transformation was the organization's decision to merge with other pro-independence groups to create the Independence Bloc in June 1949; this merging altered the nature of the intellectual debates regarding Eritrean nationalism. If the league's leadership had been more than willing to present their cause as a national struggle for Eritreans of all religious backgrounds from late 1946 through 1947, its decision to spearhead the bloc's agenda and activities demonstrated how league leaders were willing to broaden their nationalist program in even more profound ways.

In the context of these challenges, the political manifestations of Eritrean Muslim activism also began to shift. Nationalist supporters nevertheless adapted to the changing circumstances and also retained

Fig. 3.1. Muslim League demonstrators gather in Agordat, November 1947. Photograph by Kennedy Trevaskis. MSS, Brit. Emp. s. 365, box 180, file 3, folio 43.

much of their agency in articulating their political and social objectives before the wider public. This included the league's success in helping to finally establish new clan structures within the Tigre-speaking communities of the Western Province, aggressively countering the rise of rival "Muslim" political organizations, speaking out against shiftanet, and in reformulating their political advocacy before the international community.

Muslim League Troubles and the Political Lull of 1948

Although in late December 1947 the Muslim League had mobilized supporters and had drawn widespread participation during the Four Power Commission's visit, by early 1948 the league's leadership faced a series of new challenges. The first major dilemma came in January when the organization ceased printing *Sawt al-rabita*. Faced with a financial shortfall and unable to meet the publication costs, the paper's editors suspended operations from January 1948 through March of the following year. Aside from hindering the league's ability to reach a wider readership and keep its members informed of political developments, the fourteen-month gap also compromised the organization's efforts at a time when its leaders came under increasing attack from UP supporters. By early January, several issues of the unionist publication *Ethiopia* also intensified their attacks against many of the league's top officials.

In a scathing editorial published on January 4, UP writer Sayyid Ahmed Hayuti accused Muslim League leaders of embezzling the organization's funds from its general membership. Hayuti took particular aim at AbdelKebire, accusing him of being nothing more than a conceited political opportunist and the "imaginary president" of the league's Asmara branch.[1] He also accused Kebire of having once stolen funds from his friend and "life supporter" Saleh Ahmed Kekiya and that he remained a servant of Italian interests because of his former employment in the colonial civil service.[2] Before the article's publication, Hayuti even publicly accused Kebire of being born out of wedlock. Without an official media outlet to respond to the accusations, Kebire penned a response entitled "Men Are Known by Their Deeds," which he submitted to BMA officials for general distribution.

Warning that Hayuti's accusations would lead to "partial enmity" and even possibly a wider conflict between league supporters and unionists, Kebire addressed the insults made toward league leaders by saying that Hayuti's "lies" would eventually be dealt with by officials in Asmara's shari'a court. Reacting to the accusations about his own "bastard" origins, he responded, "I have nothing to say, but it is a bold, rude and impolite lie from a man who has always been known as a first class liar."[3] Kebire acknowledged his past work for Italian colonial authorities, saying that he had served as a paid employee who had earned his living by his "own honest efforts, being absolutely unlike you who have stolen public committees' money, [and that of] companies and banks—and moreover—personal cases of theft and stealing, which I am ready to prove when necessary."[4] He also defended his close friendship with Kekiya: "I am sure that your aim is to break [up] the friendship between him and myself and at that time you may be liable to gain some matterial benifit [sic] from him. I should like to tell you that he is a true friend of mine and I consider his boot to be more respectable [than] your beard. I trust our friendship will remain ever strong inspite [sic] of all efforts for breaking it."[5]

Despite the criticisms leveled against Kebire and other league officials, Hayuti's invective proved to be the most docile form of antinationalist sentiment as the year progressed. The apparent lull in the league's political activity throughout 1948 was also shared by the majority of other nationalist parties, who each suffered from varying degrees of financial trouble and political disorganization. With the Four Power Commission having postponed its final decision on the fate of Eritrea and the other former Italian colonies, the league turned its attention to addressing two troubling trends that had already begun to take shape: the growing threat of politically motivated shifta activity and the widening political division between some members within the league's hierarchy.

Shiftanet and Its Implications as an Anti-Muslim Political Tool

The hostilities that first erupted at the public demonstrations during the Four Power Commission's inquiry now gave way to a new form of violence: the use of politically motivated shiftanet.[6] Although shiftanet was certainly not without precedent in Eritrea, as family blood feuds, disagreements over land, and other conflicts had all been motivating factors in local banditry for centuries, the political nature of the attacks that erupted in 1948 represented a departure from previous "social" and "economic" forms of armed banditry.[7] N'bsrat Debassai notes that the rise in Ethiopian-sponsored shifta outlaws became one of the defining characteristics of post-1947 Eritrean politics and a major concern for all nationalist groups as well as the BMA.[8] Unlike many of the small-scale raiders that subsisted historically by raiding cattle and villages throughout rural Eritrea, this new form of banditry also developed a strong urban component. In particular, the well-documented role of Asmara's Ethiopian Liaison Office as a "guiding light and center for urban terrorism" by supporting the UP and its youth supporters with money and weaponry added to the league's dilemma during the spring and summer of 1948.[9]

Although shifta raiders were at first "directed to influence the works of the Four Powers Commission," the weeks immediately following the commission's departure brought an unprecedented level of activity against pro-independence Eritreans.[10] BMA officials noted that by early March the attacks, largely financed and "organized by elements favoring incorporation of Eritrea in Ethiopia," had caused enough worry that authorities established special anti-shifta units and patrols.[11] Not surprisingly, many shifta during this period operated out of key strongholds across the border in the northern Ethiopian province of Tigray. Moreover, both pro-unionist Christian Eritreans and Ethiopians shared a prevailing belief that these new groups of shifta activists were "not terrorists but patriots, cut from the same cloth as those who had taken to the bush to fight the Italian occupiers of Ethiopia in the late 1930s."[12] As Reid observed, the shifta insurgency during this period in part presented "the outcome of the unstable, contested borderland of some antiquity, as well as representing the tried and tested mechanism of political and social-economic protest in the region" particularly as it related to unionist attempts at breaking the will of nationalist constituencies.[13] In general, most shiftanet took the form of raids on villages and especially armed robbery along the routes between major cities such as Asmara, Massawa, Keren, and Agordat. An additional source of concern developed as many shifta also began coordinated attacks on the private homes and businesses of Italian settlers, causing panic in the rural areas.[14]

While the overwhelming majority of these early attacks were directed at prominent Italian residents and their properties, much of their "anti-Italian political character" also extended to members of the LPP, NEPIP, and especially the Muslim League. In January 1948, Mohammed Omar Abdula, a member of the Muslim League's Youth Association and the son of a prominent league official in Keren, was killed by shifta.[15] In mid-March, shifta attacked the village of 'Ad Sherraf and reportedly stole twenty-seven head of cattle owned by Muslim League members and launched an attack on the house of the district chief.[16] The concentration of early attacks in the league's strongholds of Keren and Agordat occurred with enough regularity that even BMA reports noted that with the exception of wealthy Italians, pro-independence Muslim residents almost always received the brunt of the attacks.[17]

Often lacking in financial resources, members of the league's Youth Association stepped up their efforts throughout this period to prevent further attacks. In particular, members became a potent force by helping to organize league meetings in secret so as to not draw attention to their activities. Without even a guarantee of safety at open meetings, the league came to rely heavily on the network of local branches of the Youth Association, whose members served as a protective force against possible shiftanet, particularly in the rural areas, where league supporters were most vulnerable. Apparently, some Muslim League youth even quarreled with the league's leadership over how to address the security issue. Tesfai noted that in Akkele Guzay, a number of Saho youth petitioned the league's leadership to provide them with arms to guard against attacks. Despite their concerns, Ibrahim Sultan apparently erred on the side of caution, refusing to permit their request for fear of Ethiopian reprisals and because the league lacked the financial resources to acquire arms.[18]

Fears among rural Muslim League supporters also increased as a result of the constant reports of material support given to shifta bands in northern Ethiopia. Reports of Tigrean authorities helping to organize fighters, gather arms, and help coordinate attacks increased throughout 1948 and only reinforced long-held claims that many shifta leaders maintained close relations "with Ethiopian authorities across the border."[19] Unlike the raids in the Western Province, which targeted both Italian settlers and pro-independence supporters, the attacks by "plateau Coptic shifta" were usually directed exclusively at Muslim residents and resulted in a constant state of hostility and perpetuated a series of "blood feuds" among residents.[20] Although the Ethiopian government's precise role in facilitating this rural support remains a controversial and speculative topic, the general atmosphere of apprehension remained high among residents, who often reported being threatened by shifta bands to give their allegiance to unionist authorities.[21] Adding to the growing concerns for Muslims' basic safety, league leaders were soon confronted with an additional crisis that shook its core membership during the fall of 1948 when the first major division within the league hierarchy emerged.

Al-Mirghani's Defection from the Muslim League

In late October, Muslim League representatives met in secret in Mendefera following news that their president, Sayyid Muhammad Abu Bakr al-Mirghani, had resigned his post and declared his support for the unionist cause.[22] Although British officials noted initially that both Abu Bakr and his brother, Osman, had signed over their official allegiance to the UP, reports of their dual defection from the league later proved inaccurate when Osman remained within the league membership. On October 25, Osman al-Mirghani sent a secret memo to Abdelkadir Kebire explaining the course of events. According to al-Mirghani, he had recently traveled to Agordat with Ibrahim Sultan to meet with local unionist supporters in an effort to ease the growing shifta hostilities. He explained that both men were presented with a pronouncement allegedly signed by Abu Bakr al-Mirghani stating, "To unionist[s], who are concerned with the future welfare of their country I join them together with all my followers—all past announcements made in my name by the Moslem League I hereby renounce."[23] Although Osman al-Mirghani explained that his brother's proclamation lacked his official seal, he confirmed the handwriting and in his correspondence said that he now awaited further instructions from Kebire on how to proceed.[24] In the following days, Sultan convened several emergency meetings with league officials to discuss the matter. On October 28 a gathering took place in Asmara, in the home of Berhanu Ahmedin, where league leaders actually accused the BMA of interfering in their activities by supporting the unionists. Many believed that al-Mirghani joined the UP due to direct British encouragement. Allegedly, some of the concerned league members claimed that their organization's "only hope for salvation" was to join with the NEPIP to maintain political momentum.[25]

Although the exact reason for al-Mirghani's departure remains unclear, his decision seems to have been tied to a variety of personal factors. Many accounts have noted that Ibrahim Sultan and Abu Bakr al-Mirghani had struggled to maintain an uneasy alliance, with the latter attempting to gain greater influence in the league's inner workings and financial matters. According to one BMA intelligence report, the two leaders "had a big dispute over political and money affairs" just before al-Mirghani's defection from the league, in October.[26] Others claimed that al-Mirghani, largely under pressure from family members in nearby Sudan, received instructions to switch parties because Khatmiyya authorities believed that the BMA would soon partition most of western Eritrea to Sudan anyway and they could, in the meantime, reap the benefits of Ethiopian financial support.[27] Still, other accounts have argued that al-Mirghani's motivations were based on the prodding of some Muslim merchants who wished to pursue a more conciliatory approach toward Ethiopia.

One intelligence report claimed that Massawa-born merchant and lawyer Muhammad Umar Kadi had succeeded in bringing al-Mirghani to the unionist cause. A conditional unionist himself who argued for the creation of a federation system between Eritrea and Ethiopia, Kadi became one of the more vocal Muslim League critics after the arrival of the Four Power Commission.[28] By the summer of 1948, Kadi had allegedly completed a tour of Massawa, Keren, Agordat, and other cities in an effort to convince "the influential elements of the League and other Moslems of the necessity of introducing a reform in the League." Kadi's main objective, motivated by economic concerns, seems to have been to get the league to tone down its language and become less hostile toward unionist supporters. For their part, BMA observers claimed that al-Mirghani, when faced with the likely prospect of losing a power struggle to Sultan and perhaps witness the league forge an official alliance with the NEPIP, opted for unionist support as a means of maintaining his own influence and status. Openly derided by Sultan as an "opportunist and egoist," al-Mirghani thus went about building support for union after having served for nearly two years as the president of Eritrea's largest nationalist organization.[29]

In theory, Abu Bakr al-Mirghani's shift to the unionist camp should have placed the league's mission in greater jeopardy.[30] As the spiritual head of the largest and most influential Sufi brotherhood in Eritrea, al-Mirghani and his inner circle still carried influence in many Muslim communities as khalifas and former league officials. For some BMA observers, the rebellion against the "religious chief" (al-Mirghani) left most league supporters "without a clear and capable guide" to carry on their objectives as a united nationalist force.[31] Indeed, when in the previous December the league rejected both the idea of Italian or Ethiopian control of Eritrea, some writers alluded to the central importance of the al-Mirghani family to the cause. One of the more impassioned examples appeared in an untitled poem written by an anonymous youth supporter from Tessenai under the pseudonym Nation-Child:

My Country, my Country, my Country
Wake up, listen to your enemies.
Italy claims your ownership,
Ethiopia calls for joining with you.
Since when were the Ethiopians your kings?
There isn't any reason for debate.
If you were lions in your land,
why did you leave your throne empty?
Italy, you have to be thankful
the hated son [Mussolini] was slaughtered
You were hit by thousands of airplanes,
whose fire flames you swallowed
When did you wake up and claim this?
Is your grave in such a high place?
My country, I will not let anyone claim you unless I am oppressed
and I will sacrifice my soul and my wealth for you.
I will not choose oppression for me or you

and I will not let your enemies kick you.
Our youth are our pride
we embrace the son of al-Mirghani, whom no man comes before.[32]

Nevertheless, al-Mirghani's influence among the broader Khatmiyya public did not prevent him from falling out of favor, as his "political stock slumped badly" among the league's leadership upon hearing the news of the defection.[33] For many of the more orthodox Islamic clerics, particularly those league officials closest to the mufti in Asmara, al-Mirghani was already persona non grata in terms of the league's day-to-day political activities. Before his resignation, al-Mirghani had infuriated much of the league leadership when he attempted to convene a general meeting of the executive council in Keren in October to convince other members to get behind Kadi to support conditional union with Ethiopia.[34] Consequently, al-Mirghani's defection did little to weaken the basic agenda of the executive council. If anything, al-Mirghani's switch to the UP served to validate the league's earlier claims that many prominent Muslim leaders, including most of the shumagulle in the Western Province and the merchants from Massawa, were willing to support union simply as a means to guarantee their own economic influence in any future government with Ethiopia. When in mid-1949 al-Mirghani again switched his allegiance from the UP to the Muslim League–dominated Independence Bloc, his reputation as a viable political authority was all but destroyed.

While al-Mirghani's defection appeared to further weaken the league when it already faced unprecedented challenges from shifta activity and its own financial troubles, al-Mirghani's move illustrated that collectively the organization was willing to pursue its wider objectives even if influential Muslim leaders themselves withdrew support. This attitude goes a long way toward explaining why, even at such a seemingly low point, the league's leaders accomplished one of their key aims in mid-1948 by overseeing the first steps toward legitimate tigre emancipation through the establishment of new, autonomous clan structures throughout the Western Province.

Tigre Clan Restructuring in the Western Province

By April 1948 the BMA's long-delayed process of establishing new "tribal structures' in the Western Province finally commenced in the aftermath of the Four Power Commission's inquiry. Although the previous years of unrest eased the economic burden of most tigre communities in regard to their obligations toward the shumagulle, the push to establish a new clan system reflected tigre representatives' desire to consolidate control over their respective communities. In addition to providing "adequate salaries" and "tribal retainers," the new structures also ensured that representatives could be appointed to a BMA-sponsored native court.[35]

Beyond merely appointing new clan heads, the creation of the new clan, or "tribal," units involved a close dialogue between BMA and especially league officials, whose political influence had served previously to worsen relations between tigre and shumagulle representatives even after the Four Power Commission's departure. According to British officials, the political conflicts actually delayed the clan reorganization because Muslim League and UP activists had rallied their respective constituencies to the point where any compromise to alter the preexisting clan units became "as practicable as mixing petrol and water."[36] In particular, the "close connection between the Moslem League and the movement for Tigre independence" had caused so much concern for the BMA that only when the "traditional tribal government" among the Tigre-speaking clans suffered near-total breakdown following the commission's departure did authorities finally agree to formal reorganization.[37]

With the BMA holding public meetings with new prospective "tribal" leaders, across the Keren, Nakfa, and Agordat districts, the initial meetings led to later gatherings where officials and tigre representatives actually began the process of formal reorganization. The complex process of merging and reformulating the clans presented challenges for all parties, as worries about the need to guarantee representation and safeguards against future abuses remained ongoing points of concern. Nevertheless, by summer's end BMA officials were optimistic about the extent to which the new formations had altered the tigre communities for the better: "After five months 20 wholly new tribes comprising a total population of 147, 164 have emerged as independent units, 8 former non-aristocratic tribes compromising a total population of 32,899 have been refashioned as the result of five months, the assistance of the Police was at no time required and not a single penal case has resulted from it."[38]

The peaceful and relatively rapid transition to the new clan units illustrated both the tremendous grassroots support for the new structures as well as the importance of the already-designated new clan leaders who emerged during negotiations. Organized and supported by tigre representatives within the league's leadership, the new clan heads took control in the "tribal areas" situated in the league's major strongholds across the Western Province, including the subdistricts around Keren, Agordat, and Tessenei.[39] The BMA's reference to the relatively smooth election process for the new clan chiefs suggests that the league had quite successfully worked out the transition toward these new social structures with minimal division and conflict.[40]

Beyond simply redressing the previous concerns among tigre communities, the creation of the these clan units reflected how the Muslim League leadership had succeeded in using grassroots support to establish new political units with a strong adherence to the independence cause. The reorganization, carried out with logistical support from BMA officials who hoped to finally stabilize the unrest among tigre clans, proved to be a wholesale success. Encouraged by Ibrahim Sultan and other activists, the representatives from the new clans benefited both British authorities and Muslim League leaders by presenting manageable units of authority and social organization that previously did not exist. Although some scholars have indicated that the league's leadership, particularly Sultan, desired nothing more than to acquire supreme chieftainship over the new clans, the evidence suggests that although the restructuring provided significant advantages for the league's organizational strength, it did not reflect a newfound power grab by league officials. While Ibrahim Sultan and several other emancipation leaders gained newfound status as chiefs and subchiefs in the new structures, in general their power was confined to the small local subclans, where their political influence had already made them de facto leaders of their constituencies among those that had argued that the new units needed to be based exclusively on kinship.[41]

If the league hierarchy, according to some detractors, established the organization for the sole purpose of giving opportunistic tigre leaders power over new clans, it fails to explain the continued zeal among activists in supporting the league's independence aims after the restructuring.[42] While only Eritrean independence could guarantee the continuation of the clan structures, tigre activists on the whole seem to have been particularly attuned to the larger dimensions of the league's concerns during this period. For example, the tigre political leadership, desperate to improve their revenue, began taking advantage of the financial benefits that the new clan structures presented to local authorities. With the BMA's approval of "tribal retainers" for chiefs and subchiefs as well as for "land inspectors" and elected representatives to the native court, the new clans opened up a new line of funding that leaders could use to contribute greater revenue to the league from their salaries. Unlike the previous chieftainships, where revenue could be raised through taxation and force, the new clan safeguards included preset "salaried and uniform retainers" under colonial supervision that, in theory, would prevent a return to the previous exploitation.[43] Officials also believed that bringing direct administrative oversight over the collection of tribute by the new clan heads would "provide the Administration with adequate tribute and the tribe with adequate funds" by allowing each clan group to build up its own "tribal deposit" to raise money for community expenditures.[44]

By helping solidify local power structures and clarify land ownership and financial matters among the Tigre-speaking groups, these new clan authorities represented tangible results for activists who had long sought to emancipate their respective communities from shumagulle influence. Just as important for improving localized community objectives among the tigre, the new clan structures gave the Muslim League an important victory in an otherwise bleak period. Clan restructuring secured one of its major social objectives and permanently solidified tigre-majority support for the league's efforts. This support became significant during later attempts to fracture the league and its leadership throughout the Western Province.[45] Even British officials alluded to the fact that the clan reforms were a clear advantage to the league's overall nationalist aims: "Whether the measures proposed by BMA are of a nature to commend themselves to the Ethiopians is doubtful. We feel however that the importance of this point can be discounted, particularly in view of the possibility that the administration of the Western Province will not fall to Ethiopia."[46]

When taken together, the creation of the new clans and the later loss of al-Mirghani to the UP suggest that his decision to leave the league may have also hinged on fears that the new structures also posed a threat to his traditional authority via the shumagulle. Clearly, the UP's earlier success in late 1947 in corralling shumagulle support gave little reason for tigre supporters to maintain cordial relations with many of the traditional elites, including the Khatmiyya head.

Despite al-Mirghani's earlier public support for the easing of customary payments against the tigre, many of the league's leading representatives came to resent Mirghani's perceived indifference to their plight given the inclusion of many shumagulle as local Khatmiyya khalifas. Compounding the situation, the noted rivalry between Mirghani and Ibrahim Sultan, the most prominent spokesman on the emancipation issue, suggests that al-Mirghani's decision to break from the league in the fall came once the league had finally delivered on the clan restructuring issue and solidified tigre support. Ironically, only a few months earlier Abdelkadir Kebire had alluded privately to the fact that al-Mirghani's stature and "leadership" in the Muslim League's formation had helped ensure that "999/1000 of the Muslim villagers" were allied with the league's cause.[47] Regardless of either al-Mirghani's actual motives or the concerns of many in the league's leadership, the success of the clan reorganization toward the end of 1948 helped consolidate the league's strength among both its rural base in the Western Province and the rank-and-file members in the cities. More important, the league's ability to continue its activities and address the issue of tigre representation in public demonstrated that even without the day-to-day existence of the league's press and publication resources, it remained an active force that shaped the broader dialogue of the nationalist contact zone. Indeed, redressing tigre grievances and actively working to establish the new clan structures only demonstrated that the league did not necessarily need to rely on publications to mobilize its membership. In this sense, whatever logistical challenges confronted the league, they did not impact the organization to the point where it compromised its core intellectual activities and political message. This kind of broad-based support among the general membership proved crucial when the league finally began to reengage the rivalry between unionists and other nationalist groups during in the following year.

The Nationalist Resurgence of 1949

While the Muslim League managed to keep up its momentum and retain its basic program despite setbacks throughout 1948, Eritrea's fate among the international community remained precarious throughout the rest of the year and only increased concerns that nationalist groups would not be given another chance to present their respective positions on independence. The Four Power Commission's inability to reach a consensus punted the issue of Eritrea's future status to the members of the UN General Assembly. Having been kept on standby, the UN gave notice to all Eritrean political parties in late 1948 that they would be invited to present their views to the assembly at its temporary headquarters at Lake Success, New York, for its fourth official session.

The UN's notification that the Eritrean issue would now be taken up by the General Assembly breathed new life into the league and ended the general lull in nationalist politics that had characterized much of the previous year. News that the league could send its own group of representatives energized but also troubled its leadership. Unlike the UP and NEPIP, the absence of any substantial external support for the league's activities left its officials troubled as to how to field a legitimate delegation to the UN. Still struggling to replenish its treasury and to resume the printing of its newspaper, the league found its catalyst in the form of one of its leading intellectual spokesmen.

No figure embodied the league's political tenacity better than Abdelkadir Kebire, president of the league's Asmara branch and one of its most active intellectual leaders. Since his days as a founding member of the MFH, Kebire personified the vanguard force of the urban intelligentsia in arguing for greater inclusion of Eritreans in government and in combating British indifference to local political concerns. By late March league leaders decided that Kebire would be part of the small delegation that would be sent first to Cairo in hopes of gaining entry into the United States for the Lake Success meeting. Although BMA authorities worried privately about the league delegation's departure and had initially tried to prevent their trip, Kebire announced on March 25, after conferring with the executive council that he, along with Ibrahim Sultan, Muhammad 'Uthman Hayuti, and Hajj Ibrahim Muhammad 'Ali, would represent the league at Lake Success.[48]

The Assassination of Abdelkadir Kebire

On the evening of March 27, Kebire and his colleagues met at one of the usual gathering places for league leaders, the café of the Aberra-owned Red Sea Pearl Hotel, on Asmara's Seraye Street. The meeting, called to address the agenda of the departing delegation, ended in the early evening and Kebire left for home. As he walked away an assailant with a pistol shot Kebire in the back.[49] Authorities rushed Kebire to the Regina Elena Hospital where he survived for another two days before succumbing to his wounds on Tuesday, March 29.

On Wednesday, March 30, league members observed his death by closing all offices, schools, and Muslim shops in Asmara for the day.[50] Kebire's martyrdom served to reignite the league's base of support on a scale not seen in more than a year and half. In keeping with Islamic practice, Kebire's family, friends, and league colleagues held a memorial for him forty days after his death, beginning on Sunday, May 8 at Asmara's Cinema Impero.[51] The decision of unionist supporters to target such a high-profile figure illustrated the long-held concerns that Asmara's nationalists expressed about Ethiopian involvement in unionist activity. In particular, activists throughout the previous year had focused much of their anger on the activities of the Ethiopian Liaison Office in Asmara, which they accused of sponsoring previous attacks and assassination attempts on the city's nationalist leaders. Hours after the shooting, BMA authorities raided the Asmara office of Andinet, the UP's youth wing. Investigators took note of the UP's role in the attack:

> Among the many documents discovered was one, addressed to some unknown person, asking for authority to arrange for IBRAHIM SULTAN (the Secretary General of the Moslem League) and ABDELKADER KEBIRE to be killed, as they were "enemies of Ethiopia." This document was dated 24th March 1949—ABDELKADER was shot on 27th March. The full hauls [*sic*] of documents is not yet known, as they are still being translated, but it is already sufficiently obvious that the ANDINNET and the Unionist Party proper were in constant and close communication with the Ethiopian Liaison Officer. There were also found a number of hand axes (with members' names on them) and some arsenic powder.[52]

Despite the public outcry after Kebire's assassination, the Muslim League's leadership went to great lengths to calm its members, particularly urban youth, to prevent any reprisals against unionists.

If the conspirators behind Kebire's death believed that his assassination would dishearten the league's constituency and dissipate the growing interest in the UN debate, they severely miscalculated. Ironically, Kebire's death and subsequent martyrdom actually rejuvenated the league's political momentum at a time when the organization had yet to fully emerge from its previous year of setbacks. The public interest following the assassination helped the league collect sufficient funds to relaunch *Sawt al-rabita* after a fourteen-month gap in publication. The recommencement of printing could not have come at a better time for the league, as additional reports and tributes concerning Kebire's death became one of the major topics of interest.[53] Most of the tributes to Kebire were impassioned pleas among supporters to continue honoring his memory by supporting his political aims.

Some of Kebire's admirers living outside Eritrea also made a point of praising his life's contributions to Eritrean society. Ja'far al-Sharif Umar al-Suri, a friend of Kebire's residing in Gederef, in eastern Sudan, reflected on the significance of his passing: "the news of the assassination of the hero has had the effect of a thunderstorm in the soul of every free man who respects courage and knows the worth of men. But this is God's will, that he gave cowardice and cruelty to people who could not face nations that stood for their rights. So, their cruelty pushed them to commit the worst crime ever known in Eritrean history, past and present."[54]

Kebire's martyrdom also had an important effect by galvanizing supporters just before the league delegation's pending appearance before the United Nations General Assembly. The league's UN delegation itself had left Eritrea within days of Kebire's assassination and its members could only watch the activities from abroad. Despite being short one of their most articulate and well-versed politicians, the remaining delegates wasted little time in publicizing their cause to the international community.

Sawt-al rabita's recommencement clearly signified that the league had not lost its place within the nationalist contact zone as the most aggressive articulator of the need for legitimate Eritrean independence. Yet the sudden surge in commentaries and the overall public outcry in the wake of Kebire's assassination also demonstrated that the nationalist movement, as far as the organization's Muslim constituents were concerned, had entered a new, more aggressive phase. The league's leadership thus responded to this new push by again actively engaging the intellectual discourse with a greater sense of urgency and through more direct public appeals across the Islamic world.

Presenting the Muslim League's Case

Even in the immediate aftermath of Kebire's assassination, the league's executive council continued their plans to help finance and send the delegates, now numbering three, to Lake Success. In early April the delegation arrived in Cairo and stayed several days before heading on to the United States. The delegation's stay in Egypt represented the first real opportunity for representatives to build support for their cause outside Eritrea. During their visit Ibrahim Sultan, Muhammad 'Uthman Hayuti, and Ibrahim Muhammad 'Ali made a point of seeking support from a broad range of activists. Besides visiting with clerics at Al-Azhar University, the delegates met with representatives from both the Arab League and the Supreme Committee on Palestine. Ibrahim Sultan is said to have discussed Eritrean independence with Abdul Rahman Hassan Azzam, the secretary general of the Arab League, who allegedly assured Sultan that their delegation at the UN would be "instructed to support Eritrea's demands of independence."[55]

Later, when Ibrahim Sultan meet with reporters from Cairo's *Al-Ahram* newspaper, he mentioned that he and the delegates had made a point to appeal to the Arab League as a means of gaining necessary support among other Muslim countries for their cause. During the same interview, Sultan also mentioned the contributions of pro-independence Christians in the LPP and their joint struggle to achieve sovereignty.[56] Given the context, the admission is striking for both Sultan's candor and his attempt, even when presenting the league's case in the heart of the Arab-Islamic world, to argue that Eritrean Christians were closely linked to the nationalist struggle. However, even with the league's internal agenda of supporting interreligious cooperation, its leadership clearly understood the value of linking their efforts as part of the wider struggle for independence as a predominately Muslim nation.

Eritrean representatives' visit in early April 1949 marked a new period in which the league attempted to use Egypt's prominence in the Muslim world to gain support for its objectives. More than a year after Sultan and other league delegates first met with leaders in Cairo, *Sawt al-rabita* proclaimed in June 1950 that news from coming from Cairo "suggested that the Arab League was making a great effort in supporting Eritrean unity and independence" and that the overwhelming majority of Arab League member nations at the UN, including the Egyptian government, were committed to the independence cause.[57] However, as the league's activities progressed throughout 1949 and into 1950, its leadership also moved ever closer toward the aims and mission of Pakistan in its appeals for international Muslim solidarity. If activists in Egypt became an important strategic base from which to build on sympathies in the Arab world, Pakistan embodied the ideal result of what the Eritrean Muslim League hoped to achieve.

Most league commentaries and reports about international support for Eritrea focused on Pakistan's efforts to express their solidarity with the league's cause and to build camaraderie with other nations.[58] League writers not only continued to build on Muslim solidarity in their own written tracts, but also in a substantial number of commentaries that later appeared within the Independence Bloc's own newspaper, *Wahda Iritriyya*. Many of the pieces illustrated the Muslim League's proactive role in garnering Pakistani support. For example, in August 1950 Ibrahim Sultan sent a personal message to the Pakistani government congratulating it on its third anniversary of independence. In September the paper printed the text of the Pakistani government's response from the office of Prime Minister Liaquat Ali Khan:

> Dear Sayyid Ibrahim Sultan,
>
> By his Excellency the Pakistani Prime Minister, we are thankful to you and the Eritrean Muslims for your kind wishes and congratulations included in your telegram to us on May 15, 1950, on the occasion of the third anniversary of Pakistan's independence. His Excellency the Prime Minister is very appreciative of the love and kindness and loyalty that the Muslim nations abroad have for Pakistan as a government and a nation.
>
> Yours truly, A. A. Hamid, secretary to the Prime Minister.[59]

In other instances, *Wahda Iritriyya* followed the earlier tradition of *Sawt al-rabita* by featuring articles published previously in Pakistani newspapers documenting the lives of national leaders such as Muhammad 'Ali Jinnah.[60] Later, the fascination with Pakistan and its government's support of the independence issue only increased in February 1950, when delegates from the UN Commission for Eritrea arrived in Asmara and league writers took a particular interest in the observations of Mian Ziauddin, Pakistan's representative on the commission. Beyond being merely celebrated in the nationalist press, Ziauddin's public position in opposing Eritrean partition only helped increase solidarity between the league's base and the

Pakistani government. At the end of the commission's inquiry, in late June 1950, Ziauddin also addressed the significance of Muslim unity on the issue when he acknowledged in a press conference that the idea of Eritrean partition, apart from being an "injustice" and an illegal action, also represented an affront to the Pakistani government and other Muslim nations that expressed their "total rejection in any way to divide Eritrea."[61] The idea of partition represented the most important political issue that united not only the Muslim League's membership but also the wider nationalist constituency. This visceral reaction to the idea of partition—embodied best in public outcry against the joint British-Italian plan that soon became known publicly as the Bevin-Sforza Agreement—actually allowed the league to build further support by tapping into the considerable resentment that the plan had engendered in other groups, including even some moderate unionists.

The Bevin-Sforza Agreement and Nationalist Rejection

Originally, the league delegation's arrival at Lake Success represented an opportunity for members to finally present the organization's pro-independence cause before the UN General Assembly. While league leaders remained in close contact with other nationalist delegations, particularly the LPP and NEPIP, they each came as representatives of their respective constituencies rather than as a single nationalist consortium. The political dynamics soon altered, however, after news of the Bevin-Sforza Agreement. The product of secret negotiations between Britain's foreign secretary, Ernest Bevin, and Italian foreign minister Count Carlo Sforza, the Bevin-Sforza Agreement addressed a broad range of issues on the future of Italy's former colonies, including the return of Tripolitania and Somalia to Italy as well as an agreement to partition Eritrea between Ethiopia and neighboring Anglo-Egyptian Sudan.[62]

When news of the Bevin-Sforza Agreement first reached Eritrea's nationalist delegates at the UN, it set off an unprecedented campaign among representatives to unite in opposition to the proposal. Incensed that British and Italian authorities sent the agreement directly to the fifteen-member subcommittee charged with deciding the colonies' fate, league delegates took a firm stand to denounce the secret agreement. In testimony before UN delegates, the lawyer-turned-nationalist spokesman Ibrahim Sultan charged that the agreement went against the very principle of self-determination as defined by the Atlantic Charter and requested that a new "United Nations committee be invited to decide" whether or not the agreement was even valid under the UN charter.[63] Sultan also argued that partition itself represented an affront to the majority of Eritreans, as he contended that approximately 75 percent of all Eritreans were Muslims and that the remaining non-Muslim population, being a heterogeneous mix of predominantly Christian and animist sects with an equally diverse linguistic mixture, "shared no affinities to the Ethiopian People."[64]

Although by May 1949 UN delegates had effectively neutralized the Bevin-Sforza Agreement by voting against the "wholesale disposition of all three colonies" as a viable option, the visceral reaction among nationalist delegates, and especially league representatives, ushered in a new phrase of political mobilization. As events transpired at Lake Success, the league press wasted little time in mobilizing opposition to the Bevin-Sforza Agreement and any possible plan to divide Eritrean territory.[65] Even though the nationalist delegations at Lake Success began discussions in private about their respective concerns and the need to unite against the possibility of partition, the groundswell of support for a new nationalist umbrella organization had gained traction among the league's rank and file. In a piece entitled "Solidarity Is Strength," Yasin Ba Tuq also addressed the league's fears about the dangers of both political and territorial disunion: "There is nothing better for nations in their progress than solidarity and there is nothing worse than division and fragmentation."[66]

In building support for a new nationalist coalition, he and other league writers also played on readers' feelings concerning the "glories" of Islamic civilization, emphasizing that many of the achievements and strengths of past Muslim empires could not have occurred without Muslims putting aside their differences.[67] Even the BMA reported that the league's leadership remained in close contact with activists from the other Italian colonies, particularly Libya, and had observed and understood "the lesson of the apparent success" of similar public demonstrations in Tripoli and had begun planning their own public demonstrations across the country throughout May.[68] Other reports relating the events at Lake Success emphasized the spirit of camaraderie between Muslim League representatives and delegates from the Arab League and other Muslim-majority countries.[69] Although many Muslim League writers continued to play on local affinities about a shared Muslim history and bond between Eritreans and the Arab world to build political support, the push to prevent a recurrence of the Bevin-Sforza Agreement actually encouraged the league as a whole into widening its already inclusive approach to building nationalist support, including opening up the organization to other groups, particularly Italo-Eritreans, that many league members viewed as being inherently dangerous to the independence cause.

The Formation of the Eritrean Independence Bloc

With both the UN General Assembly and the subcommittee locked in a stalemate over the future of the former Italian colonies, delegates from the nationalist parties and the UP returned to Asmara in early June 1949 without a clear verdict on Eritrea's fate. However, upon their delegation's return, two important shifts in the Muslim League's program took place. First, the perceived betrayal by the British government at Lake Success over the Bevin-Sforza Agreement permanently destroyed any remaining faith among league leaders that they could trust Britain even to mediate basic political rivalries in the region. Second, the league's leadership emerged as the principal force behind the creation of a new organization designed to bring together the respective strengths of each pro-independence faction. Barely a week after returning to Eritrea, the Lake Success delegation and other members of the executive council called a general league meeting in Keren to discuss the events at the UN. Afterward, representatives agreed to support the creation of the soon-to-be Independence Bloc. In their efforts to build support and spread the news about the impending organization, league supporters made no secret to highlight their preeminent place in the new consortium: "It is worth noting and repeating that the Muslim League was the first to call for Eritrean independence, and in their memorandum presented to the Four Power Commission, the first demand was for Eritrean independence. At the time, some of the weaker minds among the public thought that this was an impossible demand. But only time can prove our precise vision and we will see more evidence of our political success in the future."[70]

For their part, league writers made great efforts to support the bloc's objectives and clarify its position to the public. Yasin Ba Tuq argued that all of Eritrea's delegations, with the obvious exception of the UP, "were convinced after their meeting with the UN Assembly that the best way would be to unite their voices, especially when they saw how some nations pursued a complete rejection of the Eritrean people's wishes."[71] Consequently, the bloc's founding ceremony, at Dekemhare with representatives from the LPP on June 19, represented a moment of great optimism for league leaders who believed that the new organization's principal position of unconditional independence would finally gain the support of the international community. The ambitions of the bloc's leaders and Ibrahim Sultan in particular were not lost on BMA officials, who took exception to its notably "anti-British" attitudes and observed that Sultan's newfound zeal came about as a result of his "very swollen head" upon his return from Lake Success.[72]

Composed initially of the league, the LPP, the NEPIP, and the recently formed Eritrean War Veterans Association, the Independence Bloc was modeled on the Muslim League's internal structure, and its leading representatives included several members of the executive council. Ibrahim Sultan's ascension as the main spokesman for the organization also illustrated how the league provided much of the organizational apparatus to steer its agenda, particularly during its most effective period, from July through October 1949. Throughout the summer, the bloc succeeded in bringing together its diverse constituency around the independence issue, expanding its membership and even incorporating some former unionist supporters. Ironically, Sayyid Muhammad Abu Bakr al-Mirghani became one of the first unionist figures to join the bloc:

> Sayed Bakri el Morgani [*sic*] the religious leader and one time President of the Moslem League, who last November caused a stir in political circles by renouncing the aims of the League and joining the Unionist Party (See para. 754) has now caused only minor interest by reverting to the League and joining the New Eritrea Bloc in opposition to the Unionists. Owing to his previous change of front it is considered unlikely that he will exercise a great deal of influence within the Party.[73]

Regardless of the specific reasons for al-Mirghani's defection from the UP, his shift to the bloc illustrated how UP membership as a whole steadily declined during the summer of 1949, as support slipped in almost every region except in the parts of Tigrinya-dominated Hamasien and Serae Provinces. BMA reports observed that the UP had lost so much of its support that it "almost ceased to exist in the Western Province, and in addition has lost a considerable number of its supporters in the Red Sea (Massawa) Division."[74]

Even attempts by Ethiopian officials to bolster material conditions in Muslim communities often failed to ignite unionist support. For example, after the Hirgigo Islamic school, initially financed by Saleh Ahmed Kekiya through the Massawa waqf, closed down in 1947 due to lack of funds, Ethiopian officials donated money to reopen it as the Haile Selassie I School, in August 1949. However, when Ethiopian officials held a public ceremony celebrating the school's reopening, fewer than six hundred people (mostly Asmara-based Tewahedo Christians) came, even though the ministers had sent more than fifteen hundred invitations to Muslim representatives: "The affair has caused some indignation among the Moslems of Massawa and Archico [Hirgigo], who resent the blatant political maneuver and who have intimated their intention of boycotting the school."[75]

Largely because of the defection of former unionist supporters, UP officials lacked a coherent strategy for maintaining their agenda and activities as the bloc continued to expand its membership. BMA officials even took note of the diminished size of official UP gatherings in Asmara in comparison to the previous years. With the increased presence of Ethiopian delegates in Eritrea trying to rein in UP members and find new ways to stop the defections, British observers believed that the UP had actually been further weakened by Ethiopian intervention that created new tensions between Ethiopian and Eritrean officials.[76]

The Independence Bloc's Internal Challenges

Despite the weakened condition of the UP and its supporters, the Independence Bloc's quick expansion also obscured the fact that significant divisions were already beginning to emerge between its member organizations. Within the Muslim League itself, the issue of Italian participation in the bloc's activities magnified tensions between rank-and-file members and league leaders. By early July the league announced that the executive council and other officials in the Independence Bloc would accept the membership of the Italo-Eritrean community in the organization. Having been debated first among the league's executive council and later the general leadership of the bloc, the league announced on July 7 that they recognized the "mutual benefits for all Eritreans for accepting the Italian Eritreans" into the bloc. In their defense of the decision, the league made no secret of its hopes to use the economic influence of the Italian community in Eritrea to support the independence movement.[77] Despite the seemingly shrewd move to incorporate Italian influence, the decision also caused a serious disagreement within the league that ultimately helped bring down the bloc less than a year later.

At its core, the debate over accepting Italo-Eritreans into the bloc involved larger fears that Ibrahim Sultan had become too close to Italian authorities and that he had made promises that would leave Eritrea, even if independent, under continued Italian domination. Citing Italian government archives, Tekeste Negash maintains that both the Ministero dell' Africa Italiana in Rome and the secret Eritrean-based group Comitato Assistenza Eritrei (CAE) maintained considerable influence over Sultan and his inner circle. Negash infers that as early as mid-1948 both the settler community in Eritrea and the Italian government had all but achieved their initial aims by influencing the league's decision to appeal to Italo-Eritreans: "By early July 1948 the Italian organisations could report back to Rome that the political situation was moving in their favour. For example, they had succeeded in toning down the anti-Italian stand of the ML and had neutralised the anti-Italian position of Ibrahim Sultan by persuading other leaders to challenge his views. Indeed, the Italian community now felt so secure that it decided to fund the ML's newspaper as well as its editors."[78]

While considerable support and funding from such external Italian parties did work to alter the bloc's program as it related to the basic issue of membership, the true extent of Italian influence over Sultan's ultimate political objectives remains open to debate. Italian financial influence did not necessarily translate into wholesale corruption of the league's basic nationalist program or any meaningful control over the indigenous political leadership. Other members of the executive council and even many within the league's general membership were also well aware of Sultan's dealings and took the necessary precautions to address any possible negative ramifications that excessive Italian influence might have on their cause.[79]

In an emergency meeting called by officials in Keren on August 28, members discussed their worries openly with the executive council and even required Sultan to sign a "declaration on behalf of the Muslim League" that in the event of independence, no aid or support whatsoever would be accepted from the Italian government.[80] Nevertheless, concerns that Sultan and other league leaders had overstepped their boundaries by tying their fortunes to Italian settlers and Italo-Eritreans did not dissipate. By late September, Sultan and his supporters remained on the defensive and felt the need to issue a general statement to league members to alleviate fears. Written by Muhammad 'Uthman Hayuti, the announcement attempted to "remove the clouds of doubt" and reaffirm the league's commitment to the nationalist cause by stressing that its support for independence had never wavered. League leaders highlighted both their past accomplishments and their current attempts to widen the independence movement's overall objectives, including their long-held support for including their fellow Christian Eritreans. Hayuti affirmed that the league had proved that "at this important moment in the nation's history, this kind of honest behavior shows their commitment in the shared national interest."[81] Yet despite these attempts, rumors persisted that some in the league's leadership had made secret deals with the Italian government in an attempt to avoid partition: "There has been a growing fear that IBRAHIM SULTAN (para. 925) may have already compromised the position by making vague, or even specific, promises to the Italians both at Lake Success and subsequently in Rome during his visit earlier this year, in return for their support."[82]

In the short term, the bloc managed to hold together against internal rivalries well enough to worry BMA officials, who estimated by August that the bloc commanded the allegiance of at least 60 percent of the Eritrea's population if not more.[83] With a seemingly revitalized nationalist constituency, the bloc sent another delegation led by Ibrahim Sultan to the UN General Assembly in September 1949.

With its Muslim League–dominated composition, the bloc's presentation before the General Assembly largely echoed the basic spirit of the league's earlier arguments about the fundamental unity of Eritrean society in language devoid of any particular religious rationale.[84] The General Assembly's decision to eventually send its own official commission of investigation later that fall presented the Independence Bloc leadership with new challenges to mobilize for the commission's arrival, while simultaneously working to quell internal divisions. Having named representatives from Burma, Guatemala, Norway, Pakistan, and the Union of South Africa to the fact-finding mission, the commission scheduled its arrival for early February 1950. Ironically, the commission's arrival occurred at a time when the Muslim League itself faced serious challenges from ostensibly new political competitors that emerged in late 1949, particularly the Independent Muslim League (IML) and later the Muslim League of the Western Province (MLWP).

Conclusions

Beginning in 1948 and continuing throughout much of the following year, Eritrea's nationalist factions faced several unprecedented challenges. For the Muslim League, the previous gains made throughout 1947 largely stagnated when confronted by basic political competition from new organizations, internal fragmentation, economic limitations, and the notable increase in Ethiopian-sponsored political violence. On the surface, each of these challenges threatened the league's leadership with losing control of their objectives and with preventing its leaders from building their membership throughout 1948 and into 1949.

However, neither the defection of Sayyid Muhammed Abu Bakr al-Mirghani nor the league's monetary crisis seriously compromised the organization's basic objectives. Moreover, the league found new life in the spring of 1949 with the news that the UN finally planned to take up deliberations on Eritrea's future. This realization, alongside the outpouring of public grief in the wake of the assassination of Abdelkadir Kebire, had a rousing effect on the league's base. Spurred on by Kebire's martyrdom and the subsequent news of the Bevin-Sforza Agreement, the league subsequently went into high gear and led the push to establish the Independence Bloc by June 1949. Although the bloc and the core group of league officials around Sultan came under fire for their courting of Italian interests, the bloc maintained its influence over the larger nationalist movement through most of 1949. While much of their success stemmed from the ability of league leaders in broadening their program and intensifying their political campaign, they also benefited from the growing sense of collective marginalization among many Eritrean Muslims as the independence question took on more overtly religious overtones, especially in the wake of ever-expanding anti-Muslim shifta activity.

4

Maintaining Momentum

The Muslim League and Its Rivals, September 1949–December 1950

Despite the Muslim League's recovery, by mid-1949, from the previous internal challenges, its newfound success soon threatened to come undone by the end of the year. The league's struggles against political fragmentation, continued shifta activity, and the less than favorable circumstances of the international deliberations on Eritrea's future each threatened the organization's existence and agenda as never before. Yet despite the rise of counterorganizations such as the Independent Muslim League and the Muslim League of the Western Province, the league succeeded in limiting the damage of rival "Muslim" groups by maintaining significant grassroots support even in the supposed strongholds of these new organizations. More importantly, the league's challenges throughout the year ultimately helped induce further significant intellectual discussion among its members about collective Muslim responsibilities and the importance of Islam in the push to secure Eritrean independence. Ironically, the league's external political troubles actually obscured the more substantial progress within the organization in helping concretize the league's ideological foundations.

Countering Rival "Muslim" Political Organizations

By late 1949 league leaders began addressing the first major challenge to the organization's authority within Muslim-majority communities when the executive council voted to formally remove Muhammad Umar Kadi from its membership. Having been a major supporter of "conditional" union with Ethiopia and having founded the IML even before his official dismissal, Kadi's expulsion was designed largely to send a message to the other mainly Massawa-based merchants who followed his overtures to the Ethiopian government.[1] Having been one of the leading members of a delegation of pro-unionist representatives from Massawa that traveled to Ethiopia in 1949, Kadi and his supporters were publicly eviscerated for promising the Ethiopian government their support for union in exchange for certain conditions, including "a respect for Muslim institutions and an understanding that Arabic would be taught in the schools along with Amharic."[2]

Although many of its supporters claimed that the IML had developed as a result of the relatively widespread fears in Massawa that Ibrahim Sultan and his supporters would threaten the city's economic interests in an Italian-dominated independent Eritrea, the IML's program and membership estimates were highly suspect to both the league's leadership and BMA authorities. British administrators noted that IML officials were "without exception rascals who have had very chequered political careers, and who have belonged to almost all parties in turn."[3] The IML's supposed membership of sixty thousand people also caused considerable controversy, particularly among league members, who complained that authorities placed their names on the IML's membership rolls without their knowledge. More impressive than the IML's supposed entry into Eritrean politics, however, was the grassroots response that emerged to counter the organization's claim that the league had lost popular support. Contradicting Kadi and other IML leaders' claims, the league's urban members came out publicly and organized themselves politically against leaders who officially switched their affiliation from the league to the IML.

By early September, *Sawt al-rabita*'s commentary sections featured a regular series of reports from members in and around Massawa who refuted the IML's claims that they had joined the organization. One of the more notable pieces, authored by a group of Massawa residents, mentioned that while some of the local Muslim League leaders—including Umar Abdu Abbas, Muhammad Anwar, Muhammad Saleh Offendi, and Bakri Hassan—recently switched their support to the IML, their change of allegiance went against the wishes of most league members and represented a betrayal of the "covenant" that they had made with their constituents.[4] In response to their "betrayal," local members dismissed the officials and decided to elect an entirely new leadership to represent their views to the league's executive council. In addition, the new representatives stated on the record that the overwhelming majority of league members in Massawa rejected any possibility of conditional union and affirmed their support for the basic aims of the Independence Bloc. They dismissed the IML as a small, inconsequential movement of "disillusioned" leaders mainly from the prominent Na'ib family. [5] Even the BMA noted with suspicion the sixty thousand members claimed by the IML and observed that its leaders had "little or no following" in the region. Officials took particular exception to the claim that the majority of Afar-speaking communities in the Danakil, known for their historical rejection of Ethiopian influence, supported the IML's pro-unionist policies. [6]

Even with the rumblings of some leaders in the Massawa area, the IML's presence did little to alter either the league's or the bloc's basic trajectory in building support among Italo-Eritreans. Muhammad Se'id Umar, a league representative from Keren, noted that the league's efforts within the bloc to gain the backing of the Italian settlers made it increasingly difficult for Britain to stop the "widespread rejection" of the partition scheme.

Consequently, the league's efforts even pushed some former members of the UP to join the bloc and allegedly gave the nationalist parties support among at least 75 percent of the population. [7] At the very least, the movement against the UP continued well into 1950 and pushed the balance of influence in political affairs to the pro-independence groups. Despite Muslim concerns regarding possible Italian domination within the bloc, several former unionist Muslim clan heads publicly endorsed the bloc throughout early 1950. In late February, at least eight shaykhs from the Bet Musa and Bet Sereh clans came out publicly against the UP, renounced their previous membership, and promptly joined the Independence Bloc. [8] The steady trickle of former unionist Muslim clan heads and merchants into the bloc throughout late 1949 and early 1950 suggests that Italian influence in the bloc did not encourage a significant number of members to abandon the independence cause.

Part of the reason for the continued shift away from the UP also involved the growing instability caused by shifta activities in both urban and rural areas. Attacks continued throughout the summer and fall of 1949 against Italian settlers and leading Independence Bloc officials, and the league reported that homes and business establishments of several league members in the Muslim-majority cities along the coast were the primary target of the continued attacks. [9]

Challenges from the Muslim League of the Western Province

Despite the relative success in containing the IML and even in building greater nationalist support among former unionist Muslim leaders, the most pressing challenge within the bloc and particularly for the Muslim League occurred when Shaykh 'Ali Musa Radai, a prominent league member, announced the creation of an entirely new political organization, the Muslim League of the Western Province (MLWP). Although much of the momentum for creating the organization has been attributed to the alleged secret actions of BMA administrators, many league members on the ground also believed that Ibrahim Sultan and his supporters had overplayed their hand by allying with Italian elements and still expecting support for their actions from among the clans across the Western Province. For their part, BMA officials reported that the league's decision to court Italian influence via the bloc had caused considerable unrest, observing in late November 1949 that there were "indications that the inarticulate masses of the Moslem League in the Western Province may be becoming restless; there is talk of them throwing Ibrahim Sultan (who has not yet returned from New York) over board."[10]

The MLWP's creation continues to be debated in terms of the actual degree of support that its leaders commanded across the Western Province. Lloyd Ellingson supports the claim that the group broke away over widespread fears that Sultan had allowed for too much "Italian influence in the Moslem League" and sought to tie its fortunes to British administration for at least ten years.[11] Ellingson also argues that the MLWP's worries were, in part, grounded in the historical fears that clan fighting between Beni-Amer and Hadendoa groups along the Sudan-Eritrea border would only increase if British authorities suddenly annexed the Western Province to Sudan. However, Alemseged Tesfai has observed that the MLWP's origins were directly tied to the efforts of some British officials to break up the Independence Bloc and halt the nationalist momentum during the UN Commission for Eritrea's stay in country. The main actor in the drama surrounding the supposed creation of the MLWP was British diplomat Frank Stafford. A career officer with experience in diplomatic postings across the Middle East and who later served in the Ministry of Foreign Affairs, Stafford worked as a British delegate during the previous Four Power Commission before returning to Eritrea as a British adviser for the UN commission.[12]

Indeed, Stafford had gone to great lengths to thwart Eritrean independence by trying to encourage an internal split in the bloc since late 1949. In the previous months, his efforts to "infiltrate" the Muslim League's leadership by encouraging division had failed. Stafford found little if any support for a separatist movement among either Asmara's league leaders or the senior leadership within the LPP, and by early 1950 he turned his attention to the disaffected clan leaders across the Western Province.[13] Certainly Stafford's decision in part reflected his calculated reading of the growing dissatisfaction with Ibrahim Sultan by some tigre who felt that he and the Muslim League leadership would abandon its rural base for the largely urban Italo-Eritrean and merchant communities. Moreover, some league representatives maintained a long-held rivalry with Sultan and his faction regarding the league's overall direction. By late 1949, Shaykh 'Ali Musa Radai emerged as one of the more notable critics of the bloc's activities. Although a founding league member, Radai maintained an ongoing rivalry with Sultan. According to several members of the executive council, his relationship with the secretary general was "by no means fine" and was plagued by mistrust and disagreement.[14]

Radai appeared most receptive to Stafford's encouragement. By February 1950, Stafford and (allegedly) Kennedy Trevaskis visited with Radai and other concerned shumagulle and *nazeraat* (chiefs) who had previously joined the bloc. Apparently, Stafford stoked fears that Sultan had planned to remove them from their positions in the clans and "keep power for himself among the tigre."[15] In his study *Aynfelale*, Tesfai cites the testimony of the one chief, Shaykh Umar Nashif, who claimed to have attended a secret meeting between several of the clan leaders and Stafford in mid-February at a village in Gash-Barka. At the meeting, even many of the local shaykhs had complained to Stafford that most tigre remained loyal to Sultan and that their own support did not carry beyond more than ten chiefs in the Western Province. According to Tesfai, either Stafford or Trevaskis responded to their concerns by saying, "ten is enough for us," and later even suggested to the chiefs that they name their organization the Muslim League of the Western Lowlands.[16]

Called *teksum* (division) by its members, the MLWP elected 'Ali Musa Radai as secretary general and Qadi Hamid Abu Alama as president in late February, dealing a major setback to the league's morale. The perceived betrayal by Radai represented one of the "lowest moments" for many league leaders who had steered the organization since its founding.[17] Ahmed Kusmallah recalled that this period represented the darkest hour for many league officials who were "financially, physically and emotionally drained" during the previous months, and many feared that the league as a whole was heading toward greater fragmentation.[18] Nevertheless, the MLWP's actual membership numbers suggest that its creation represented more a symbolic protest than a strategic blow to the league. Ultimately, estimates that only ten of the more than twenty-three clan chiefs in the Western Province joined the MLWP support Tesfai's earlier argument that despite the defection, the league's efforts were not fatally compromised.[19]

While the MLWP's general failure to mobilize in part reflected Ibrahim Sultan's own skills as a nationalist leader who continued to be admired as the primary defender of tigre interests, it also illustrated that both the Muslim League and the Independence Bloc succeeded in undercutting possible support for the MLWP by continually rejecting partition when authorities first proposed it under the previous Bevin-Sforza Agreement. Although the defection of any group from the Independence Bloc could have been considered a new source of strength for the UP, its own weakened state in the Western Province and the MLWP's rejection of union with Ethiopia made its cause even more vulnerable. Consequently, the MLWP never developed into a political force that could seriously compete with the league, even among the majority of clan leaders in the Western Province. Ultimately the MLWP's claims of more than 215,000 members proved so exaggerated that both pro-union and pro-independence delegates within the 1950 UN commission dismissed such estimates as fanciful.[20] In addition, the MLWP's inability to field a steady stream of representatives during the commission's six-week stay further revealed that even in areas supposedly dominated by Radai's new group, the Muslim League maintained a commanding influence and membership across the Western Province.[21] By August 1950 the MLWP faced another setback when much of its already negligible non-shumagulle membership abandoned the organization after Radai's shumagulle supporters requested that local British authorities abolish the recently implemented "tribal councils" that had previously been enacted during the clan-restructuring movement.[22] The league's ability to rally tigre support again demonstrated that the success of its nationalist program rested on broader issues than simply elite concerns over the strategy of league leaders in working with Italian settler interests. Ultimately, both the bloc and the league maintained their relative strength against internal divisions. Instead, the major challenge to their agenda and basic safety came largely as a result of external factors tied to the continued threat of shiftanet.

Muslim Responses to Shifta Activity

Ironically, the increased shifta presence seemed only to encourage greater camaraderie among the various political and social factions within the Independence Bloc. This unity between the bloc's disparate groups again demonstrated how the Muslim League remained the primary authority within the association in terms of shaping its basic agenda. This influence also revealed itself when the league, in conjunction with the LPP leadership, launched the bloc's own newspaper in late January 1950. Appearing in both Arabic and Tigrinya, *Wahda Iritriyya/Hanti Ertra*, became the bloc's most effective tool to articulate the consortium's broad aims. Featuring a front-page illustration of a Muslim lowlander and a Christian highlander shaking hands in friendship, the newspaper represented the most tangible example of the bloc's push to stem threats of sectarianism. In its inaugural issue, on January 22, 1950, editor Woldeab Woldemariam expounded on the importance of the bloc's three primary directives, which included a rejection of partition, complete Eritrean independence, and the implementation of a "free and democratic" government of the citizens' choosing.[23] Yet beyond repeating the Bloc's basic positions, both the Arabic and Tigrinya commentaries addressed the growing crisis of shiftanet across the country. Bloc members used the paper to condemn Ethiopian-backed attacks as well as to provide updates on the status of injured nationalist supporters. The league, and especially the LPP leadership, began authoring pieces in which bloc members pledged financial contributions to members whose homes, cattle, and personal possessions were stolen or destroyed by unionist shifta.[24] For the Arabic-literate public, commentaries and reports in *Wahda Iritriyya*, under the supervision of section editor Hassebela Abdel Rahman, became increasingly preoccupied with addressing shifta attacks against Muslim communities and especially those living in and around the league's stronghold, in Keren.

By late 1949 and early 1950 the attacks developed with far greater intensity and precision when compared to previous years. While the previous reports of political shiftanet were categorized by robberies and shootings against many of the more well-to-do pro-independence supporters, the attacks, first reported in late 1949 and into the following year, took on an entirely new dimension of targeted raids and even political kidnapping.[25] The precision and intensity of the campaigns dispelled any speculation that such activities were somehow based exclusively on "personal grievance and feud."[26] Indeed, the overtly political nature of the attacks represented a clear challenge to the league and the broader Independence Bloc's ability to maintain momentum and organizational structure in areas where armed attacks became commonplace.

Despite the increased hostilities, both Independence Bloc and Muslim League members across the Western Province began addressing wider concerns for reform beyond just the immediate threat of the raids. Part of the explanation behind their calls for radical societal change even in the midst of intensified shifta activity rested on the fact that the ongoing political violence represented one of several concerns for the health of Muslim communities across the region. With critics arguing that Muslims had failed to live up to their calls for independence, many of the subsequent commentaries within the nationalist press interpreted Muslim victimization at the hands of shifta as merely as an indication of how they, collectively, had remained in a state of social lethargy. These criticisms, coming on the heels of the broad surge of shifta activity in the heart of the league's and bloc's base of support, served to fuel increasing self-doubt that Eritrean Muslim nationalists had kept pace with unionists in achieving their ultimate objectives.

As they had done before the creation of the Independence Bloc, league activists used the growing political momentum to address the perceived deficiencies in Eritrea's Muslim communities. In this respect, some writers continued to emphasize the need to develop education within their communities to meet the challenges of their coming independence. However, many of the commentaries appearing in late 1949 and 1950 also differed from earlier efforts. While previously writers had encouraged and expressed their hope that Muslim youth would take advantage of their situation and increase their interest and overall enrollment in schools, many of the later commentaries derided students for their alleged intellectual laziness and inability to "progress" from their current situation.

In one article, an anonymous author who claimed to be a student at Asmara's Islamic institute wrote that Muslim youth had ignored calls by their elders to "get education."[27] The writer berated his colleagues for not having prepared to meet the requirements for independence: "Now independence is here and you will be slaves for the Ethiopians. We told you that the prerequisite for freedom and independence is education."[28] Disheartened by the comparatively low enrollment of Muslim students in most cities, the author also positioned intellectual development as an integral component for moral well-being:

> God truly reveals himself, and his perfect art is the human mind. So if you look at any human being and look at their movement, stillness, and daily routine, you can observe that they are guided by a supreme being . . . and that is the mind.

The mind actually manages the body and moves it the way it wants . . . guiding the body to avoid the bad and pursue the good. So if the mind is enlightened and executes God's commands carefully, then it will avoid failure and be granted success by wise actions.[29]

Disenchantment with the state of Muslim education took on even more aggressive and seemingly "bold" pronouncements by students. One of the most significant student contributions occurred in a September issue of *Wahda Iritriyya* when editors published the first article authored by an Eritrean Muslim woman.

One author expressed her disappointment with the "cultural backwardness" that had resulted from denying Muslim girls education and not encouraging their participation in political activities.[30] Having decided to end her silence and "break her chains," the student, allegedly a young girl from Ghinda writing under the initials F. M., called upon all Muslim fathers and brothers to help "elevate" the Muslim female. Her pleas for assistance were overshadowed only by the frankness of her discontent at the situation: "Dear fathers, I'm telling you, in truth, you are in darkness. How can you live? You see the daughters of competitors [unionists] making constant progress and you see your best-educated Muslim sons chasing after the least-educated Christian females and leaving behind the ignorant and uneducated Muslim females. And the reason is you, because you ignore the education of your daughters; that is why any educated man does not want to associate with them."[31]

In a manner similar to many of the previous commentaries, the author chastised those whose failure to embrace education illustrated, in her view, the inability of Eritrean Muslims as a whole to keep up with the perceived accomplishments of Eritrean Christians, particularly girls living in the major cities. She continued her prodding, "Look at the Christians, compare yourselves to them, and you will find that you are greater than them in wealth and money but that you don't have the motivation. You don't understand the importance of education."[32]

At a deeper level, the student's anger also tied into a recurring concern prevalent among some activists by 1950: that Muslims' collective inability to take advantage of educational opportunities under the BMA revealed a deeper, moral deficiency among community members. For F. M., this moral stagnation had direct consequences for political realities. She warned Muslim elders, "You spend your money on entertainment and worldly things, forgetting what is going to happen when we get independence."[33] One of the most striking aspects of the piece was the author's own apology to readers: "I conclude by asking the readers to forgive me if there are any mistakes because I do not really speak very good Arabic and the reason is my father. He did not make any effort to educate me, but I read the Qur'an and some stories, and with the reading of the Qur'an I learned a little Arabic."[34]

Surprisingly, the first instance of a Muslim female addressing the educational shortcomings among nationalist supporters resonated positively with most officials. Hassebela Abdel Rahman welcomed the inclusion of F. M.'s commentary and claimed publicly that he hoped more Muslim women and girls would contribute pieces to *Wahda Iritriyya*. One week later, a commentary appeared in *Sawt al-rabita* that also supported the broad goal of Muslim female education, albeit in a much more conservative manner. The author of the piece claimed that although many Muslim fathers supported female education in both Qur'anic schools and primary institutions, many had forbidden their daughters from receiving an education because they rejected the idea that any non-Qur'anic school would have mixed classes.[35] Downplaying F. M.'s previous accusations about the resistance to female education among Muslim elders, the writer instead argued that the lack of Arabic-language Muslim schools "stood in the way of future progress" for *all* students, not just girls because they did not provide the necessary institutional support for the youth.[36]

Other contributors proved even more sympathetic to the cause of Muslim female education. One writer from Keren said that he agreed with F.M.'s argument for the simple fact that "the daughters of today will be the women of tomorrow" and that it was in Eritrea's interest for women to become educated and benefit society.[37] In spite of the ongoing struggles in ascertaining how Muslim women with both the league and the Independence Bloc contributed to the political events, there seems to have existed a large enough base of support among many league writers and officials that were willing to entertain serious questions about why, unlike Christian unionists, Muslim women were continually kept out of both educational and political involvement. However, the question of women's exact place in the nationalist movement represented only one of several questions on Muslim collective responsibility that the league began to address on a more internal level.

Guarding against Islamists while Defending Islam

If some nationalist supporters believed that Eritrea's Muslim elders had become too lenient in adhering to their faith and in ensuring the education of the youth, others seemed to hold an even greater fear that the recent politicization of religion would invite the threat of Islamic radicalism into Muslim communities. In June 1950, Shaykh Hamid al-Emin, a league supporter from Agordat, penned a public warning against the "followers of Muhammad Ibn al-Wahab" and warned Eritreans about the growing danger presented by such Salafi supporters, calling them "kaffirs" (infidels) for having spoken ill of their mainly Sufi-oriented brethren: "We understand that you, a group of rebels, who pervert the text and misinterpret the Qur'an and cheapen the blood, wealth, and honor of the Muslims, you totally embody the satanic agenda; you are the satanic party and the party that will lose."[38]

Although al-Emin's accusations about the influence of Salafism did not materialize in any significant degree within the Muslim League's leadership, some supporters did occasionally rally under a more rigid interpretation of Islam and its significance to Eritrea's cause against Ethiopia. Beginning in mid-1949, some contributors to *Sawt al-rabita* reflected on the growing attacks against Muslims by shifta and openly questioned the league's decision to continue to embrace non-Muslim nationalists in their movement. Some members even objected to its editors' inclusion of occasional Tigrinya-language texts as an "invasion of the newspaper" and a grave insult to "all Muslim peoples."[39] In some supporters' view, only Arabic could be used to unite all "East African Muslims" because it represented the most effective means to achieve political success.[40]

In most instances, the more hardline Islamist opinions appeared only when the league editors included publications from other Arabic newsletters in their own tract. An article by Egypt's Ahmed Hassan al-Ziyad (taken from that country's *Al-Rassala* magazine), discussed the importance of establishing a broad and forceful Islamic movement across Africa and the Middle East, noting that within this movement "Arabic is its tongue, which silences all others."[41] The rigid promotion of Arabic's supremacy, in combination with the inferred distrust of non-Muslim nationalists, represented the most common form of Islamist-themed commentary.[42] Yet in spite of these occasional commentaries, al-Emin's previous attack on Wahhabism and other forms of Salafism echoed the league's overall defense of interreligious cooperation. At best, the majority of the league's discussions on Muslim unity and "Islamic culture" manifested not in attacks against non-Muslims but in describing the historical oppression of Muslims in Ethiopia.

Fig. 4.1. Muslim League members shout slogans during a rally in Agordat, November 1947. Photograph by Kennedy Trevaskis. MSS, Brit. Emp. s. 365, box 180, file 3, folio 42.

Almost immediately after the league resumed operations of its newsletter, in April 1949, activists attempted to connect the plight of their own Muslim communities with the historical legacy of Ethiopian suppression of Islam. Yasin Ba Tuq highlighted the historical oppression of Ethiopian Muslims, particularly those in and around the Tigray region that became "dispossessed of all means of resistance and defense and choked in such an unimaginable way."[43] He elaborated in detail on many of the supposed instances of mass killing and "forced conversion" of Muslims during the late nineteenth century under Ethiopian emperor Yohannes IV and warned that "the crisis of Islam in Ethiopia cannot be equated with any crisis in any of the other nations of the earth!"[44] In spite of its alarmist tone, the piece illustrated how many within the league watched with trepidation as Muslim communities came under direct physical threat from pro-unionist elements and Ethiopian-supported groups. Beginning in April and May 1949 and continuing throughout 1950, other league writers intensified their efforts by playing up the anti-Muslim policies of the Ethiopian government and arguing that only independence could spare Muslims from the same fate in Eritrea.[45] Set against the backdrop of Muslim League apprehension at both the activities of some conservative Islamist groups and especially the prospect of Ethiopian political authority being imposed over Eritrea's Muslim communities, the league's leadership in general seemed only to further embrace an inclusive nationalist agenda to build political momentum.

The continued rationale for including Italo-Eritreans in the bloc thus reflected the basic aims of Sultan's careful, if often frustrating, strategy to avoid partition by promoting an even broader, inclusive view of Eritrean nationalism. The Muslim League's continuing financial struggles throughout this period also support the idea that Sultan's courting of Italian influence was largely an act of political necessity that ultimately revealed the fragility of the bloc's leadership as a whole. The most succinct observation about Sultan's strategy came in an August 1949 BMA intelligence report regarding a meeting between Sultan's faction and worried league members just before the Independence Bloc delegation's trip to New York:

> At this meeting IBRAHIM SULTAN was required to sign a declaration on behalf of the Moslem League to the effect that in the event of independence being achieved aid of any sort would not be accepted from Italy. After considerable hesitation he signed and he is now in complete harmony with his former critics. He has been astute enough to explain to them that he was only keeping in with the Italians in order to be sure of the votes of the Latin-American States in U.N.O. The Italo-Eritreans and the local Italians apparently do not yet know of these proceedings.[46]

Ibrahim Sultan's actions, as well as those of the Muslim League leadership in general, support the idea that their agenda remained open to program changes if deemed practical. Yet for all the talk about Sultan's increasingly friendly relationship with Italian authorities, he continued to seek, even at the height of his supposed alliance with Italo-Eritreans, the official backing of nationalist supporters in the Arab League as well as from representatives of the Pakistani government in residence in Cairo.[47] His uncompromisingly nationalist language both in public and private suggests that the BMA provided an accurate picture of Sultan's careful politicking between Eritrean and Italian supporters during this period. His ability to walk a sometimes dangerous line between these constituencies culminated in September 1949 when Sultan, along with Woldeab Woldemariam, Yasin Ba Tuq, as well as Eritrean War Veterans president 'Ali Ibrahim and Dr. Vincenzo Di Meglio of the Italo-Eritrean Association pled their case again before the UN as members of a united Independence Bloc. In doing so, they presented a new dilemma for the General Assembly, whose delegates remained still deeply divided on the independence issue.[48] Unable to reach consensus, the UN body agreed in November to establish and send its own commission of inquiry to Eritrea and decide on its fate.[49]

International Deliberation and the UN Commission for Eritrea

Representatives of the five-member UN Commission for Eritrea arrived in Asmara on February 9, 1950, and commenced their duties less than a week later, eventually holding more than sixty public hearings with political representatives in Eritrea's major cities and towns. Their arrival represented the culmination of international engagement on Eritrea's future.

The commission's stay also occurred at a time when tensions within the Independence Bloc had increased more substantially than in earlier months. Muslim League leaders had spent much of the previous five months chastising many of the smaller merchants groups who had rallied to the Massawa-based IML, calling their actions a "betrayal" against the Muslim masses. At almost the same time, the league downplayed rumors about the growing discontent among some members in the Western Province who viewed the inclusion of Italo-Eritreans in the bloc as a threat to Muslim interests. However, the bloc's quarrels were not confined exclusively to members of the Muslim League. During the public hearings with bloc representatives, members of the UN commission noted that several Tewahedo Christian members within the LPP and NEPIP claimed they were "excommunicated because they did not hold the same political views as those of the Unionist Party."[50] Carlos García Bauer and Mian Ziauddin, the commission's delegates from Guatemala and Pakistan, respectively, also recorded that in several instances "priests and monks complained that they had been threatened or actually excommunicated by the Abune of the Tewahedo Coptic Church for refusing to support the Unionist Party."[51]

Deciding Eritrea's Future and the League's Subdued Reaction

When the UN Commission for Eritrea submitted its final report on Eritrea, in late June 1950, the previous months of political

mobilization again shifted as the groups within the bloc again returned to their day-to-day operations rather than attempting to
organize massive, nationwide activities before an international audience. With the commission members presenting a split verdict of
supporting complete union with Ethiopia (Burma, Union of South
Africa), independence (Pakistan, Guatemala), and a compromise federation system (Norway), the debate on which option to approve
continued in the General Assembly. For their part, the league tried
their best to rally support for a sustained lobbying effort to UN
delegates. Their efforts received a particularly bitter blow in October 1950 when the league published a news report from Cairo
explaining that the Egyptian government had abruptly reversed its
previous position in the General Assembly by publicly calling for
Eritrea to be united with Ethiopia.[52] Despite the news, the league's
leadership pressed on, and Ibrahim Sultan requested in early November that the public once again rally behind both the league and
the bloc as the leadership planned to send yet another delegation to
the UN in late November.[53]

Despite the success of Sultan and other leaders in again reaching
the UN and presenting their appeal in late November, the ultimate
passage of Resolution 390-A, on November 2, 1950, which created
a broad federation between Eritrea and Ethiopia, effectively ended
nationalist hopes of an unconditionally independent Eritrea. Ironically, news of the UN's decision did not initially seem to register
on the public discussions among most Muslim League writers.
Throughout much of December 1950, *Sawt al-rabita* largely focused
on issues related to the league's ongoing political activities in the
major cities. In particular, the league devoted several issues to no-
tices and commentaries celebrating the beginning of its fifth year
of existence. Throughout the first week of December the league's
executive council, in conjunction with Independence Bloc leaders,
sponsored celebrations commemorating the league's anniversary
in all major cities.[54] When representatives returned to Eritrea, on
December 13, most league reports continued to omit any discussion of the actual decision to establish the federation system between Eritrea and Ethiopia and instead continued to focus on the
speeches and celebrations taking place in Eritrea itself. Only details
of the league's final appearance before the UN received mention. In

particular, league writers expressed admiration for Sultan's decision to provide his closing argument in Arabic, a point to which both unionist and Ethiopian representatives took exception. League writers commended Sultan on his statement and its symbolism for the nationalist cause and provided an explanation of the secretary general's actions:

> This is actually a point of pride, not one you can feel or understand, and you cannot attain it from your leaders because you are all parasites. You live off the foreign languages but the leaders of al-rabita, with his true nationalism, his noble self, could do nothing less than speak his national language in front of sixty nations. And after that, he talked in a European language to prove he could speak in another language.[55]

Other reports of the delegation's appearance also noted Sultan's confrontation with Ethiopian delegates and his insistence that only complete independence could guarantee Eritrean security. In dramatic foreshadowing of the abuses that later surfaced within the yet-to-be established Ethiopian-Eritrean Federation, Sultan told the assembly, "We demand Eritrean independence and we are here requesting this entity to do the necessary justice. We are not asking for an artificial agreement whose harm will be guaranteed in the future."[56] Although the league's leadership as a whole did not initially address the political implications of Resolution 390-A, some commentators took heart by placing the recent course of events in a broader perspective and offered a mildly optimistic picture of Eritrea's "historical" success in resisting outside control. One anonymous piece explained that various empires had claimed Eritrea as part of their own territory through conquest and that all had ultimately failed to control Eritrea.[57] Other smaller commentaries that did address the UN decision implied that Eritreans' autonomy as a whole had not been compromised by the plan to create a federation government. Indeed, as 1950 gave way to 1951, league leaders themselves came to rally behind assurances of local control and cultural autonomy in the federation as evidence that the league itself had succeeded in guaranteeing many of the basic objectives of the nationalist movement.

Conclusions

Only with the coming of the UN Commission for Eritrea and the creation of splinter groups such as the MLWP in early 1950 did the Independence Bloc truly fracture and lose its advantage in the political rivalry. Yet despite the setbacks that plagued the nationalist movement throughout the year, both the Muslim League and other groups within the bloc continued to embrace their broad nationalist message and maintain their core membership. Much of the evidence also illustrates that the league's leadership remained vigilant and aware of the dangers of inviting too much Italian influence.

In both their public testimonies and private actions, league leaders preserved the core elements of their program and even began to shape new understandings about Muslim "identity" in an increasingly hostile environment. Even more than in previous years, league supporters began to focus on Muslim oppression as both a fundamental element of the unionist cause and as a reflection of their own past failures to rally their constituencies. Members also continued to embrace the organization's main objectives of defending tigre emancipation and the protection of broad Muslim interests—including developing educational institutions and the promotion of Arabic—from Ethiopian influence. Through these strategies, league writers reframed the debate by placing the focus on Ethiopia's historical oppression of Muslim peoples to argue against the unionist cause.

While the UN's passage of Resolution 390-A effectively neutralized the independence issue, it placed the league and its allies in the bloc in a new position where they began to shift their tactics from focusing on unconditional independence to ensuring Eritrean autonomy in a federal system. In addressing the status of Muslim rights, religious autonomy, and political freedom within the impending federation, league activists remained focused and proactive in their operations by challenging the public discourse on Muslim activism even as the nationalist community prepared for Eritrea's still-vague status as an autonomous region within the federal system with Ethiopia.

5

Holding the Line

*Institutional Autonomy and Political Representation
on the Federation's Eve, December 1950–September 1952*

I ask the members of this committee why European colonialism
is being fought and opposed. Is it in order to replace it by an
African form of colonialism?

—chairman of the delegation of the Muslim League of Eritrea (1950)[1]

In the aftermath of the UN's passage of Resolution 390-A, which established the guidelines for a federation government between Ethiopia and Eritrea, the Muslim League and other nationalist groups began salvaging their program by moving away from supporting outright independence to charting a new course toward protecting regional autonomy within the new federal structure. In the brief period between January 1951 and the inauguration of the federation government, in September 1952, the league also struggled to adjust to the changing circumstances of nationalist politics.

In its cause, the league intensified its efforts in arguing that autonomy for Eritrea's religious and educational institutions represented the cornerstone of a viable, functioning federal system. Consequently, the focus on Muslim institutional integrity became its main rallying cry as league members more overtly promoted Muslim representation and political rights as the federation's implementation drew closer. While embracing a more aggressive defense of Muslim rights and cultural representation within the planned government, the league also branched out from its previous efforts in the nationalist dialogue by working with Eritrea's fledgling labor movement, remaining pro-independence Christian elements, and other segments of civil society to strengthen its agenda.

Despite the transformation in the political situation, much of the league's actual tactics and language remained consistent with its previous efforts. Its leaders continued to appeal to the Muslim grass-roots, particularly those across the Western Province as well as in the cities, through carefully crafted arguments that went to the heart of Muslim civic and religious concerns. The preservation of Arabic as an official language and the need to guarantee viable Muslim representation in the expanding civil service remained major points of contention, as did the league's argument that it still represented the true voice of Muslim interests rather than "opportunists" in rival organizations such as the IML or the MLWP. Yet league leaders and the organization's wider membership also confronted the realization that its principal aim of unconditional independence could no longer be achieved. This recognition forced the Muslim League to embrace the federation while carefully working to ensure that the still vague promises of autonomy and religious freedom would be protected. Ultimately, the league's shifting program and tactics contributed to a more aggressive defense of Muslim rights in the political system during the crucial period after the UN's passage of Resolution 390-A and before the federation's actual implementation, in September 1952. This brief period also represented the last true era for unrestrained pro-independence discourse among league intellectuals engaged in the nationalist contact zone, as Arabic and Tigrinya publications attempted to sound the alarm about the dangers of Eritrea being merged with the Ethiopian government. In doing so, the league and its affiliated writers engaged both constituents as well as the organization's political rivals in proclaiming that the UN's ruling did little to fundamentally alter their course for autonomy. Thus the political language employed by nationalist leaders aimed to limit the perceived damage caused by Resolution 390-A as much as it tried to reframe the nature of the debate on the new course toward legitimate Eritrean sovereignty.

Muslim Responses to Resolution 390-A

For league officials and the broader nationalist constituency within the Independence Bloc, news of the UN's decision did not immediately discourage their hopes that the basic objectives of independence were still attainable by the new proposed federal system. In light of the alternatives of partition or full-scale incorporation with Ethiopia, league leaders appeared ready to embrace the federation in spite of its shortcomings. By early December league officials began to publicly embrace the UN decision and did their best to frame the resolution in positive terms:

> The United Nations' decision and its declaration concur with the rights and capacity of [the people of Eritrea's] governance and administration of their own country. As a result of such a decision and declaration, the fear and terror of "partition" that was posing a threat to all Eritrean people and the country, which the Independence Bloc strongly fought against, and sacrificed many lives and properties, has completely disappeared!

> . . . based on the United Nations resolution and declaration, we know that we did not receive the complete independence of Eritrea that we asked for. However, we believe that we have the right to claim that the victory of the people of Eritrea is our victory, as we were the ones who were able to avoid partition and brought blessings to the people of Eritrea to govern their own the land.[2]

Other reactions were nothing short of jubilant. One bloc supporter, Degiat Sebhatu Yohannes, claimed that the general population received the UN decision with "overwhelming happiness" because people were finally relieved that the long-awaited decision promised to bring both "success and freedom" to all Eritreans.[3] Such commentaries support the idea that for the Independence Bloc (and consequently the Muslim League), true victory had meant "the non-partition of Eritrea, not the federation and its rights that came with it."[4] Nevertheless, the sudden about-face in both the league and the Independence Bloc's rhetoric regarding the merits of an autonomous federal system ran counter to the ideas that representatives had espoused only weeks earlier. In his final appearance before the UN committee, on November 24, Ibrahim Sultan had laid out the bloc's firm opposition to the very idea of a federation government, stating that representatives refused to accept such an "ambiguous scheme" on any level.[5] He added that "a federal union, as we understand it, can only arise willingly between two independent states of equal sovereign rights, and not between an independent state and one which is being denied independence."[6] Largely because of the league's recalcitrance in even considering the possible merits of a federal system, the tone in most of *Sawt al-rabita*'s commentaries throughout late 1950 and early 1951 suggests that the league's leadership struggled, at least initially, to find a way to articulate a response that could acknowledge the decision's shortcomings but also to encourage its members to look to the future.

Having mobilized an extensive network of branches and affiliated members of the Youth Association throughout the country, the initial responses to the decision did little more than describe the details of the UN resolution rather than speculate on the political ramifications for Muslims. Echoing the executive council's previous efforts, most league leaders carefully avoided any talk of possible sectarianism and instead redoubled their efforts to present a united front with the other member groups within the Independence Bloc. Nearly a month after Sultan's unilateral rejection of the federal system, he and other members of the executive council publicly joined with other Independence Bloc representatives to embrace Eritrea's future status as an autonomous region within a federated Ethiopia.

In framing their response to the UN decision, the league and its allies claimed that the approaching federal system could achieve the basic demands that nationalists had sought in the previous years. Bloc representatives went so far as to meet with the other political parties on December 30 in Asmara and agreed to establish an Evaluation and Peace Committee.[7] According to *Sawt al-rabita*'s editors, the news of the committee's creation had already helped ease political tensions in the weeks following the UN vote as "the news started spreading that all Eritrean nationals and their leaders realized that it is for the benefit of the nation that people disregard their differences and receive this new chapter in Eritrean history with peace and harmony."[8] At a celebration held in Asmara's Cinema Impero, the league's executive council and several of Asmara's Muslim religious clerics commemorated the recent course of events. Days later, representatives of all the major political parties issued a joint declaration that outlined where they intended to take the political debate as the transition from the British to federation rule approached:

> All of the political parties emphasize the importance of brotherhood and peace among the public and in light of the UN decision regarding the future of Eritrea decided the following:
>
> 1. To respect the federal system between Eritrea and Ethiopia in all aspects, according to its principals and objectives and its formulation.

2. To do their best in cooperation with the UN envoy to work toward the formation of the Eritrean government

3. Make the mission of the British administration easy in regards to the security of the country.

4. To promise to direct all Eritrean peoples' efforts to achieve objectives toward the mission of prosperity and progress of the Eritrean nation.[9]

Taking their public commitment even further, the Independence Bloc, allegedly due to Ibrahim Sultan's encouragement, announced on January 11 that their umbrella organization had decided to formally change its name to the Eritrean Democratic Front (EDF) to "suit the times" and to serve as an act of faith in supporting the approaching federation's legitimacy. Representatives proclaimed that they looked forward to the "uncorrupt implementation of the UN decision" as a means to guarantee "peace and prosperity to the Eritrean people."[10] And while the league's leadership still claimed that many of the other unionist groups represented nothing more than "the tools of special interests and motives which are contrary to the wishes of the people," its leaders now seemed poised to embrace their former rivals and prepared to make the best of Eritrea's political future.[11]

By stressing above all "cooperation" with the authorities in creating a tenable federal system, both the league and newly named EDF appeared willing to engage in the next stage of political dialogue. In fact, much of the Muslim League's reports and commentaries already began reflecting on its leaders' successful attempts to avoid partition and set the stage for meaningful autonomy in the new government. During a speech commemorating the league's fifth anniversary, Massawa member Hussein 'Ali Nehari noted that the executive council had worked with "selflessness and efficiency" in fighting for Eritrean independence and boasted, "It will be written in gold that they did their best for their country."[12]

Yet in the midst of celebratory reflections by representatives, Ibrahim Sultan and other league leaders in Asmara worried privately that the news of the impending federation would only encourage British efforts to create further divisions in the nationalist consortium as officials had done with previous groups such as the MLWP. On January 2, 1951, Muhammad and Adem Kusmallah hosted a secret meeting called by Sultan and other EDF leaders in their Asmara compound. Attendees were especially concerned about the possibility that Degiat Abraha Tessema would be appointed by the BA as the first indigenous governor general of Eritrea. Although the league and other EDF leaders had previously approached Tessema to join the front (of which his father, Ras Tessema Asberom, remained a highly regarded leader), fears that his pro-unionist sympathies would lead to further infiltration of unionist elements only stiffened nationalist leaders' anti-British sentiment, particularly among the league. One BA intelligence report noted that part of the EDF's reservation about Tessema included his alleged connection with other "disloyal" political opportunists that had broken away from the bloc/EDF in previous years: "Degiac [*sic*] Abraha Tesemma has been suspected as being a tool of the British Administration from the day he was sent to Addis Ababa during the stay of the U.N.O. Commission. Furthermore, he is accused by the Eritrean Democratic Front of conniving with Ali Redai of the Western Province with a view to forcing partition— accepted as the basis of British policy in Eritrea."[13]

In part because of fears that the EDF and especially the league's base could again fracture under pressure from the BA in the aftermath of the UN decision, Ibrahim Sultan embarked on a targeted campaign to rally league constituents while explaining the ramifications of the UN decision for Muslim communities in general. From late February through mid-March, Sultan traveled across the country, visiting the organization's major branches in Agordat, Keren, Tessenai, Massawa, Ghinda, and elsewhere. League writers reported optimistically that "the news coming from these places was very well received, which indicates that people's feelings were high [not frustrated] and shows their attachment and loyalty to the Muslim League."[14] Beyond merely meeting with branch leaders and members, Sultan's trip also demonstrated the league's continuing efforts to build a more supportive coalition beyond its core membership in the cities; he participated in several celebrations among Muslim religious leaders in many of the smaller towns and villages throughout the Western Province and along the Red Sea coast, where he met representatives from the regional khalwaat, zawayaat, and various other civic groups.

In addition to meeting with clan chiefs, merchants, and Sufi authorities allied with the league, Sultan also took the time to discuss the impending Ethiopian-Eritrean Federation with the NEPIP and other organizations that he felt could help ensure greater Muslim representation in the new government. On February 28, 1951, Sultan even met with representatives from Massawa's Na'ib family, long a thorn in the side of the league's leadership, to discuss the stipulations of the federation in an effort to garner additional support for the EDF's platform.[15] If Eritrea's unionists had reasoned that Resolution 390-A would once and for all resign the league and its leaders to a silent role as a minor opposition party, they failed to appreciate the extent to which Sultan and the executive council attempted to redirect the nationalist discourse in arousing support for regional autonomy among Muslim citizens. Tesfai argues that this urgency helps explain why league leaders from the outset of the UN resolution began a "campaign for their members to work toward guarding the internal independence or autonomy given to Eritrea from dwindling."[16] He also noted that in a public address given by Sultan in late 1951 the league's general secretary remained adamant about the need to protect against continued threats to Eritrean independence as the federation government took shape. He noted that the real work still lay ahead, as supporters needed to guard against the political obstacles that could prevent a legitimate, self-reliant government from forming. In Sultan's view, political autonomy could be assured only if citizens "remained vigilant" against ongoing unionist efforts to derail the federal plan by dividing the population.[17]

Although Sultan's warning addressed Eritreans of all faiths, it carried particular meaning for his closet adherents within the league, who represented the heart of Muslim awareness against possible compromises to Eritrean autonomy. Consequently, the league redoubled its political efforts, including a revitalized push to emphasize that "Muslim culture" be protected in the federation. The very fact that activists believed that Muslim interests needed to be protected also spoke to the relative success within Eritrea's wider Muslim community during the previous period, as the expansion of educational and legal institutions, youth associations, charity organizations, and Islamic cultural groups all revealed to what extent civic life had flourished during the mid- and late 1940s. Although their focus on safeguarding Islamic interests included a wide discussion about how religious and cultural life would be secured, activists' most forceful arguments developed through the league's emphasis on protecting Arabic as an official Eritrean language.

Protecting Arabic

In the midst of shifting political debate from one of outright independence to Eritrean autonomy as an equal partner in the federation,

league writers continued to defend Muslim rights and cultural practices as an integral part of regional sovereignty. Not surprisingly,
concerns over the preservation of the use of Arabic only increased in
the months after the UN decision. In written commentaries, branch
meetings, and public gatherings, Arabic's centrality again resurfaced
as a key issue among supporters. Yet what also emerged included the
basic belief that Eritrea's national identity and character would be
compromised if the federation failed to allow Muslims to use Arabic
in any official capacity. One commentary boasted that Arabic could
and must be protected solely for the fact that "the language of every
nation is the spring of its life and the source of its strength, and a
space in which the degree of civilization this nation has reached is
manifested."[18] Likewise, league writer Ahmed Muhammad Haji Ferraj
concluded that, as one of the leading international languages, Arabic
represented a way to "open doors" for Eritrean Muslims' success in
the wider world.[19] Recalling previous arguments by league leaders
and branch representatives, supporters also defended Arabic as one of
the major cultural hallmarks of Eritrea's unique historical experience:

> The Muslims in this nation, in spite of their diverse dialects,
> realized this and adopted Arabic as a lingua franca in which
> they can communicate. This is because they realized that it
> represented the sacred heritage of their ancestors and that
> they should maintain it in the same way that they maintain
> their own lives, and they know that both their lives and the
> lives of their children depend on it. They were so adamant
> about this that even the Italians had no choice but to consider
> Arabic the official language of the Eritrean Muslims.[20]

As many league commentaries illustrate, the rationale for promoting and protecting Arabic was directly linked to supporters' embrace
of a nation-state both unique and separate from Ethiopia. It also
reflected the growing fears about threat of "Amharization" against
Eritrea as a whole. Indeed, long-standing fears that the Ethiopian
government would force residents to learn Amharic, Ethiopia's official
language, were expressed in many previous commentaries in *Sawt al-
rabita*. Concerns that Eritreans would be forced to learn Amharic in
the schools and speak the language in government institutions only
strengthened Muslim resolve that Arabic be given the status of an official language as a means of ensuring their separate "national" identity.
Echoing this spirit, the league's post-1950 efforts continued to follow

this same trajectory while also downplaying the historical connections between Eritrea and Ethiopia. This de-emphasis also helps explain why the league's most forceful proponents of protecting Arabic also showed a relative open-mindedness in accepting that other indigenous Eritrean languages such as Tigre and Saho be included in the federation government, thereby demonstrating how the region's linguistic and cultural diversity ran counter to the Ethiopian government's own attempts to force the full-scale "Amharization" of its subjects.

By late July 1951 even the mufti Ibrahim al-Mukhtar began to engage more forcefully in the public discussions over Arabic's centrality in an autonomous Eritrea. *Sawt al-rabita*'s editors began publishing a serial of his work, "A Detraction of the Traitors Concerning the Arabic Language in Eritrea and Habesha," from its July 23 issue until October 28.[21] Although published anonymously, the mufti's widely recognized efforts to explain the historical significance of Arabic as a viable national language demonstrated that both the league and the wider Muslim populace perceived Arabic as far more significant to daily life and communication than simply serving religious ritual. The mufti's serial revealed the widespread fears within the league and among Muslims in general that the Ethiopian government would, if given the chance, interfere in Eritrea's Islamic affairs, just as authorities had done previously in Ethiopia. In particular, the mufti described the various ways in which Emperor Haile Selassie's ministers had outlawed the use of Arabic within Ethiopia's Islamic courts and replaced it with Amharic. He also noted the rapid decline of Arabic in public schools across Ethiopia when the Emperor reestablished his authority after Italy's defeat in World War II.[22]

Although the league's executive council and Ibrahim Sultan in particular continually embraced the idea of a dual language policy, the tone of the mufti's serial also reflected the growing feeling among many league supporters who were increasingly resentful of the perceived historical advantages of Tigrinya speakers during both the Italian and British periods.[23] Specifically, the mufti's writings addressed the widely held belief that Muslims were largely "shut out" from any institutional advancement because of both the BA's neglect of Arabic and its failing to incorporate a greater number of Muslims into its administrative ranks. As a result of the supposed "privileging" of Christians, English gradually "overtook Arabic as the dominant language in most institutions," which ultimately benefited Tigrinya speakers, who "convinced the British that Tigrinya was the language spoken in Eritrea."[24] According to the mufti, Muslims in Eritrea were effectively "marginalized" for much of the 1940s due to the general lack of English-speaking Muslims available to work with the BMA and the relative ignorance among the majority of Muslim political leaders concerning the "conspiracy against their language and rights" that many of the leading Tigrinya Christian intellectuals pursued.[25]

In late June 1951 the mufti met with the UN envoy, Bolivian-born Eduardo Anze Matienzo, to discuss his concerns and composed a letter the following August again defending the use of Arabic as the ideal language to articulate Muslims' "conditions and history." The mufti reminded Matienzo that in the past, "the Turkish and Egyptian rulers of Eritrea wrote and published documents for the Eritrean population only in Arabic, as there were no other written languages during that era." Reflecting the league/EDF's position on the language question, he argued that Arabic was "the language of all real Muslims in Eritrea and Abyssinia, and the oldest of all languages now in Eritrea and the only one in which Muslims can understand each other and communicate with the peoples and nations of Asia, Africa and other continents than by using dialects."[26]

The mufti's discussion was also noteworthy because of his mentioning of Arabic's essential role in disseminating Islamic law and regulations within communities. He emphasized that Arabic's official status remained a necessary reality because of its significance to Eritrea's "judicial Islamic courts" relating to the "issues and judgments, records and other correspondence" among the local population. He also noted the historical precedent for Arabic's use in "all Islamic organizations, whether cultural, sporting, political or national."[27]

Beyond the mufti's efforts to recall the supposed inequities among Arabic speakers during the early BMA period, his accusations also reflected a growing discontent among Eritrean Islamic clerics in general, who feared for the viability of Eritrean Islamic institutions even before the federation. On May 19, 1951, the mufti helped organize a meeting of all regional clerics in Asmara and established the Ulama Front. Composed of Islamic scholars, jurists, and community leaders (including several members of the league's executive council), the front was primarily designed to "refine Islamic institutions" in Eritrea by expanding the participation of all Muslim scholars in religious affairs and rituals beyond the immediate circle of qadis.[28] In the organization's seven-point charter, representatives made their pledge to ensure that first and foremost the organization would serve to "monitor the situation of public and religious affairs" among all Muslims. Moreover, the front allegedly tried to strengthen Eritrea's ties with instructors and officials at Cairo's Al-Azhar University. Building on the mufti's previous efforts, the organization's members sought to renew the steady trickle of Arabic teachers and jurists that had traveled from Egypt to improve Islamic education, particularly in the major cities and towns.[29] In bringing together Islamic clergy, former Al-Azhar students, and community leaders to strengthen Islamic education, the organization reflected the growing political nature of Muslim civic activism even before the federation's inauguration.[30] The group's aims were also largely an extension of the mufti's earlier efforts in bringing greater standardization and continuity to Islamic practices, and many of the front's basic objectives called for both the autonomy of Muslim institutions such as schools and courts and a broader protection of religious rights. The organization's reliance on legal precedent also reflected another general pattern of protest that emerged from those within the Muslim League.

Despite the particular differences between these religious and political organizations, their mutual suspicion of the perceived Ethiopian marginalization against Muslims further illustrated how religious and political concerns increasingly merged as leaders challenged such "intrusions" into community affairs in the months before the federation's inauguration. While the Ulama Front attempted to publicly defend Islamic practices as well as protect the Arabic language, some league members also went on the offensive, even going so far as to attack the legitimacy of Tigrinya. In one commentary, Adem Musa Berhanu openly ridiculed proponents of a Tigrinya-only policy, observing that their proposals were irrelevant since Tigrinya represented "only one of many regional dialects" and lacked any legitimate claim as a language appropriate for official use: "This language only reached this point because of the care of the Italians. Until today, Tigrinya speakers do not have a script to write numbers, but instead have to write them in Latin. Despite efforts to promote the language, it has failed to be anything more than one regional language, let alone to be a national language."[31]

Echoing this spirit, one commentary that appeared in November 1951 derided critics of Arabic's official use by charging that those against its implementation were part of a wider "conspiracy against the Arabic language" that sought to merely privilege Tigrinya over others that had an equal, if not greater, claim to be official languages.

The article's anonymous author observed that those who supported implementing Tigrinya merely wished to elevate their own status over "equally legitimate" languages such as Arabic, Saho, Afar, and particularly Tigre.[32] Pushing the debate even further, the writer concluded, "If we really think about this language question, we should conclude that justice requires that Tigre be the first language, and Saho and Danakali (Afar) the second languages," and that those who spoke Tigrinya simply did not want a "Muslim language" to take precedence in the federation.[33] While most league members' defense of Arabic mirrored earlier efforts before the passage of the federal resolution, many of the commentaries during this period took on a more aggressive and at times even prideful attitude that Arabic represented the spiritual cornerstone of Eritrea, as one writer conveyed:

> *You are the sun and others are stars,*
> *With your light our nights became light*
> *Upon the light of your lamp we worship God in the mosques*
> *And using you in the sermons like a bell ringing*
> *You are sugar for writers; they cannot find anything similar.*
> *Your life spring gives us clarity and eloquence*
> *So let us go forward, we are behind you*
> *We swear by God to protect you.*[34]

Another major influence on this growing attitude revolved around the widely held belief that although not indigenous to Eritrea, Arabic essentially performed the function of a "local" language because of its significance in regional history among Muslims and non-Muslims alike.[35] As early as January 1951, Ibrahim Sultan declared in a meeting with the then BA governor general, Duncan Cumming, that Arabic should be protected within the federation because of its already de facto status as the "official language" of all Eritrean Muslims.[36] Throughout 1951, several of the league's branch representatives submitted several memoranda that often included references to the importance of Arabic and the need to designate it as one of the official languages within the federation. One September 1951 memorandum written by league representatives from Akkele Guzay also claimed that of the "83 tribes of the Arabic Islamic Saho," official meetings and press releases among its constituents were conducted exclusively in Arabic.[37] Only days earlier, on August 21, members of the league's executive council cosponsored a general meeting along with representatives from other parties within the EDF with Matienzo in which attendees demanded that Arabic be declared as at least one of the official languages.[38]

The concerns of the league and its allies over the language issue continued well into the following year, when Matienzo finally presented his draft of the proposed federal constitution. When meeting with representatives at the 32nd Assembly, in Asmara in June 1952, to discuss Article 40, which concerned the language issue, the majority of league supporters and other Muslim representatives from the affiliated EDF groups expressed support for a dual-language policy, provided that the constitution include Arabic.[39] Rejecting claims that Arabic represented a foreign language that should be excluded from official use, Qadi 'Ali Umar 'Uthman, an EDF representative from Akkele Guzay, reiterated the Muslim League's argument that Arabic "was no more foreign than Tigrinya" and that both languages deserved official status based on their supposed common origins in regional history.[40] Other league representatives echoed this basic spirit of an Arabic-Tigrinya policy, while the majority of unionists supported Tigrinya as an official language alongside Amharic.[41] Although Matienzo had hoped to reach a compromise on the issue, the continuing controversy in addressing Arabic's precise place in the new government demonstrated that the language question developed parallel to other apprehensions among Muslims, who believed, as a matter of principle, that they would not be given equal footing in the federal system with Eritrean Christians.

In a memorandum composed by the league's executive council in October 1951, officials conveyed to Matienzo their anxiety that unionist elements were already threatening the integrity of Eritrea's Islamic communities within the proposed government.[42] League members rejected the proposal to allow the use of the Ethiopian flag simultaneously with the flag of the federation on the grounds that, in addition to "having the colors of the Coptic flag, it bears the Lion of Judah, symbol of the Hebrew people and the said lion carries a cross over one shoulder."[43] The council demanded that the "flag of the federation must be far removed from any religious or racial symbol" as a necessary measure to guarantee that "all forms of religion will be respected by all sections of the population."[44] Although they largely supported Matienzo's initial proposals during the previous June, the executive council also took exception to several additional stipulations within a sample booklet of proposals that the UN envoy had distributed, including vague assertions to Ethiopian oversight of the federal judiciary and national defense. The council's fears thus mirrored Sultan's belief that Matienzo, by way of his concessions to unionist elements, helped ensure that "the threat of annexation to Ethiopia" remained a reality.[45]

As with their previous efforts, league officials demonstrated their knowledge of the historical legacy and possible implications of federation-style governments, explaining that, unlike other variations of similar systems found in Europe and North America, the Ethiopian-Eritrean Federation could be implemented in such a way as to ensure a "wide autonomy" and thus guarantee a way for their government to thrive well beyond other supposedly successful federation systems.[46] However, in responding to the UN envoy's booklet, the league also noted that its executive council had recently "decided energetically to oppose such interpretations which, should they materialize, would surely and rapidly reduce Eritrea to a status of vassalage and domination by Ethiopia."[47]

Representatives also cited the preamble to Article 15 of Resolution 390-A, which prescribed that the federation would "guarantee the inhabitants of Eritrea the fullest respect and safeguards for their institutions, traditions, religions, and languages, as well as the widest possible measure of self-government" as a necessity for all sections of the population.[48] In drawing attention to the shortcomings between the rhetoric and the reality of the institutional safeguards, league leaders again placed their primary focus on issues of language and cultural identity. Continuing with their previous arguments, league representatives again made a simultaneous effort to respect the "wishes of the Tigrinya-speaking population" while reiterating their long-standing position of guaranteeing Arabic's place in the new system. Taking a slightly different approach than the previous efforts of league writers and even the mufti, the executive council provided a justification for using Arabic based less on its religious importance than on its stature as an international and common vernacular: "Arabic is not only a language for religious use, as it is claimed, but is a language spread widely throughout the whole world and used as an official language by Christian people, as for instance in Lebanon (Middle East) whose population is about 90% Christian. On the other hand, it is the language used by the majority of the Eritrean people."[49]

Although the memorandum proved to be only the latest in a series of public statements on the part of its leaders, the league's efforts to challenge Matienzo on maintaining an autonomous administration within Eritrea demonstrated that the language issue also addressed wider concerns about the underrepresentation of Muslims at all levels of Eritrean political and civic life.

The Eritreanization of the Civil Service

Widespread concerns that Muslims would be denied access to employment within the government also developed as a result of the fears that Ethiopian authorities wished to exploit the cultural and religious connections with Tigrinya-speaking Christians as means of limiting Muslim influence within the federation.[50] In the context of the growing debates about the very structure and character of the federal system, the political ramifications of the Christian-Muslim imbalance within the civil service only increased throughout 1951.

Although by April 1951 British administrators began increasing their public recruitment drives across the country to fill vital "administrative, technical and clerical positions," the actual results of their efforts to incorporate Eritreans into the civil service only seemed to confirm the mufti's earlier accusations about the underrepresentation and marginalization of Muslims by the BA. Lloyd Ellingson notes that although "between July 1951 and July 1952, 1,973 Eritreans were inducted into various departments," a substantial majority of the new recruits within the civil service came from exclusively Christian backgrounds.[51] In light of the fact that the majority of the new postings for Eritreans continued to be under the authority of the small but influential group of British and Italian managers in the "high-level administration," any particular Muslim influence within the federal government was limited to workers in clerical and especially translation services.

Ultimately, most of the "Eritreanization" of the civil service occurred by mid-1952, just three months before the planned official transfer of power, in September, as "the total number of Eritreans employed by the Eritrean Government, either salaried or hourly, was 7,947 (96%)," with approximately 354 non-Eritreans employed in the aforementioned "high-level administration and technical positions."[52] Yet despite the success, the religious imbalance within the administration only confirmed to the league that its members' apprehensions about the lack of Muslim representation were justified. Although in conversations with BA officers Matienzo had "stressed the importance of endeavoring to induct Moslems and Christians into the Administration in approximately equal numbers," the numerical imbalance proved considerable.[53] Indeed, the overall estimates revealed that Christian Eritreans were represented at almost three times the rate of Muslims in the civil service. For example, a June 1951 clerical training course in Asmara began with only 40 of the 189 attendees coming from a Muslim background after an initial candidate pool in which only 24 percent of the 1,140 considered applicants were Muslim.[54] In spite of British efforts to integrate the civil service and Matienzo's own belief that the federation would invite broad participation from the public to eventually "guarantee of the rights of free expression, habeas corpus, religious belief and political organization," the religious imbalance in the civil administration only increased perceptions both within and outside the league that Muslims were heading toward permanent second-class citizenship.

Based in part on these fears and the continued rivalry with several of the Massawa-based leaders, the league again expressed its resistance to conditional unionist Muslims who tried throughout mid-1951 to chart a new political course for wider Muslim "interests" at the expense of the league. When news reached the executive council that IML president Muhammad Umar Kadi and several colleagues had organized their own "Islamic Conference" in Massawa in June 1951 to challenge the league's policies within the EDF, supporters launched a public campaign to discredit the meeting as nothing more than a power grab that would only instigate further division among Muslims. Yasin Ba Tuq argued that the June conference had less to do with any genuine concern for Islamic practices than it did with establishing a new counterorganization to the league. Composed of Kadi, Muhammad Hassan Na'ib, and several other longtime league opponents, the meeting represented—for the league's leadership— little more than the most recent attempt to surrender Muslim protection by tacitly accepting an Ethiopian-dominated federation rather than establishing a legitimate, sovereign system. Putting the group's motivations in context, Yasin Ba Tuq observed, "Saying that this movement is an instigation is something without doubt, and the fact that we are calling it thus is not because of our bias against it but because in the past the leaders of this movement have indicated that they are against Muslims' interests. So we have no choice but to call this instigation. Because sooner or later it will lead to the division, distrust, and weakening of the Muslims of this nation."[55]

In later weeks, other league supporters went to great efforts to discredit the Massawa gathering, stating that the overwhelming majority of members in the regional branches were "deeply opposed" to Kadi's actions.[56] Additionally, several high-profile Islamic clerics within the league purportedly came out against the conference and refuted Kadi's attempts to speak on behalf of the region's Muslims.[57] Ironically, the league's aggressive treatment toward the "Islamic Conference" organizers, particularly the conditional unionist leadership within the IML, occurred at a time in which many other former Muslim League rivals began to finally take a more aggressive position against both the broader unionist sentiment and the vagaries of Matienzo's promises regarding Muslim representation.

Even IML president Kadi voiced skepticism in June 1951 about the planned government's ability to provide viable safeguards needed to guarantee the autonomy of Muslim religious institutions and schools. Kadi's emergence as a skeptic of Muslim "protection" evolved gradually from the generally optimistic tone that he and his organization expressed as late as November 1950, which embraced union between Eritrea and Ethiopia provided that Muslims be given assurances, including the "recognition of the Arabic language as our own language, the recognition of the personal rights of Moslems, and with appropriate guarantees for their protection."[58]

The growth of political tension between "conditional" Muslim unionists and the wider UP membership developed largely as a result of the inherent contradictions in establishing a federal system that would supposedly allow Muslim religious and cultural institutions to thrive under the auspices of an Ethiopian-dominated government.[59] Matienzo noted that during initial discussions with Muslim representatives throughout June and July 1951 about developing the structure of the federal system, IML members and representatives from the Massawa-based National Party submitted a joint memorandum petitioning for the creation of two wholly independent administrations in Eritrea based on religious affiliation. For their part, MLWP representatives also submitted an "identical" tract calling for two administrative units while the capital Asmara would fall under its own special administrative unit.[60] Both tracts proposed that the administrations include legal guarantees to protect religious institutions among the respective minority population.[61] Yet despite Kadi's and other unionist Muslims' efforts to address these religious and cultural concerns, their inability to articulate a coherent policy in the aftermath of the UN resolution only encouraged the league to take the initiative in leading calls for greater Muslim autonomy. This became especially evident as Matienzo began meeting political representatives in mid-1951 to develop Eritrea's constitution.

The growing tensions between representatives reflected the extent to which Muslim fears of exclusion within the coming federation became major points of contention in both domestic and political life. That these pressures actually encouraged further divisions within the country's broad Muslim nationalist community also illustrates how several emerging interpretations of what constituted "Muslim interests" emerged among the different factions. These varying interpretations also influenced the ways in which nationalists began to confront the challenge of crafting the Eritrean constitution, as both the league and rival organizations sought to establish a viable constitution that could protect their respective Muslim constituents from possible marginalization.[62] In the context of this apparent political stagnation, some league members began expanding their initial activities with more broadly based reform efforts, particularly in regard to the country's fledgling labor movement.

Muslim League Participation in Labor Activism

Complementing the league's attempts to embrace the new political realities in the aftermath of the UN decision, several members also involved themselves in early efforts to unite workers and improve general labor conditions in the country. While their involvement developed amid Eritrea's deteriorating economic conditions, labor activism also represented a key aspect in protecting Muslim community interests during the early 1950s, particularly among merchants in the major cities. While most of the league's leadership participated since the early 1940s in business organizations such as the Asmara Chamber of Commerce or had publicly addressed concerns about workers' rights and wages, 1951 represented a marked increase in both the scale and political nature of labor mobilization among league members.

When Asmara-based activists formed the labor organization Hara zekhone semret kefletat serahatenyatat eritrawiyan (Syndicate of Eritrean Workers), in November 1951, Muslim League members contributed to the syndicate's early efforts to mobilize the various segments of the economy and to establish religious harmony within the organization. In their respective analyses of Eritrean labor activism, both Tom Killion and Tesfai rightly note that the impetus behind the syndicate's creation involved workers' previous attempts to procure equal employment opportunities for both Muslim and Christian laborers. They also allude to the high degree of interreligious cooperation within the group and the ability of labor activists to avoid sectarian rivalry, even when faced with potentially volatile labor disputes. That "ability" revealed itself best when a group of mainly Christian workers affiliated with the syndicate tried to secure employment with job recruiters from the Arabian American Oil Company (ARAMCO).[63] After failing to arouse interest and support from leaders in Asmara's "Arab" (Hadrami) community, labor activists received the support for their cause from Woldeab Woldemariam, who used his influential position as *Hanti Ertra*'s editor in chief to help the group publish an editorial in November 1951.[64] In their public testimony against the group carefully aired its grievances about being discriminated against while continuing to embrace the need for religious unity in their cause:

> In writing such words and notifying the people, we, the Christians who are writing [this] complaint, are not doing so because we envy our Muslim brothers. Because they are also our Eritrean brothers, their harmony is our harmony and their happiness is ours, too. However, as the people understand deeply, those Arab people who could be close to us through lineage, and geography, are very close neighbors. As we have been since ancient times, we will seek to be cooperative in the future as well; however, although they come to our county, freely work in peace, and get rich, the moment a few [Christian] Eritreans go to their country and request permission to work . . . we are extremely saddened and astounded that [the Arabs] ordered the company [ARAMCO] . . . to deny any Christian from Eritrea to enter their land.[65]

Although several delegates from the syndicate did eventually engage in a bitter public quarrel with representatives of Asmara's resident Hadrami community, the group managed to avoid turning the spat into a sectarian dilemma by arguing that the resident "Arab" merchants had demeaned all Eritrean workers by not assisting them in their efforts to gain employment abroad. Syndicate representatives accused many of the Hadrami leaders of simply extracting Eritrea's resources and wealth through their own merchant activities and of having allegedly lied about their influence in ARAMCO's hiring process.[66] The situation escalated to the point where *Hanti Ertra*'s editorial staff announced that they would temporarily stop printing individual commentaries so that the feuding parties could address the issue among themselves in an "appropriate manner."[67]

Labor activist Tsegaye Kahsay alluded to the fact that despite the initial conflict with the Hadrami community, Woldemariam's encouragement of the group precipitated the wider involvement from other nationalist "intellectual Eritreans" who helped advise the group on how to go about strengthening their organization.[68] The group also received considerable support in many of the commentaries featured in *Hanti Ertra* by late 1951, as EDF supporters reasoned that the "severe economic situation" across the country required more proactive involvement from the labor section to address the public's needs.[69] By seeking to unite both Muslim and Christian merchants, business owners, and workers, the very spirit of the labor movement ran parallel to the political ideals among the EDF and especially the league's urban-based branches. Its large youth base also reflected Sultan's previous discussions that a robust civil society needed to be harnessed from among the country's youth, whom he believed were the ones with "the most responsibility and challenges regarding the federal plan" and whose success would determine whether or not the federation would survive.[70]

Several editorials implored the syndicate to continue its efforts to build unity to help remedy the employment crisis that faced most workers, especially in the major cities.[71] With Tsegaye Kahsay and Muhammad Abdelkadir Kiyar appointed as the main representatives to facilitate worker negotiations with the BA, the labor leadership received considerable support from Asmara's Muslim community and Jabarti leaders in particular.[72] The group attracted widespread support from among the wider pro-independence population and even among some unionists, although "there was not any clear understanding" among the movement's leaders about what specifically constituted a legitimate worker to qualify for the organization.[73]

Although some unionist leaders, particularly Tedla Bairu and Haregot Abbai, participated in and supported labor activities throughout 1951 and 1952, the syndicate's internal organization was largely built around the leadership-affiliated LPP and Muslim League officials. This resulted in the labor movement essentially "becoming an institutional base for an emerging pan-Eritrean nationalist movement."[74] In an effort to stem possible religious divisions, the syndicate's founders opted to elect an eighteen-person executive council composed of an equal number of Christian and Muslim members, with each group consisting of five labor representatives and four advisors, respectively. Among the members of the syndicate's first advisory board, league leaders Suleiman Adin and Adem Kusmallah held formal positions on the executive council, while several other league veterans, such as Degiat Hassan 'Ali, served in informal roles as outside advisers and facilitators between merchants, workers, and British authorities.[75] Later, league official Muhammad Seraj Abdu served as the syndicate's vice president.[76]

The syndicate's wider objective of encouraging the participation of broad segments of civil society to "preserve and enlarge not only workers', but all Eritreans', democratic rights under the Ethio-Eritrean Federation" also conveyed the basic spirit of both the EDF and league's basic platform.[77] Although the full ramifications of the league's participation in the labor movement did not materialize immediately, its contribution to the formation of the syndicate demonstrated that its core agenda of building a viable consortium for both Muslim and Christian activists across civil society remained alive and well despite the growing political challenges.

Muslim League Troubles in the Constituent Assembly Elections

Compounding league members' concerns over the language issue, civil service employment, and labor unrest, the impending election of the Eritrean Constituent Assembly also represented a further challenge to wider Muslim concerns across the country. In theory, the BA's decision in early 1951 to proceed with the UN resolution's demand for a popularly elected Eritrean legislature should have represented a significant step toward regional autonomy and a triumph for the league's supposed grassroots strength. The establishment of 238 administrative units, to be represented ultimately by sixty-eight assembly seats from across the country, also held promise for the league that it would have a strong chance to influence much of the legislature's agenda. Ellingson notes that twenty-three of the planned assembly seats were set aside for constituencies in the Western Province, offering the league an opportunity to capitalize on its self-proclaimed appeal across the region.[78] In addition, league candidates running under the EDF banner also sought election among large Muslim electorates in Asmara and especially Massawa and along the major coastal communities.[79] Yet despite the apparent advantages for the league and the EDF more broadly, the results of the assembly elections demonstrated that despite its rhetoric and proactive measures to rally supporters, the league faced major challenges in fielding official support across the Western Province due to the ongoing divisions between its leadership and former supporters now aligned with the MLWP.

While BA officials claimed that the MLWP benefited from "a large number of supporters" across the province, particularly in the Agordat, Tessenei, and Nakfa Districts, the inability of the league to field a stronger showing in part resulted from both the considerable influence of a small number of religious and clan leaders from across the Western Province whose own personal histories revealed a mixed rationale for their opposition to the league.[80] For example, MLWP president Qadi Hamid Abu Alama had maintained a long-standing rivalry with both Ibrahim Sultan and several of the leading Islamic clerics affiliated with the league, particularly the mufti.[81] MLWP leaders, especially those in positions of authority as clan chiefs such as Saydna Saleh Mustapha and others leaders affiliated with 'Ali Musa Radai, continued to use their influence to pressure their respective constituencies into voting against league/EDF candidates. Moreover, BA interference also seems to have played a role in explaining the league's electoral troubles in the months leading up to the elections.

Although he eventually secured a seat in the assembly, even Ibrahim Sultan faced unexpected difficulty in his election to the legislature. According to Ellingson, BA officials had attempted to block Sultan's nomination by misinforming electors from Sultan's own Rugbat clan about the correct date to cast their ballots. Later, some of the Rugbat electors were allegedly bribed into switching their votes. Even American consulate officials stationed in Asmara suspected that members of the BA, chiefly Frank Stafford, were involved in pressuring some of the Rugbat electors into switching their votes from Sultan to other candidates during the three-week period before the election.[82] Although Sultan managed to win a seat in the elections by a narrow margin, his experience reflected the broader challenges among the league's core constituency in showcasing their electoral strength.

For example, beginning in February 1952 more than twenty thousand members of the Bet Asghede clan complained to BA officials that they had not been provided with their own candidates for the assembly elections. Finally, the clan representatives "were told by the UN Commissioner that the BA did not regard the Bet Asghede as a tribal unit" and subsequently dismissed their objections and partitioned the clan members with representatives from outside their own communities mainly affiliated with the pro-unionist and BA-backed MLWP.[83] Edward Mulcahy, an Asmara-based American official, accurately summarized the dilemma of the Bet Asghede representatives when he stated that their renunciation of the MLWP candidates had effectively incurred the wrath of BA administrators concerned only with limiting league/EDF support from expanding across the Western Province.[84] He even professed his belief that Stafford "was not beyond rigging the election results to advance the Ethiopian cause."[85] Beyond revealing the still considerable gap between Sultan's faction and former league members now embracing the MLWP, the election results across the Western Province also demonstrated that the league largely failed in its efforts to reassure a significant portion of its constituents through the spirited debates both within the nationalist press and in the public discussions. For all the league's bold proclamations about being at the forefront of protecting Muslim interests and still remaining the most sizable nationalist force, its position by April–May 1952 revealed that its previous influence within the intellectual parameters of the nationalist contact zone had dropped considerably. The league's problems during this period demonstrated that for the first time its history, the organization lost much of its ability to shape the nationalist contact zone because of the perceived weakness of its leadership. While in previous years Ibrahim Sultan and his inner circle succeeded in maintaining control of the overall debate and direction among the intellectual nationalist Muslim class, the 1952 elections signaled the decline of the league's influence within the wider nationalist discourse. Coming at a time in which the very ability of nationalist groups to address their political concerns in public became increasingly difficult, the league's decline as the main facilitator within the contact zone developed in conjunction with the rise of its political rivals. Consequently, the overall direction of the discussions within the nationalist contact zone demonstrated how leading pro-independence intellectuals were less and less dependent on the Muslim League's leadership for ideological guidance and more concerned with the wider "Muslim" struggle to preserve Eritrean autonomy.

And yet, despite the league's continued difficulties in fending off the MLWP and IML and its own failure to subdue grassroots concerns across the Western Province, the growing apprehension among some conditional unionist Muslims provided the organization with a much-needed boost. In a commentary in the April 27 edition of *Sawt al-rabita*, longtime league rival Muhammad Umar Kadi expressed his own concern that although a significant number of Muslim representatives were elected to office, many of the new representatives lacked the political experience, ability, and willingness to safeguard Muslim rights. He even questioned whether or not the new Muslim delegates "would have the same rights as others" once the assembly began its official session.[88] Later commentaries also suggested that the equal number of Christian and Muslim seats within the assembly (thirty-four for each) did not reflect the actual demographics in the country and that the lack of real Muslim representation in the assembly only revealed a concerted effort to limit Muslim input within the federation's legislative body.[89]

Consequently, league writers increasingly tried to focus on how the assembly's actions sought to further relegate Muslims to second-class citizenship. In *Sawt al-rabita*'s coverage of the assembly's weekly activities throughout the late spring and early summer of 1952, writers often made note of the rising hostility between Muslim and Christian representatives, especially in regard to the language issue and when representatives debated laws perceived as being too favorable to Muslim interests.[90] During the assembly's first day in session, the language controversy erupted in full force when authorities removed Qadi ʿAli Umar ʿUthman, an EDF representative from Senafe, after he tried to shout down the Ethiopian government representative Andemikael Dessalegn for beginning his introductory remarks to the assembly in Amharic rather than in one of the assembly's working languages—Arabic, Tigrinya, English, or Italian.[91] Another report took note of Ibrahim Sultan's alleged attempts to get the assembly to approve a land reform law that would have allowed Muslim communities across the lowlands and the Western Province to purchase small private plots of land rather than continue to pay rent and reside on government-owned property.[92] Despite Sultan's efforts, league writers lamented that many of the Christians in the assembly rejected the motion and refused to even call for a vote before they adjourned from their session.[93]

Other contributors worried openly that the assembly's unionist majority and public proclamations to minimize Eritrean autonomy had already created an atmosphere in which Eritrea's most "fanatic" unionist supporters were attempting to marginalize Muslims from government offices, schools, and other institutions in the same way that the Ethiopian government had done to Muslims living in Ethiopia. For league observers, this sudden and pronounced encroachment into Eritrea's cultural and political life revealed how extremism "was now so apparent in our country that it appears just as the sun in the middle of the sky."[94]

Eroding Sovereignty on the Federation's Eve

While the months following the assembly elections brought additional concerns about the curtailed autonomy within Eritrean political institutions, the weeks both preceding and following the formal transfer of power from BA to federation rule, on September 15, 1952, revealed the extent to which Ethiopian and unionist authorities had already crushed several mediums of nationalist discourse. The suppression and ultimate banning of *Sawt al-rabita*, in early September, represented a major blow to the league's strength and influence. Discontinued initially because of recurring funding difficulties, the paper's death knell came ironically after Muslim League writers complained that Ethiopian and federation officials were attempting to forcibly close its printing press.

Given the nature of much of the content in many of the paper's latter issues during August and September, its discontinuation could not have come at a better time for the Federation's most ardent unionist supporters. Reports began surfacing in late August in *Sawt al-rabita* about the presence of Ethiopian troops already within Eritrea's borders. The paper's August 24 edition featured several commentaries about the military's arrival at various points in Serae and Akkele Guzay Provinces, including one editorial authored by Imam Musa that discussed the possible ramifications of Ethiopian soldiers' presence in the still supposedly independent federal government.[95] Just weeks later, the league's worst fears were confirmed when Haile Selassie issued Proclamation 130, stating that the Ethiopian Federal Court would supersede the authority of the Federation judiciary. Apart from directly contradicting Articles 85 and 90 of the Eritrean constitution, the ruling also represented a troubling turn for league constituents by limiting the ability of Eritrea's Islamic courts to operate without direct Ethiopian interference.[96] Validating the earlier concerns of the mufti and many of the qadis that came together and created the Ulama Front, Eritrea's Islamic clerics soon discovered the proclamation's implications for Ethiopian intrusion into the inner workings of Eritrean Muslim religious institutions, including the appointment of qadis as well as the management and oversight of the various waqf administrations. By late September, even rank-and-file league members emerged as vocal critics of the federation; members protested and sent written complaints to the assembly about the already apparent violations against the constitution, including the refusal of several government offices to raise the Eritrean flag—protesting Ethiopian control of key industries and properties within Eritrea—and especially in voicing concerns about the presence of Ethiopian armed units across the major cities and towns.[97]

The federation's very beginning coincided with the end of one the most powerful and effective political tools available to the league and other nationalist groups. Although some scholars have since argued that there remained "ample opportunities" for the organization's members to continue to voice their objections to the perceived inequalities of the federation, both the league and the wider EDF constituency suffered almost immediately in the aftermath of the clampdown.[98] Coupled with the earlier discontinuation of *Wahda Iritriyya/Hanti Ertra*, the closing of *Sawt al-rabita*, and the departure of Woldeab Woldemariam from Eritrea after having barely survived the seventh (and final) attempt on his life, in early 1953, the federation's establishment represented the virtual end of Muslim League activism within the dynamic intellectual exchanges of the nationalist contact zone. Previous discussions about how Islamic religious institutions and Arabic could serve to build a viable, independent Eritrea now gave way to more defensive posturing about the need to insulate Muslims from the already apparent state-sponsored discrimination.

Although some critical Arabic and Tigrinya commentaries by league supporters continued throughout much of the next two years following the launching of *Hanti Ertra*'s successor paper, *Dehay Ertra*, in late September 1952, most of the league's leading intellectuals found themselves forced to operate within an unprecedented atmosphere of political repression. Operating with merely the symbols of a functioning independent government, Eritrea's nationalist factions faced the challenges of an already gutted federal system in which Eritrean autonomy, particularly for Muslim residents, existed in name only. The virtual annihilation of the nationalist contact zone, in late 1952, also had a profound effect on the league's ideological trajectory in the coming years, as its constituents' concerns for protecting Islamic educational and religious institutions and the official recognition and use of Arabic took on even greater urgency after the transfer of official power.

Conclusions

The brief but tumultuous period between the UN's passage of Resolution 390-A, in December 1950, and the formal transfer of power from British to federal authority, in mid-September 1952, witnessed a considerable transformation within both the nationalist movement and especially within the Muslim League. Having lost the wider battle for unconditional independence, the nationalist camp, led largely by the league and its affiliates within the newly formed EDF, redoubled its efforts aimed at guaranteeing the greatest possible autonomy for Eritrea within the future federation government. While the league's leadership continued to embrace an inclusive nationalist vision, its constituents began concerning themselves with what the federation would mean specifically for Muslim fortunes. Set against the backdrop of deteriorating political autonomy, even before the federation's actual implementation, many league activists only intensified their efforts by publicly working to ensure Arabic's survival as an official language, involving themselves in the growing labor movement, and encouraging greater inclusion of Muslims within the civil administration, as well as by consistently challenging UN authorities to guarantee greater autonomy to Islamic leaders and religious institutions.

Despite the league's efforts to remain relevant, its broader political influence continued to decline amid growing unionist and even direct Ethiopian pressures. By the time of the Constituent Assembly elections, in March–April 1952, the Muslim League's leadership had lost its ability to formulate a coherent policy to combat the wholesale demolition of Eritrea's autonomy. While the league remained a vocal force of political opposition, its minority standing in the assembly, coupled with its diminishing resources and the weakened state of its political allies, ushered in a period of decline. By September 1952,

Sawt al-rabita's discontinuation signaled the virtual end of the league's place as the center of formal Muslim nationalist intellectual discourse. Its closure, coupled with Ethiopia's already palpable military presence, the reduced authority of the Eritrean assembly, and the still unresolved issue of Muslim underrepresentation in the civil service and federal government, challenged the league to continue its agenda as political freedom further eroded. Still, the deteriorating political situation also presented the league with an opportunity to rework its previous failings by redirecting much of its program from political to more religious-based issues. Consequently, the league's reformation in subsequent years, as an outlet to address concerns among both the religious leadership and the wider Muslim public, demonstrated how the organization's leaders reacted to increased Ethiopian domination by learning "the political value of their Islamic connexions."[99]

6

Struggling for Autonomy

The Disintegrating Federation, October 1952–December 1957

For the Eritrean Muslim League and nationalist supporters in general, the official transfer of power from British to federation rule, in September 1952, offered little reassurance that violations against Eritrean sovereignty would dissipate. At the outset of federal rule, long-standing concerns among nationalists that the new government represented little more than a rubber stamp for Ethiopian policy only increased. Indeed, many league members as well as Eritreans in general feared the implications that the supposed Ethiopian "backwardness and feudalism" would bring. Their apprehensions only increased throughout the decade, as the federation's executive, legislative, and judicial branches transformed from independent authorities into quasi extensions of the Ethiopian government.[1]

The Muslim League nevertheless continued pursuing a policy that emphasized the need to protect Muslim religious freedom by highlighting the cultural autonomy of the Islamic religion from Ethiopia as its main "political" message. While their approach represented a continuation from the previous period before the federation's implementation, the virtual collapse of nationalist intellectual dialogue in the public sphere by late 1952 limited the organization's ability to direct a new course of activism. The league's actions after September 1952 reflected the general consensus among Muslims that their respective constituencies now needed to put aside their previous differences about independence and conditional union to develop a new strategy aimed at preserving the integrity of regional autonomy. As a result, the league rallied around the question of Eritrea's legal status as an "autonomous unit" by emphasizing its own jurisdiction over regional institutions and public affairs. According to Tekeste Negash, league leaders developed this strategy through a "scrupulous defence of the United Nations Resolution of 1950 and of the Constitution of Eritrea which emanated from the UN Resolution."[2]

Surprisingly, the league both survived these challenges and even reshaped itself as the general membership pushed for organizational reforms to adapt to the realities of the federation. At the heart of this push was the league's investment in what Kibreab terms the "associational life" of federal-era Eritrea. This proved especially true in regard to the broad mobilization against the exclusion of Muslims in the political process and dissatisfaction over the country's continuing economic troubles. As Eritrean Muslims' collective political misfortunes merged increasingly with economic instability, many league members began to take more proactive measures in addressing how the federation represented both an affront to their religious freedom and a hindrance to their economic progress.

League Participation with the Syndicate of Eritrean Workers

Even before the federation's official inauguration, activists across the country expressed their apprehension about possible Ethiopian interference in Eritrea's economy through the new government structures. While two years before, the Muslim League began to address its members' apprehensions about the country's economic future, critics now voiced specific opposition to Ethiopia's takeover of key aspects of the country. Activists both within the league and in Eritrea's Constituent Assembly also worried that Andargatchew Messai, the emperor's first designated representative to Eritrea and son-in-law, now exercised direct influence over institutions that were designated originally as joint federal enterprises, including regional telecommunications, railways, defense forces, and even customs.[3] Beyond the initial complaints of members within the Federal Assembly, discontent with Ethiopian dominance in the economy and the obstinacy of the federation's chief executive, longtime unionist leader Tedla Bairu, also contributed to the climate of emerging labor activism.

On November 23, 1952, more than six hundred members from the Syndicate of Eritrean Workers met in Asmara to inaugurate their new organization after Woldeab Woldemariam finalized the group's draft constitution. Two weeks later on December 7, Syndicate leaders held a ceremony at Asmara's Cinema Impero commemorating their recent accomplishments and pledged to use the organization to "better their moral, social, and economic conditions" as a united force.[4] The subsequent celebration of the first Eritrean Workers' Day, on January 1, 1953, represented both the high point of the organization's activities and its position as a legitimate "pan-Eritrean" organization, one that even reached across the unionist and nationalist divide and fielded more than twenty thousand supporters in its first public demonstration.[5] Nevertheless, the syndicate's operations also benefited from league constituents' input, both at the executive ranks and the grassroots.[6] When the syndicate staged labor strikes in early 1953 to protest low wages and to petition for the implementation of a federal labor code, the league supported striking salt workers in and around Massawa, even as many of the syndicate's more hardline unionist members began doubting the merits of labor protests. By mid-January, as Woldeab Woldemariam recovered from injuries after he survived another assassination attempt, league member Muhammad Seraj Abdu took over the syndicate's leadership until federation authorities closed the organization's main office the following November.[7]

Through the syndicate's activities in late 1952 and 1953, league members began aligning their political program with the widening labor unrest. During the celebrations, in early December 1952, commemorating the seventh anniversary of the Muslim League's founding, members addressed the ongoing economic troubles and praised those who had begun to organize and protect Eritrea's internal interests. In Asmara, branch president Shaykh Ahmed Saleh gave a speech to supporters alluding to the need to address the material conditions of the country along with the ongoing political struggles. Likewise, speakers in Keren, Agordat, Massawa, and other major cities stressed the league's official position that meaningful employment and decent wages for all workers remained a priority that both the Constituent Assembly and the Office of the Chief Executive needed to address.[8] Commenting on the chronic unemployment, inflation, and lack of government action on the economic crisis, *Sawt al-Iritriyya* editor Muhammad Saleh Mahmud argued that Eritrean Muslims faced a two-front crisis in that both their economic and political livelihood were threatened by the lack of available work across the country. Consequently, the newfound "economic reality" represented just as much of a danger to the well-being of the Muslim community as it did to the survival of a truly independent federal system.[9]

Addressing Muslims' Rights as Federal Citizens

Labor concerns across Muslim-majority communities contributed to the league's reemergence, by late 1953, as the main political organ able to address the federation's already apparent failures. In October, the league led a delegation of several organizations in writing a memorandum to the Office of the Chief Executive. That document included opposition to key issues still being debated within all branches of the federation government, including the supposed primacy of Ethiopian courts over federal jurisdiction, the continued presence of Ethiopian soldiers in the country, and concern for the overall autonomy of the various departments and bureaus within the federal civil service.[10] Nearly a month after the groups presented their grievances, the Muslim League sent a separate memorandum directly to Ethiopian ministers in Addis Ababa offering a similar list of complaints and noting that now under federal authority, Eritrea's Muslim population was now "deprived of its civil and religious rights" in much the same way that Ethiopian Muslims had historically been marginalized by the imperial government.[11] In their discussion of these violations, members now linked the previous British administration with Ethiopian authorities as being complicit in transferring Eritrea's wealth and resources outside the country.[12]

Yet despite the league's efforts within its various memoranda to recast the federation as a prearranged prelude to annexation, much of the actual protests and objections to federal control between 1953 and 1955 reflected the still widely held belief that the federation could provide the basic mechanisms of independence for Muslims if given the chance. These attitudes emerged throughout the first year of federal rule in the pages of *Sawt al-Iritriyya/Dehay Ertra*, which also served as the last legitimate outlet for public dialogue for both the league and other concerned Muslim residents.

The Last Gasp of Muslim Nationalist Media

Within the news reports and commentaries of *Sawt al-Iritriyya/Dehay Ertra*, federal autonomy appeared as a constant topic of discussion among writers who argued that Ethiopian interference represented the main impediment to regional autonomy. Although printed as a joint Arabic-Tigrinya publication, the Arabic commentaries within

Sawt al-Iritriyya gradually assumed a fixation with the historical conditions of Muslim "self-governance" and the need to adhere to the local autonomy guaranteed in the original Eritrean constitution. While often highly critical of the political developments, much of the Tigrinya literature within *Dehay Ertra* remained focused largely on the day-to-day mechanisms of government and usually excluded commentaries concerning how violations against the federation's constitution explicitly targeted religious freedom. This dissimilarity aside, the dual news coverage also reflected the reality that for the Muslim League, *Sawt al-Iritriyya* served, for a brief period, as the only major available outlet for members to address the ongoing political developments. Yet even then the paper's limited circulation in and around Asmara had the effect of minimizing much of the organization's press releases at a time when the public discussions about the need to protect Muslim rights and institutions against government overreach increased. By early 1953, the atmosphere that previously encouraged such lively intellectual exchanges within the nationalist contact zone devolved into little more than a sounding board for addressing ongoing "violations" of Islamic religious and political rights. In this sense, the publication of *Sawt al-Iritriyya*, while significant, ultimately did not represent a direct continuation of the previous era of active nationalist intellectual dialogue.[13]

Despite league members' discussions of such constitutional violations within *Sawt al-Iritriyya/Dehay Ertra*, authorities silenced Eritrea's freedom of the press by May 1953 as result of the official crackdown against the paper's editors for publishing critical commentaries and petitions against the alleged "abrogation" of the federal system. Nearly two months earlier, federal authorities first shut down the paper against the legal objections from its editor in chief, Muhammad Saleh Mahmud. In the midst of the controversy, Muslim leaders defended both the newspaper and the need to safeguard autonomous federal institutions for the benefit of Muslims and non-Muslims alike. Shaykh Saleh Karrar, the headmaster of Asmara's King Farouk Islamic Institute addressed the controversy, and argued that Eritrea's "autonomous" status as a partner within the federation necessitated the continuation of a free and independent media.[14] Although Asmara's district court eventually sided with the paper's editors and nullified the government's actions to block publication, the paper nevertheless remained closed under government pressure and only occasionally recommenced with printing until the paper ceased operations permanently, by August 1954.[15] *Sawt al-Iritriyya/ Dehay Ertra*'s closing represented, for Eritrea's Muslim communities, only the latest in a series of intrusions by authorities to effectively limit criticism against the federation's increasingly anti-Muslim, blatantly annexationist policies. Thus, while the formal political discussions within the nationalist contact zone had all but ceased to exist by 1953, activists attempted to revive and continue on with some semblance of independent media for more than a year afterward. The active and relatively accessible nationalist discourse that emerged during the late 1940s came to an unceremonious conclusion by direct political pressure. The end of formal and open nationalist dialogue among Eritrea's intellectual activists ultimately had several repercussions on the very direction of the independence movement. With fewer resources to actually engage the political and cultural concerns among the public, the league's leaders and its grassroots membership in particular entered into a period of tremendous turmoil as the very pillars of Islamic life in Eritrea became targets for further government suppression. Even more significant than the destruction of independent media, the government's push to take control over the country's Islamic religious, legal, and educational institutions struck at the heart of one of the core concerns among both pro-independence and even conditional unionist Muslims.

Government Intrusion into Islamic Religious Institutions

Although several of Eritrea's leading qadis expressed concern about the future of Islamic religious institutions even before the formal transfer of power, clerics intensified their efforts throughout late 1952 in objecting to Ethiopia's intrusion into the regional waqf administrations. Arguing that the waqf system previously existed under the control of Italian administrators, Ethiopian-backed federation officials assumed authority for the regulation, administrative duties, and distribution of waqf funds against Muslim leaders' objections. Most prominently, mufti Ibrahim al-Mukhtar decried the actions and proclaimed that the waqf's administrative authority belonged solely in the hands of religious authorities, as defined by Eritrea's constitution.[16]

Islamic officials' indignation against government intervention only increased throughout the federation's first two years, especially following the mufti's failed efforts to petition federation authorities through written protest. Following a dispute in August 1954 in which a government inspector forced the qadi of Assab to transfer the city's waqf endowments to government officials, the mufti intervened, examined the qadi's complaints, and appealed in a letter to the federation's interior minister. In his correspondence, the mufti made a point of accentuating the waqf's legal autonomy, pressing the minister to "abolish these conspiracies committed by the inspector and order back all documents, endowments, and accounts that have been taken by the alleged committee to the judge's authorities."[17] Muslim leaders' defense of the inherent autonomy of Islamic legal institutions represented an effort to continue the tradition of relative autonomy that Eritrea's Islamic clergy experienced since early Italian colonialism, when local leaders thrived under administrators who provided "subventions to Mosques and monthly stipends to Muslim community leaders and granted sharī'a [*sic*] courts autonomy in matters of personal status, family and inheritance" in exchange for local political allegiance.[18]

Fears of federal subversion against the affairs of regional Islamic religious authorities only increased throughout 1953 and especially 1954, as the government began restricting foreign teachers and instructors from carrying out religious missions across Eritrea. The relatively steady trickle of missions from Al-Azhar University that came into the country throughout the BMA era now slowed to a crawl as the federal government's denial of licenses to delegations became so frequent that it made entry into the country virtually impossible for non-Eritrean Islamic scholars. The mufti became so concerned about federal authorities' involvement that he pleaded for assistance directly from the Egyptian government. In a May 1954 letter written to Egyptian authorities, the mufti revealed his worry about the threat of losing total support from Al-Azhar. Despite previous government attempts to keep out the Al-Azhar missions, he affirmed that the current mission "found a great acceptance, turnout, and appeal from Muslims" that he believed "must be further developed" so as to not deprive the community of Islamic education.[19] The mufti also requested that Al-Azhar officials delay calling back the representatives that were still inside Eritrea before their replacements could be guaranteed admission, as he believed that federal authorities would again try and prevent their entry.[20]

The mufti's concerns reveal a great deal about the perceptions among Eritrea's leading Islamic savants in how they linked the repression of Muslim activities and marginalization against institutions with the transfer of independent federal authority to Ethiopian control. The waqf controversy and the struggle to allow religious teachers and Arabic instructors into the country only served to highlight the league's objections to the growing institutional interference. Despite the assault against Muslim religious officials and their respective administrations, most of the public statements and writings by Muslim League members lacked divisive language concerning the privileging of Christians. Even violations against Islamic protocol, including the above-mentioned intrusions into the waqf system, were argued by emphasizing the institutional autonomy of the waqf and omitting any direct reference to the supremacy of Islamic practices. Officials instead highlighted the connection between independent Islamic institutions and the laws established by Eritrea's constitution. As early as 1953, Muslim complaints of federal interference even extended beyond the previous controversies surrounding the waqf, as some activists complained that many Eritreans were even being prevented by officials in the major coastal cities from leaving the country to participate in the Hajj.[21]

Federal Political Institutions and Muslim Marginalization

Even when effective in passing its own legislation, the federation's Constituent Assembly, activists argued, seemed only to further infringe on Muslim economic livelihood and political freedom. Even well-known conditional unionists like Muhammad Umar Kadi could no longer ignore the reality that the unionist-dominated assembly had produced an aggressive political program that sought to eviscerate regional political autonomy by targeting Muslim rights. In Kadi's handwritten, self-published monograph *Tarikh hagerkha meflat* (*Knowing the history of your country*), the president of the IML laid out a detailed account of how throughout the early and middle years of the decade the assembly had devolved from its supposed independent role as Eritrea's legislative branch into a virtual arm of the Ethiopian state, focused almost solely on limiting regional autonomy by pursuing an explicitly anti-Muslim program with help from "the dictatorship" of the federation's chief executive, Tedla Bairu.[22] Observing the developments, Kadi argued that the legislative body, as early as 1953, did not encompass "pro" or "anti" unionist factions as much as it was split between "standard members," who confined their official duties to the legislative sessions, and those whose main political dealings occurred in the "secret meetings" outside the assembly with Ethiopian officials and the chief executive, which focused on finding ways to explicitly use the legislature to further erode Eritrean autonomy.[23] Apart from revealing the dramatic turnaround in Kadi's political thinking, his monograph demonstrated that even in the absence of an active nationalist press such widespread concerns emerged within the public discourse. In this way, some of the more accomplished Muslim activists still reached a core nationalist audience despite the severe limitations.

After Ibrahim Sultan's failed attempt to introduce a bill allowing for Muslim residents to purchase government-owned land across the lowlands, the assembly passed the Eritrean Land Tenure Act in July 1953. While in principle the law now merely required that the government extend "the traditional seven-year cycle" of private land ownership to twenty-seven years and include the payment of tribute to the government, it also created another troubling issue by encouraging young farmers, "especially those from the highlands, to take up permanent residence on government-owned lowlands" by expanding their plots and effectively monopolizing much of the property across the predominantly Muslim territories. In response, mass opposition among Muslims "who feared that lands which had been considered their own would be taken away" erupted, and in conjunction with resistance even among some Jabarti residents across the highlands, officials in the assembly eventually decided against putting the act into effect.[24]

While the Land Tenure Act served to only reinforce perceptions throughout Muslim communities that the assembly represented nothing more than an abuse of government authority, other legislation conveyed to Muslim activists the idea that the legislative body represented a direct extension of the chief executive's unionist program. This included Tedla Bairu's attempts to remove the Eritrean flag from government offices, monitor political meetings among Muslim League supporters across the Western Province and the major cities, openly promote Amharic as the working language of government, and ultimately override Eritrea's constitution as a means to further restrict Muslim political power. While during Bairu's tenure (1952–55) each of these aims became central pillars of unionist policy, they reached unprecedented levels with the election of Asfaha Woldemikael as the second chief executive of the federation government, in August 1955.

Ironically, Bairu's longtime status as a committed unionist did little to endear him to either the Ethiopian government or other unionist supporters. Although as the federation's first chief executive he oversaw the dismantling of Eritrea's independent press, privileged Christian unionists in civil employment, and increased police surveillance and the imprisonment of pro-independence activists, his ultimate refusal to "expedite the dismantling of Eritrea's autonomy" lead to his downfall by mid-1955. Woldemikael's subsequent election demonstrated the full extent of Ethiopian control over the legislative and executive branches and also illustrated the degree to which unionist leaders capitalized on the league's "inherent weakness" as a fragmented force by late 1955.[25]

While serving simultaneously as Eritrea's deputy representative to Haile Selassie, Asfaha Woldemikael's appointment as chief executive increased the speed by which Ethiopian officials and unionists liquidated Muslim citizenship; he achieved this by first removing Muslims from Eritrean political society through decree by prohibiting the use of Arabic within the federation's institutions and government offices.[26] This attempt to ostracize Muslims represented the most destructive step, as it forced Muslims from administrative positions and encouraged their replacement with government-trained Amharic speakers. Even officials at the American consulate observed that by late 1956 Asfaha Woldemikael's measures to eradicate the official use of Arabic and his refusal to address religious leaders' concerns were the primary reason behind the "increasing dissatisfaction on the part of the Moslem population" with federation officials at all levels of government.[27]

The new chief executive's actions also severely compromised Muslim youth education. The growing dominance of unionist Christian officials within the Ministry of Education resulted in an uneven allocation of funds to the training and hiring of qualified teachers to schools in Christian-majority areas. With Arabic eliminated from the public-school curriculum and most government funds channeled into predominately Christian institutions in the major cities, Muslim schools fell into considerable disrepair and employment opportunities for Muslim teachers both in the cities and rural areas were restricted.[28] In a May 1956 memorandum directed to the chief executive, the Muslim Mosques Committee of Asmara pressed Asfaha Woldemikael's administration on the aforementioned violations, arguing that the administration by law needed to adhere to Article 38 of the constitution, guaranteeing the promotion of Arabic (and Tigrinya) in all Eritrean government departments, offices, and schools, and that the chief executive's office was obligated to punish those found in violation of the law.[29]

More significantly, the committee expressed its desire to see the government rectify inequalities in the education system by working to "encourage the Muslim students to have instruction in the Arabic language." Echoing the mufti's wishes, representatives also asked the government to allow for the invitation of Arabic teachers from abroad. In addressing the issue of education reform, the committee also commented on the dire circumstances that government discrimination had produced regarding the lack of employment opportunities for Muslim youth. Committee members requested that federal authorities give consideration to "all applications submitted by the Muslim-educated youth who want to obtain employment. It is understood that such applications were all discarded."[30] While most of the committee's concerns were related to issues that touched everyday concerns within the wider Muslim community, the later actions of the Muslim League's leadership attempted to redress the core issue of political representation and its adverse effect on almost every aspect of public life for their constituents.[31] The growing dissatisfaction with the prohibition against the use of indigenous languages, the destruction of independent media, and the worsening economic realities all fostered a "deep national resentment" that in turn became "the midwife of a flourishing national consciousness" during the latter federal period.[32] Before the league could capitalize on the widening Muslim discontent, its leadership first needed to address many of the long-standing internal conflicts that had plagued much of its political program after 1952.

Political Contention between League Leaders and the General Membership

At first glance, the Muslim League's ability to influence the course of federal politics by 1955 suffered from several major disadvantages. Having gone nearly three years without a viable media outlet to replace *Sawt al-rabita*, and with *Sawt al-Iritriyya/Dehay Ertra*'s cancellation the previous year, the league, by the middle of the decade, failed to even reach its constituents and inform them on several of the organization's policy decisions. The continuing economic crisis across the country left the league on the verge of bankruptcy, which limited its ability to organize. However, the most significant issue that challenged the organization's internal operations during the mid-1950s developed out of the wide gap between the league's leadership and its rank and file members.

Ibrahim Sultan in particular became a major target of the growing frustration, especially among his former base of tigre supporters, who began resenting Sultan's status as a supposed "stooge of the Italians" and for focusing more on the league's urban-based constituencies. Sultan's partnership with Italian settlers and his previous acceptance of CAE-backed funding increased suspicions that the league's agenda had veered far off course from its original populist aims. His long-standing association with the league's more prominent Jabarti members also became a source of tigre discontent. Although the MLWP's leadership had accused Sultan as early as 1950 of being a tool of Italian interests with autocratic tendencies, his alleged transgressions against the predominantly tigre masses by the mid-1950s revealed the extent to which his loss of stature reflected the league's overall weakened condition.

The rural-urban divide within the league also extended to concerns over the close relationship that Sultan had developed with former conditional unionists since his national tour of Eritrea in February and March 1951. Having begun to mend fences with many of the Massawa- and Hirgigo-based merchants throughout 1951 and 1952, as federal rule loomed, the secretary general now made overtures that incurred the hostility of many tigre outside of Sultan's own Rugbat clan. Despite the public rhetoric against rival groups such as the IML within earlier commentaries in *Sawt al-rabita* and *Wahda Iritriyya*, Sultan's later courting of IML officials such as Muhammad Umar Kadi demonstrated how the league leadership's newfound emphasis on building support from the coastal, merchant-dominated class in an around Massawa became a major priority as the federation progressed. Sultan's exploits, in combination with the league's overall stagnation in the rural areas in the aftermath of the federation's establishment thus paved the way for wider internal dissatisfaction.

Beyond the mainly rural and tigre-based discontent with Ibrahim Sultan, their grievances spoke to the larger disconnect that plagued the organization by the mid-1950s. Although the league's executive council and regional branch leaders held prominent positions as religious, civic, and economic leaders across the country, the organization's top-down approach, coupled with the never fully resolved concerns about Italian-settler influence during the Independence

Bloc era, nurtured a relative lull among many general members, who largely shunned the league's new direction. Even in the likely event that Sultan and other league leaders continued accepting Italian funding during the federal period, the funding proved to be a nonissue in that it failed to alleviate the organization's overall funding crisis that challenged both the executive council and the general membership. By the mid-1950s, the new economic realities limited the leadership's ability to organize opposition to the federation government's actions and thus increased dissatisfaction with the league's leadership. The league's troubles only increased in the months before the second Constituent Assembly elections, in August 1956, as renewed antinationalist crackdowns in districts across the Western Province further constrained the organization's activities and ability to mobilize. Beyond facing personal threats from unionist-backed leaders and continued shifta attacks, league officials running for public office also had to contend with nearly daily harassment from police. Some candidates were jailed after making public announcements that they would seek positions within the Federal Assembly. Even Ibrahim Sultan, despite his apparent falling out with many constituents, expressed concern in his discussions with officials at the American consulate about reports that police agencies were now beginning to arrest civilians for "expressing opposition to government chosen candidates."[33]

In spite of the league leadership's increased troubles by the middle of the decade, the general membership still maintained an informal network of political dialogue across Muslim communities, as groups under the league's broad authority began to push for internal reform even as the organization's leadership appeared on the verge of complete fragmentation. The fact that the league's grassroots members managed to influence major changes within the organization came about, in part, as a result of the still broad consensus that the league still had the ability to address Muslim concerns against the federation government's abuses. Thus, the league's weakened position by 1955 and its leadership's troubles actually obscured the organization's remaining strength. For example, in spite of its past rivalries with the MLWP and Ibrahim Sultan's falling out with many tigre constituents, lower-level officials maintained a strong following across the Western Province, particularly in the rural areas, where constituents still looked to local league representatives to help address their grievances as the government's neglect of the rural areas worsened. Likewise, the combined weight of rural dissatisfaction and the economic stagnation in the cities also helped diminish much of the previous hostility between the league and conditional unionist Muslims, whose once bright hopes for economic prosperity under federal rule diminished in light of the "shortage of liquid capital, the failure on the part of the Ethiopian authorities to provide adequate attractions for foreign investors and the continuing difficulties created for foreign business men by the customs authorities."[34]

The growing frustration and desire for political change ultimately carried over into the league's national conference in Keren in December 1955. The conference not only allowed the league's various subgroups to come together and voice their complaints on a national level, but it represented the beginning of several significant internal reforms that carried the league through the remainder of the federal period. For all their present faults and past mistakes, many members of the executive council apparently recognized the urgent need to restructure the league as a viable opposition force. With the support of Suleiman Ahmed Umar, Imam Musa Abdu, and other members of the executive council, planning for the league's national conference in Keren developed with an understanding among officials about the need to reform the organization at all levels.

Reshuffling the League

On December 1, league leaders convened the national conference with affiliated branches from every province in an attempt to address the federation's growing authoritarianism and to reconfigure the organization's precise role as an organ of opposition. The conference adjourned after several days with a nineteen-point memorandum designed to stem the tide of unionist influence within the federation government. Although much of the league's concerns echoed their earlier efforts to safeguard autonomy for Islamic religious practices and community institutions, the memorandum also represented the sum total of the league's anxieties about the economic and social hardship that their constituencies now faced. In particular, representatives requested that federal authorities provide immediate subsidies for "public consumption materials including gas, oil, electricity, and water" because so many residents remained in a state of chronic poverty.[35]

Reflecting delegates' broader economic distress, the league also requested that the Federal Assembly finally agree to fully implement

Article 84 of Eritrea's constitution, thereby establishing an Eritrean advisory council to help develop key issues of "public health, budget, and infrastructure" across the country.[36] The memorandum even demanded that the federal government ease "trading regulations" in the major coastal cities to address the ongoing economic depression facing both merchants and residents in cities such as Massawa and Assab. If many of the league's complaints related to tangible economic concerns, the league nevertheless managed to also address how the deteriorating conditions had impacted their lives as Muslim citizens.

As the executive council members expressed previously, other representatives articulated their disapproval of Proclamation 130 alongside other fears about Eritrea's institutional viability. In particular, attendees expressed concern about the exclusion of Arabic and Tigrinya in government offices, federation authorities' refusal to fly the Eritrean flag from all government buildings, and their desire to support meaningful educational reform. Indeed, the need to develop a comprehensive and modern education system for the younger generation represented one of the league's primary concerns: "Because the future of the nation is based on education and educating future generations, special attention is needed for the construction of schools in all areas of the country. This kind of [practical] education is not going to produce strong men to lead the nation immediately, so we are calling for further efforts, including a portion of the federation budget for sending Eritreans outside Eritrea to receive foreign education."[37]

Taken together, the league's conference and its subsequent memorandum revealed how the organization addressed the concerns of its increasingly distressed constituents. Perhaps not surprisingly, the executive council's proposal two months later to outline the league's new internal organization and broaden its membership demonstrated the leadership's written acknowledgment that the league needed to adapt its strategies.[38] Beyond serving merely as a political announcement about the new restructuring, the league's February 1956 internal memo also represented the first major attempt since the closing of *Sawt al-rabita*, in 1952, to reaffirm the league's status as the vanguard for federal autonomy and in bringing Eritrea out of the "dark nightmare of foreign colonization" during the previous years.[39] Citing their contributions in helping steer the creation of the federation, league representatives proclaimed that the country's "Islamic elements" were responsible for ensuring this "first stage" of Eritrean autonomy and that now no observer could ever deny their "material, intellectual, and political efforts" in the nationalist struggle.[40]

Composed of a three-member commission from the league's central planning committee, including Yasin Ba Tuq, Muhammad Omar Akito, and the current league-affiliated activist Muhammad Umar Kadi, the February memorandum also went well beyond simply an historical overview of the organization's contributions to the nationalist movement; it included a draft of the league's new constitution. Expressing the executive council's long-standing claims that federal rule meant the protection of Muslim rights at all costs, the commission echoed their insistence that all members contribute to the restructuring of "Muslim solidarity under the banner of the league" to insure their overall objectives.[41] Article 1 set the tone by presenting a more overtly religious rationale in the organization's program. Beyond reiterating calls for autonomy and defending "the Muslim Sect," it affirmed that the league worked "for the diffusion of high and true Islamic values and principles between Eritrean Muslims and educating them about their national duties and rights."[42] With the creation of the new constitution, the league offered its general membership increased access to the mechanisms of political power by decentralizing much of the authority from the national executive council and channeling it through direct, popular consensus within the district branches.

Despite the new turn toward decentralization and increased grassroots input, league leaders remained concerned that defections would undercut overall support. Weary of past conflicts with rival groups such as the IML and MLWP, the league also made an effort to instill loyalty by requiring that members first take a solemn oath of allegiance before other branch representatives: "I swear by God, the almighty, the great, that I will follow the Eritrean Islamic League's principles, and I will sincerely make every effort to realize its goals and to follow directions of the league's authorities and to be a good, gracious member and to avoid anything or any act that contradicts or harms the league's principles. May God be my witness."[43]

Ultimately the new stipulations illustrated that the league, now completely deprived of any direct political influence within the federation government, sought to reclaim its strength by revitalizing its own ranks. And while the organization failed to fully address the root causes of its fragmentation in previous years, the restructuring laid the groundwork for much of the broader grassroots activism that developed throughout the federation's latter years. More important, the reforms demonstrated the extent to which meaningful dialogue and ideological debate could still develop, even within the context of a suppressed Muslim nationalist media. The fact that the general membership successfully petitioned for such internal restructuring demonstrates that even though the broader debates within the nationalist contact zone remained severely limited, the Muslim League's grassroots exerted meaningful agency in regard to their own political agenda. Such aggressive tactics later proved instrumental to the league's remaining a relevant force in the absence of formal, public intellectual discussions. In sum, the league's internal reforms displayed the extent to which intellectuals altered the parameters of the Muslim nationalist contact zone to suit the new political realities of the late federal period.

The December conference helped reposition the league to address members' concerns that federal institutions were now being summarily cleansed of "Islamic" influence by the new chief executive. Apprehensions about Muslim representation had emerged since 1951 with the BA's previous efforts to incorporate Eritreans into the civil service. Now league members claimed that Ethiopia increased its authority inside all branches of the federation government by promoting the Christian identity of its employees, effectively helping to "Christianize" the administrative ranks.[44] These concerns echoed Ibrahim Sultan's earlier warnings, which claimed as early as October 1952 that Haile Selassie and his representatives had placed their allies in influential positions to guarantee Christian control of the administration, even as federation authorities "beat down and imprisoned" politically active Muslims.[45] The erosion of Muslim rights thus developed with Ethiopian efforts to appeal to the perceived religious affinity between the monarchy and those sympathetic Christians from the highlands.[46] During the second half of the decade, government discrimination against Muslims "gradually led to their treatment as *quasi* foreigners or second class citizens at best."[47]

State-sponsored privileging of (unionist) Christians had the added effect of worsening the already dire economic situation among Muslims. With unemployment having reached "an all-time high" of fifteen thousand in Asmara and with the newfound momentum in the wake of the internal reforms, the Muslim League began to field candidates in preparation for new Constituent Assembly elections in 1956. Apart from displaying the league's newfound self-confidence, the campaigns demonstrated a surprising degree of trust in the legislative branch despite the previous years of political maneuvering by unionist assembly members to undermine their own authority to the chief executive. As recently as October 1955, just weeks after Asfaha Woldemikael's election as chief executive, the assembly tried to modify the Eritrean constitution and secure key changes in the federal government's structure, including the adoption of Amharic as the official language of government, abolishing both the Eritrean flag and official seal and allowing the emperor to appoint the future chief executive.[48]

By late 1956 officials from the office of the chief executive also began taking more proactive measures to neutralize the league's political leadership. As secretary general and still one of the loudest remaining voices of opposition in the Federal Assembly, Ibrahim Sultan became the first target of Woldemikael's purge of nationalist sympathizers. In the midst of the league's reformation and reenergized campaigns, in mid-1956, both Woldemikael's administration and Ethiopian authorities "were determined to keep Ibrahim off the Second Assembly in any way possible."[49] In July officials found their opportunity when authorities accused Sultan of "insulting a Sudanese diplomat" during his stay in Asmara, "for which Ibrahim was hauled to court and was fined $600."[50] However, after Sultan appealed the ruling and federal authorities transferred his case to the Ethiopian imperial court in Addis Ababa, authorities "converted" the fine into a one-year prison sentence. Sultan ultimately received three years' probation on condition that he abstain from federal politics. Living under virtual house arrest by August 1956, Sultan's troubles represented only the first in a series of attempts to decapitate the league's leadership.

Likewise, league central planning committee official and assembly member Muhammad Omar Akito became a prime target of federation officials, who successfully voided the results of Akito's electoral victory in the Assab District, which led to further unrest among league supporters in both Asmara and Asseb: "There are continued reports of increasing dissatisfaction on the part of the Moslem population with Ethiopian activities in Eritrea including one report that a Moslem meeting held in Eritrea after the general assembly declared the election of Sheik Mohammed Omar Achito invalid had been broken up by the police."[51]

Fortunately for the league, the previous organizational reforms did allow many supporters to redirect their efforts even as federal authorities intensified their crackdown against the leadership. Throughout late 1955 and 1956 Jabarti merchants from Asmara and Massawa under the leadership of Imam Musa established an auxiliary group, the Muslim Youth League, to offset the growing political limitations faced by many in the league's leadership.[52]

The new group formed after harassment by federal police against the league increased throughout mid-1956, as authorities even began prohibiting league officials from holding local meetings among branch members.[53] Accordingly, Imam Musa and other Jabarti leaders "began organizing party groups in Keren, Massawa, Agordat and Tessenei" throughout the next two years that in turn helped coordinate pro-independence activities with local merchants and youth. As with the league's leadership, "the members of the club were concerned not only with the gradual loss of Eritrean autonomy but also about Eritrea's weak economy."[54] Several of the association's affiliates, including Massawa-based leaders such as Muhammad Umar Kadi also began to aggressively make personal appeals in Jeddah to enlist Saudi political and financial support as nationalist activities spread.[55] Ellingson observes that the organization's rapid expansion across the major cities and even throughout rural areas in the Western Province demonstrated the group's considerable success in siphoning off support from former conditional unionist elements, including many former MLWP supporters.[56] The combined pressures of widespread disenfranchisement with federal rule and the youth league's newfound popularity thus remobilized broad Muslim discontent as members also began to formulate activities with frustrated segments within Eritrea's Christian communities.

By 1957 government repression against the official use of Arabic and Tigrinya, continued violations against the internal operations of the waqf committees, the suppression of Muslim schools, and the deteriorating economic conditions throughout the country had all merged to induce a particularly aggressive atmosphere of nationalist discontent among urban residents in Asmara and Massawa. The prior banning of nationalist media outlets also contributed to public outrage even as the government-backed media painted a portrait of a complacent population. The government's refusal to address any major issue concerning rising political tensions proved so transparent that even American officials in Asmara observed the notable disconnect between social realities and the picture painted by the government-sanctioned media. In one June cable, officials went so far as to compare the federation's media programs with the Soviet Union's *Pravda:*

The Government controlled press in Eritrea seldom prints any real local news. For example, not a word appeared in the local press in regard to the recent school strike and riot by the students at Haile Selassie I Secondary School. In the same manner, nothing is ever published in the press about the numerous and increasing attacks being perpetuated on the highways by Shifta bandits.[57]

The American consul's reference to the student strike at the Haile Selassie I Secondary School also illustrated that the urban discontent among the youth reflected how the growing ranks of activists shared a high degree of religious solidarity. While the strike that first erupted in mid-March had originated after the school's Indian headmaster allegedly made disparaging remarks about both the Islamic and Christian religions to the students, it occurred at a time in which student activism itself became a major element of nationalist-antifederal politics.[58] Moreover, the very composition of the student strikers revealed the extent to which disillusionment with the now hollowed-out federation system angered youths from among Asmara's political elites:

Another significant factor in the student strike is that the students of the Haile Selassie School are the sons of prominent Eritreans, mostly government officials, and represent rather the cream-of-the-crop of Eritrean youth. According to two American teachers who are employed at the school, the great majority of the students are very sophisticated in their political thinking. And the majority of them resent saluting the Ethiopian flag and the efforts of the school to instill Ethiopian patriotism into them."[59]

Although the students eventually ended the strike and returned to class in the following weeks, its occurrence amid the wider public opposition to Asfaha Woldemikael's administration and the virtual destruction of any true remaining political sovereignty broadened protests to the point where the Muslim-Christian divide, at least among the urban youth, proved to have little if any relevance to the general discontent. The American consul in Asmara, Earle J. Richey, reported to the State Department in June 1957 that "the Moslems and the Coptics are joining forces in opposition to the Ethiopians" as the urban "young people" from both communities were now "taking over the political opposition movement."[60] The scale of urban discontent among several key groups, including students, merchants, unemployed workers, and rank-and-file league members helped set the stage for the mass protests that eventually broke out across several major cities throughout early 1958. By then, localized opposition to government policy gave way to nationwide discontent over the perceived abuses to Eritrea's institutional autonomy and economic fortunes. In the process, this new period of intensified public mobilization signaled an important shift in how the league and other activists used the concept of "Muslim identity" to address their criticisms. As many of the activities and protests throughout 1956 and 1957 suggest, concerns over Islamic institutional freedom and autonomy from among the league leadership and religious clerics transformed into more genuine dissatisfaction among the wider membership that swelled and created an atmosphere of chronic social unrest by late 1957.

Conclusions

From its inauguration, in September 1952, and continuing through 1957, the Ethiopian-Eritrean Federation government served largely as a staging ground for the dismantling of the kind of genuine institutional autonomy that both conditional unionists and even many nationalist groups had begun to support after the UN's passage of Resolution 390-A. For Eritrean Muslims as a whole, this period represented a full-scale assault against the foundations of community and religious life at a time when residents across the country looked to their respective religious and educational institutions to address political failings. Ultimately, Muslim leaders' efforts to preserve cultural and institutional strength met with the realization that the federation's very existence served as the major impediment to Muslims' collective security.

For its part, the Muslim League, damaged by fissures between its leadership and the grassroots and also compromised by Ibrahim Sultan's continued associations with Italian and urban-based interests, experienced increased fragmentation by the middle of the decade. Beyond simply being an inconvenience for its leadership, dissatisfaction and distrust toward Sultan and his inner circle shook the very foundations from which the league had first emerged. Lack of support among the organization's once solid base of Tigre-speaking clans across the Western Province only added to the league's political difficulties throughout the middle of the decade and led to a further loss of influence. Only with a dramatic restructuring of the league and its authority did supporters begin to reengage the nationalist program through grassroots organization. Ultimately, the reforms carried out by the league allowed for its revival as an important force in nationalist activism. And even though the league remained in a relatively weakened position in comparison to previous years, officials continued to focus on broader issues beyond the immediate political crisis by working to address religious anxieties and the growing economic concerns within their respective communities. Building upon the long-standing links between league members and Muslim clerics, activists made a concerted, albeit unsuccessful, effort to prevent continued institutional interference from federation authorities.

The federation government's exclusion and marginalization of its Muslim subjects thus helped the league and its allies shape religious identity as a political vehicle. Abuses against Muslim rights and institutions solidified popular notions about the federation's inherently "anti-Islamic" character. Ironically, the broad dissatisfaction among Eritrea's Muslim communities, regardless of ethnic or regional composition, developed in spite of the league's failure to dominate nationalist activity as it had in the past. In particular, Asfaha Woldemikael's increasingly authoritarian measures succeeded not only in helping rejuvenate the league and its cause, but also in killing hopes among most of the Tigrinya-speaking Christian population that the federation remained a viable option for their own freedom and prosperity. In the next three years, the league's place in the nationalist movement gradually merged with the broader restlessness that swept across the country, as discontent among both Muslim and Christian communities carried well beyond the league's traditional support base.

7

New Beginnings at the Federation's End

Muslim Mobilization, Popular Resistance, and Diaspora Activism,
January 1958–September 1961

By 1958 the steady erosion of Eritrean autonomy within the federation created enormous challenges for nationalist supporters in discussing their objections to the growing authoritarianism. For activists and Muslim League members in particular, the previous years since Asfaha Woldemikael assumed authority as chief executive, in 1955, only confirmed their anxieties that the federal administration represented the main impediment in addressing Eritrean political, economic, and cultural concerns. For the majority of Muslim communities, the previous years also illustrated the unprecedented degree of encroachment by the Ethiopian government in both religious affairs and educational institutions. By the end of 1957, widespread abuses against Muslim religious and educational institutions had become so commonplace that even former unionist Muslim supporters of the federation could not overlook the scale of Ethiopian domination in religious affairs.

Although the Muslim League attempted to stave off Ethiopian encroachment by rallying around nationalist representatives in the Constituent Assembly and by reorganizing its own internal structure and outreach efforts among the grass roots, the consolidation of power by the chief executive left legislators devoid of any real authority. Consequently, the movement for legitimate autonomy took on more aggressive forms of public protest by the end of the decade. As a result, the Muslim League and its affiliates' actions contributed to the full-scale *remobilization* of independence activism that had remained largely dormant since late 1950. This reemergence also signaled how the precarious nature of nationalist politics during this late period encouraged a marked increase in diaspora-based political activity, particularly among communities in Egypt and Sudan.

Asfaha Woldemikael's policies as chief executive had set both the Muslim League and the general public on a collision course with federation authorities. Specifically, the growing concerns of chronic unemployment and unrest in the major Eritrean cities helped facilitate the growing camaraderie between league authorities and the broader labor movement. Although the league and labor activists had worked together closely since the beginning of the federation to address economic concerns, the general push for a national labor code that had begun in 1956 succeeded by 1958 in establishing a "broad anti-government coalition of urban Eritreans which included both the already alienated Muslim population and the increasingly disillusioned Tigrinya/Christians who made up the majority of the Asmara working population."[1] While much of the turmoil that developed in late 1957 and early 1958 resulted from the growing anxiety among both Christian and Muslim urban youth, several veteran Muslim activists also proved to be a major driving force in harnessing the unrest for political gain.

Asmara's "Muslim Trials"

Although he served for several years as one of the most ardent champions of conditional union, Muhammad Umar Kadi emerged by late 1957 as an aggressive spokesman against the abuses of the federation government. Kadi targeted Asfaha Woldemikael and his administration in particular for attempting to "destroy" Muslim religious and cultural autonomy. Consequently, the league's past efforts to discredit pro-unionist Muslims like Kadi and other mainly Massawa-based leaders gave way to greater cooperation between the league and many former conditional unionists.[2] Although now marginally affiliated with the league, Kadi arrived in New York in the fall of 1957 still professing himself to be the IML president as well as the UN delegate for the EDF.[3] Regardless of his particular political affiliation, Kadi proved less than successful in accomplishing his ultimate goal of turning UN delegates against Ethiopia's "black colonialism" in Eritrea.[4]

Despite his claims of the widespread support for autonomy in Eritrea, Kadi admitted privately to members of the United States' UN delegation that his recent attempts to build support for Eritrea's cause among most of the leading Muslim states, including Pakistan, Saudi Arabia and Iraq, fell short.[5] Although Kadi managed to deliver his pamphlet, "The Complaint of the Eritrean People against the Ethiopian Government," to several delegations, his trip ultimately failed to bring any substantial international attention to the issue. Nevertheless, the league's executive council continued to support Kadi's efforts to speak out against the federation government's abuses.

When Suleiman Ahmed Umar met with representatives of the American consulate in Asmara in late February 1958, he noted that the league approved of Kadi's actions despite the fact that he was not officially part of their organization. He added that "Kadi had now been accepted by them as their spokesman only because of his increasing prominence and that he was not an initiator of the movement; that if he were to disappear, another spokesman would be found."[6] Further complicating the relationship, several league officials and Muslim religious leaders joined Kadi's public declaration against the Ethiopian government and federation authorities by signing their names to the pamphlet. Among others, the cosigners included league executive council members Adem Kusmallah and Imam Musa; Shaykh Muhammad Seraj Abdu, the administrative director of the Asmara Islamic Institute; Suleiman Ahmed Umar; and Saleh Naser, former president of Shuban al-rabita.[7]

After being arrested in November 1957, Kadi was put on trial by Ethiopian authorities at Asmara's federal court in March 1958 on multiple charges of treason against the federation government. Other Muslim League members also faced prosecution; all individuals were charged with at least one count of "dealing with a foreign government" without the consent of the emperor. Although most of the cosigners were jailed for a short time and later released on $2,000 bail each, Hajj Imam Musa and Suleiman Ahmed Umar both received sentences of four years imprisonment for their actions, while federation authorities sentenced Kadi to ten years in prison for sedition.[8] Although the group tried collectively to bring the UN's attention to the abuses taking place at all levels of the federation government, the trial against Kadi and his colleagues quickly took on strong religious overtones.[9]

Observing the course of the "Muslim Trials," American consulate official George Moore noted that the Islamic leadership in Asmara reacted strongly to the initial charges and attended "in great numbers sessions of the trial, and making dire verbal threats of civil disobedience if the accused were found guilty."[10] He added that the defendants received support from a diverse segment of Eritrea's Muslim population: "That the trials were viewed by many as a form of religious persecution is evidenced by the open interest of leading representatives of the 6,000 person Yemeni-Hadrami group resident here, who normally do not appear to take any position regarding the political activities of their Eritrean brothers in Islam."[11]

The coalescence of religious and political interests during the trials also illustrates the degree to which Muslim leaders intensified their efforts in calling for effective protection of sovereign religious institutions within the federation. Accordingly, officials noted that Asmara's Muslim community was greatly disturbed even weeks after the trials and incensed over what residents considered "travesty justice."[12] As a result, community members began to mobilize through their religious institutions:

> As a token of complaint, the majority of mosques in Eritrea were closed for the evening prayer of April 3 and many remained closed part of the following day, a Friday. They were reportedly reopened later in the day following an order from the Chief Executive to the Mufti, but many did not hold the formal Friday noon service. The significance of this form of religious protest is heightened when it is realized that it took place in the middle of the Muslim holy month of Ramadan.[13]

Beyond the broad support of Muslim leaders during the trials, many league representatives had already involved themselves in Kadi's cause in the previous months. In late January representatives from Keren sent a memorandum to authorities expressing both their support for Kadi and their objection to his arrest and forced return to Asmara. Moreover, the league's memo alluded to the recent activities of Kadi and his supporters as being part of a broader campaign to protect political freedom and expression.[14] The league's anxiety only increased in the following months. On February 14, league members staged a peaceful demonstration in Asmara in which they protested the government's announcement of a ban on public gatherings and cited their right to assemble as defined by Article 7 of Resolution 390-A and Article 32 of the Eritrean Constitution. Gathering after Friday prayers, a group of representatives composed a memorandum that again addressed the need to enforce the stipulations of the constitution and delivered their signatures in person to the chief executive's main office.[15] Less than a month later, in early March, one Muslim

League protest in Keren grew so large that police opened fire on demonstrators, injuring a dozen people and arresting more than one hundred.[16] In response to the crackdown against the city's protesters, residents responded by refusing to open shops or to go to work. By the first week of March, "the entire Western Province" had gone on strike in protest of the recent government actions.[17] The widespread response to the "Muslim Trials" also revealed the extent to which the long-standing discourse within the nationalist contact zone had seemingly been replaced by a new, more urgent articulation of Islamic religious freedom. While previous actions by both the league and other predominantly Muslim groups had long addressed concerns over the security and integrity of Islamic institutions, the outcry that emerged in the wake of the trials demonstrated that immediate concerns about the safety and welfare of Eritrea's Muslim communities redirected the Muslim intellectual class to more pressing issues. In short, the previous years of debate and discussion about Eritrea's right to self-determination withered away in light of the deteriorating situation facing the league's leadership and Muslims more broadly. This dramatic shift in part explains why for much of 1958 Muslim political activism became increasingly aggressive and less academic.

In the context of the widespread resentment, both the league's protest and the "Muslim trials" occurred simultaneously and with greater unrest from all segments of the urban workforce. The general strike, which included approximately one hundred thousand participants in Asmara and effectively paralyzed the capital city in March 1958, reflected the high level of coordination and mutual support that the Muslim League and its members shared with urban activists. Leaders from the league's Keren branch had already directly petitioned Emperor Haile Selassie during his visit to Eritrea the previous January to finally address their "six-year-long unanswered pleas for correct implementation of the UN Federation Decision" as a means to "invigorate the economic life of Eritrea, and alleviation of the brutal situation."[18] Indeed, several of the league members who were tried along with Kadi also had considerable experience in Eritrea's labor movement.[19]

Accordingly, the relationship between Muslim political activism and economic concerns could not be ignored. Even the American consul, George Moore, warned that if the Ethiopian government could not succeed in "ameliorating economic conditions in Eritrea," then the trials of Muslim activists could lead to even more violent disturbances. For his part, Suleiman Ahmed Umar also took the time to explain to American officials about the league's concerns that the lack of Eritrean autonomy compromised the economic interests of all citizens, claiming that Ethiopian encroachment into federation affairs both discouraged foreign investment in local businesses and placed an unfair burden on Eritrean workers seeking stable employment.[20]

The 1958 General Strike and the League's Disintegration

Although the massive civil unrest that erupted in March and April of 1958 was attributed chiefly to the efforts of Asmara's heavily Christian labor base, the Muslim League also claimed to have played a major role. In a March 25 meeting between Ibrahim Sultan and officials at the American consulate, Sultan claimed that Asmara's striking workers were both inspired by and advised on their activities by the league after workers observed "the Muslim partial strike of the previous week in Keren and elsewhere in the western province."[21] For their part, league leaders coordinated activities both across the Western Province and in Asmara in late February and early March. As early as January, league and Muslim religious leaders from across the Western Province provided a detailed memorandum about their growing concerns in relation to several of the "violations of our constitutional rights," including the government's barring of political parties from attending meetings and the increased suppression by the police force.[22] The league succeeded in convincing merchants to close most Muslim-owned businesses throughout the Western Province for four days during the week before the Asmara strike. Beyond giving "moral support" to laborers in Asmara, the league leadership also encouraged merchants and laborers in the capital to rally behind Christian labor activists.[23] Sultan even predicted that unless both the economic and wider cultural concerns were addressed by the government, the general strike could quite possibly lead to even greater instability among Eritrea's Muslim population that could spark intervention on the part of the nationalist supporters across the Arab world.[24]

Despite this apparent warning about possible external influence, both British and American officials in Asmara seemed unconcerned about the role of outside agitators in causing the urban unrest. Sultan himself later went on record to affirm that the strike erupted solely from the widespread public discontent: "There was absolutely no foreign organization or participation in the strike, it being an entirely local effort, with the major organizing elements coming from former Unionist party members, the bulk of whom have become disillusioned with the IEG's [Imperial Ethiopian Government's] failure to insure basic human rights granted to the Eritreans under their Constitution and the Federal Act."[25]

Even prominent unionist leaders in the Federal Assembly such as Shaykh 'Ali Musa Radai confided to the American consul that the activities were orchestrated without any assistance from supporters outside Eritrea.[26] Nevertheless, the intensity of the unrest even before the general strike in Muslim communities did cause concern for some interests, particularly among some within the Italo-Eritrean community. When rioting broke out in Massawa on March 13 and more than eight thousand protesters took to the streets, some settlers blamed the unrest on support for Egyptian nationalists and "Nasser's propaganda" and worried that the rioting in Massawa would spread to other major cities.[27]

Although intervention from "outside" elements proved virtually nonexistent, the general strike witnessed an unprecedented degree of cooperation between the league and many former unionist Christian elements. Attempts to show the Muslim-Christian solidarity of the demonstrators took many forms besides the public declarations from the league and labor leaders. According to Kibreab, the strike's main architects chose the compound of Asmara's Enda Mariam Orthodox Church as the staging ground for their protests because "the organizers wanted to make a powerful statement to the effect that all Eritreans, including the previously staunch supporters of the unification project, had undergone a change of heart and mind."[28] Additionally, many Christian labor activists tried to illustrate to federation authorities that discontent did not rest exclusively in "Muslim elements" who were supported by outside backers in the Arab world.[29] Former unionist and labor leader Blaata Kidanemariam even noted that tigre frustration with the federation government had increased so much that by the time of the strike most tigre communities "were in great sympathy with their linguistic brethren in Eritrea and could be expected to join in future Eritrean-instigated disorders."[30]

Although the general strike illustrated that the majority of Asmara's Tigrinya/Christian population had largely turned against the unionist position that many had supported in previous years, it also revealed that the Muslim League continued to exercise considerable influence within the broader nationalist coalition. Moreover, it showed that its religiously inclusive leadership continued to push its agenda and mobilize on a wide scale in its urban strongholds to work with the mainly Christian-majority composition of the approximately one hundred thousand protesters that gathered in Asmara. The fact that the government's repression of the general strike resulted in both the destruction of the Eritrean labor movement "and the suppression of all public anti-unionist organizations" testifies to the fact that the political and economic crises impacted a broad segment of the public, including much of the league's base in the major cities.[31]

Taken together, both the league's support for the protests and Asfaha Woldemikael's later decision to abolish all Eritrean political parties while giving federation security forces extraordinary powers "by which the commissioner could put in jail anyone for up to ten days without bringing any charges" suggests the large-scale social dimensions of the league's involvement.[32] For the league, the general strike represented its final act of broad political action within Eritrea. Under the threat of imprisonment as a result of the new ban on all political parties, the league's leadership fragmented in the months after the strike, as several executive council members sought refuge outside Eritrea or were jailed. Although members continued to meet in secret in urban enclaves in Asmara, Keren, Agordat, and elsewhere, the league's remnants looked increasingly to diaspora communities in neighboring Sudan, and especially Egypt, to facilitate future efforts.

Nationalism Goes Abroad

In March 1959 the Muslim League's symbolic end in Eritrea came when Secretary General Ibrahim Sultan and his colleague Idris Muhammad Adam fled in secret across the western border to Sudan.[33] Having heard rumors that federation police had begun rounding up several of the "elderly" nationalists, Sultan and Adam purportedly made their way from Keren in a frantic escape. When their car broke down as they headed west, the pair resorted to more drastic measures:

> On the road, we stopped and threatened a Habesha driver with a gun and made him drive us. We passed through check-points in Barentu and when we reached Haykota, police asked us where we were heading and we told them that we were going to Haliste to attend a wedding. They let us go. When

we came near Tessenei-Haliste, we jumped off the car and warned the driver not to say a word. From there, we met Hadi Musa Hussein (from the Maria Tselam Rugbat) and Abdella Idris Mohamed (a teacher from the Ejud-Kassala school) with camels, and they took us to Kassala.[34]

After being kept hidden for several days by Sudanese ex-soldiers in a "Khatmiyya Village" on the outskirts of Kassala, Adam's contacts arranged for a taxi to transport both him and Sultan to Khartoum.[35] Following a brief stopover in the city, the pair eventually made their way to Cairo, where Sultan claimed he soon met with Eritrean students at Al-Azhar to explain the situation. Afterward, "the students spread the word to all of the embassies and news of their arrival was soon heard in Addis Ababa." In response, Haile Selassie purportedly passed an order for a search squad in Asmara to gather information about their activities.[36]

Sultan's arrival in Cairo as a "political refugee" also signaled that the generation of early Muslim activists who had worked for Eritrean independence since the end of World War II were now giving way to a new, younger cohort of activists whose transnational dimensions would fundamentally alter the course of nationalist mobilization.[37] The demise of the Muslim League and the beginning of the exile of Sultan and his colleagues represented a significant new phase in which both the nationalist movement and broader ideas about Eritrean "identity" developed as part of a truly "transnational entity."[38] Ironically, this new diaspora-based political climate has remained to this day the primary vehicle by which ideas and debates regarding Eritrean nationalism have taken place. As a result, nationalists across the diaspora became even more aggressive in their articulation of Eritrean independence not simply as a political movement but as a quest for true national liberation. Sultan himself alluded to the changing circumstances of the crisis when he argued in a telegram to Edward Mulcahy that because Eritreans had finally learned "to understand the truth of the subjugation and slavery of Haile Sellasie [*sic*]," the independence movement had to now find a new way to survive despite the dire circumstances. For his part, Sultan sounded to American officials less like a defeated, exiled politician than a reinvigorated leader boasting of his readiness to engage the next stage of the nationalist movement: "We must struggle until the achievement of our goal, and we Eritreans shall make friends with whoever helps us or at least whoever does not oppose us and help Haile Sellassie, and we shall be the enemy of all those friends of Haile Sellasie who help him or hurt us."[39]

Sultan's confidence reflected, in part, his apparently sincere belief that broader social mobilization, particularly among the youth in the diaspora, held the key to Eritrean liberation. As Sultan's testimony illustrates, both his and Idris Muhammad Adam's escape succeeded only with the help of sympathetic networks of Sudan-based Eritrean Muslims mainly in Kassala and Khartoum, especially groups of former soldiers and teachers. Two years earlier, a group of exiles formed the Committee for Eritrean Nationalists in Khartoum. Apart from developing as a social network for Eritreans in the city, the original group followed political events in Eritrea and often sent correspondence to politicians still in Asmara inquiring about the situation.[40] By mid-1957 a subcommittee under the same name developed a more concentrated program centered on assisting newcomers in Khartoum to find food, housing, and employment. When Sultan and Adam traveled to Sudan, members of the Khartoum committee received them to discuss the political situation and helped collect money to send them to Egypt.[41] Beyond the Khartoum committee, the growing diaspora networks benefited from the involvement of Eritreans who were former Sudanese army soldiers. According to organizer Saleh Heduq, the rise in the soldiers' activity in Eritrean affairs grew out of the wider political transformations occurring in the region: "In the 1920s many Eritreans reached officer rank in the Sudanese army, but after the revolution began they did not reach these ranks. Then the Sudanese started to know who is a real citizen and started to screen more effectively for enlisting and promotions. Actually already after the British left and Sudan became independent, life became very difficult for us inside the army."[42]

Having joined the Sudanese military in larger numbers during the 1940s and early 1950s, many Eritrean soldiers found themselves unemployed after the British withdrawal, in 1955, and many were encouraged to participate in the liberation movement by virtue of their location.[43] Former soldier Adem Gendifel described how after he left the Sudanese army he began placing posters across border towns in western Eritrea advocating an armed struggle.[44] As clandestine political activity increased in the wake of the 1958 general strike, many of the former soldiers took on new roles as transport guides to take activists across the border.[45] For the organizers of the networks that sprang up throughout Kassala by the end of the decade, contact with their colleagues in Eritrea usually came without difficulty, as their proximity to the towns along the porous border between the Western

Province and Sudan made contact so routine that often there was "no difference between inside and outside."[46] As a result, an intensified nationalist impetus developed organically as "public awareness reached into Sudan" and encouraged active interest in addressing the deteriorating situation within the country.[47]

The Eritrean Liberation Movement

While the Kassala- and Khartoum-based groups facilitated activists' movements across the border and procured safe passage to other locations, Eritreans in the northeastern city of Port Sudan formed another core group of activists that eventually became the Eritrean Liberation Movement (ELM), the first major opposition group to emerge from the diaspora. The main thrust of political activism in Port Sudan came from Muhammad Se'id Nawud and a group of urban professionals. Born in the western Sahel in 1936, Nawud spent much of his adolescence in Port Sudan and eventually found work for the Eastern Telegraph Company. His interest in nationalist politics caused him to briefly join the Sudanese Communist Party before becoming involved in Eritrean affairs. According to colleague Saleh Ahmed Eyay, Nawud first approached a group of colleagues in Port Sudan in November 1958 with the idea of establishing a new organization to liberate Eritreans from Ethiopian control.[48] With a population of approximately five thousand resident Eritrean students and workers, the organization benefited from an energized youth base.

The success in promoting the ELM, or Haraka as it became known, as a force among diaspora youth enabled the group to organize across the country during the next two years, including in Gerba, Gederef, Medeni, Khartoum, Toker, and Kassala.[49] Nawud recounted that initially many concerned Eritreans in Sudan and Egypt did not set out to create their own organization but simply to find ways to support in secret those political organizations "which were prohibited to work inside Eritrea" due to the government crackdown.[50] Nevertheless, most members by late 1958 came to the conclusion that the virtual evaporation of organized political parties inside Eritrea and the jailing of most nationalist and labor leaders required the establishment of a new political entity to impact the situation.[51] The secretive, cell-based organization of the ELM developed from the uniquely "Eritrean experience" of the late 1950s in which clandestine activities became the only recourse for activists.[52] Consequently, the ELM's policy of recruiting new members through cells of seven people revealed a basic strategy in which members infiltrated various institutions within the country, including schools, police departments, and others by gradually increasing membership through political education. At its heart, the ELM's operation reflected a grassroots educational program in which activists emphasized three basic aims: the political liberation of Eritrea, the complete unity of Eritrean population, and the "creation of democratic political power" within the country.[53]

While the process of building the movement took several months, Nawud claimed that the ELM's success developed once branches in most major cities and towns established their own "local program according to its situation" which in turn led to considerable grassroots support.[54] Known colloquially as Mahber shewate, or the "Association of Seven," the ELM activists inside Eritrea also made important inroads and "achieved great success" by tapping into the discontent in the Eritrean police force and especially the Central Investigation Department in Asmara.[55] In addition, the broad support for the ELM's activities among secondary-school teachers also served as an important base to interact with students and encourage their increased involvement in the movement

Although influenced by the ideology of socialist-inspired movements taking place across Africa, espousing a rigidly secular program and having a leadership that genuinely supported ethnic and religious unity among all Eritreans, the ELM's heavily Muslim composition cannot be overlooked in exploring how members achieved their initial success. Even its secular-minded leaders in Port Sudan made a point of beginning their first official meeting with a group prayer in which each of the eight original members swore an oath upon the Qur'an to support the cause.[56]

The ELM's almost exclusively Muslim composition both in the Sudanese branches and in most of the Eritrean cities beyond Asmara demonstrated the organization's particular appeal to disenfranchised Muslim youth.[57] While the ELM made explicit efforts to reach out to Christian youth and segments of urban labor to emphasize religious cooperation within their cell structures, the organization's prominent Muslim membership only increased as the economic situation worsened by the end of the decade. According to Nawud, the religious imbalance in some ways benefited the ELM's activities due to the strategic location of many prominent Muslim supporters who used their connections across the Red Sea region to garner support among the Eritrean communities outside Sudan, particularly in places such as Saudi Arabia. Eritrean merchants and workers in Jeddah provided one of the more important bases of support both in raising funds for the organization and in disseminating information about the new nationalist movement through Arabic political tracts and letters. Yet regardless of its heavily Muslim composition, the ELM's leadership in Port Sudan proceeded from the belief that Ethiopia's past efforts to divide Eritreans along religious lines as well as to encourage "the regional and tribal sensitivities" required that one of the organization's central goals be "removing the wall of doubt and suspicion among the Islamic and Christian sects" by uniting them around the independence cause.[58] Ironically, the ELM's new and seemingly radical message of religious unity owed much to the league's efforts during the previous twelve years.[59]

The Muslim League's Ideological Influence on the ELM

The ELM's success in developing clandestine communication networks both in Sudan and western Eritrea relied heavily on the participation of former Muslim League elements. Specifically, the ELM's initial growth benefited from the active support of urban-based Muslim merchants in Asmara, Keren, and Massawa, many of whom used their contacts to secure communication and supply lines along the coastal cities and across the Eritrean interior. Support from Jabarti leaders in Asmara and other major cities also represented a key source of aid to the organization. Despite the economic situation, several Jabarti supporters allegedly helped ELM cells raise the necessary funds for many cross-border travels.

The ELM also found support from several remaining members in the now powerless Eritrean Constituent Assembly who were previously affiliated with the league, including Osman Hindi, Muhammad Omar Akito, and Muhammad Saleh Musa.[60] Some former officials, such as newspaper editor Muhammad Saleh Mahmud also lent their services to the group.[61] Like the Muslim League before it, the ELM allegedly received the private backing of Eritrea's Islamic religious elites, particularly Ibrahim al-Mukhtar. According to Nawud, the mufti worked "behind the scenes directing and agitating through individual communications" even though he continued to refrain from official membership because of his "sensitive religious position."[62] Additionally, several Khatmiyya khalifas in Keren and Agordat contributed their services by instructing their supporters across the Western Province to provide material assistance and shelter to ELM cell leaders during their travels.[63] According to ELM founding member Saleh Ahmed Eyay, several of the "old politicians" in and around Keren that helped organize the initial cells were themselves experienced activists within the Muslim League, including several teachers and tradesmen.[64] In Asmara, the ELM also benefited from the involvement of a large number of former members of the Muslim League's Youth Association, some of whom eventually served on the ELM's executive council in Asmara.[65]

Although the ELM helped organize a new generation of activists that came of age with increasing frustration at the injustices during the federation, their broad nationalist objectives filled a political void that resulted in many members viewing the new organization as a needed successor to the league. Moreover, the ELM's program was almost indistinguishable from the league's earlier proclamations, especially the ELM's "redefinition of a politically distinct, pluralist, and secular Eritrean State; a reassertion of the Eritrean demand for independence on the basis of Ethiopia's violation of Eritrean constitutional rights" and a "rejection of Pan-Ethiopianism."[66]

While the ELM's leaders may have viewed themselves as overtaking the "elite nationalism" that had, in their eyes, failed to address the demise of Eritrean sovereignty, its basic ideological thrust represented a validation of the previous efforts of both league leaders and other groups within the Independence Bloc.[67] Apparently, even Ibrahim Sultan believed in the continuity between the two organizations. Former ELM official Muhammadberhan Hassan claimed that Sultan sent a secret telegram in 1960 addressed to Haraka supporters stating, "we *al-rabita* are one with you in our mission and we are going around the countries [throughout North Africa and the Middle East] to tell them to support and stand by the people of Eritrea."[68] Even before Sultan's alleged statement of support, ELM leaders had made efforts to gain the support of established nationalist leaders in Cairo through letter-writing campaigns and by sending some of their leading representatives, such as Tsegaye Kahsay, abroad.[69] Regardless of its leaders' behind-the-scenes efforts, the basic strategies, arguments, and aims of the ELM illustrated its connection to the league's ideological legacy.

Although ELM leaders espoused an aggressively secular program, they nevertheless benefited from the apprehensions among Muslim communities in a similar way to the league's previous base. In addition, the ELM's agenda to liberate Eritrea through covert organization and aggressive diaspora-based activism represented a new avenue for the nationalist movement. By tapping into the discontent of merchant communities, clerics, and especially Muslim youth, the ELM demonstrated that political activism against federation abuses could continue even without the presence of formal political parties. Despite claims that the ELM developed its urban base by using a newfound "secularization" as a strategy to "reconcile the Moslem-Christian schism," these religious-based divisions among Eritrea activists were largely mitigated by the growth of Christian discontent that characterized much of the support behind the labor strike in March 1958.

The ELM's particular organizational strategy, coupled with the composition of its membership, helped sustain its early outreach efforts despite the logistical limitations. According to Ruth Iyob, the organization's success came largely from its substantial investment in Eritrean civil society: "The use of the cultural arena as a vehicle for national reconciliation and mobilization was one of the most significant developments of this period. Social gatherings, sports, and tea houses were transformed into mobilization centers for youth, workers, and small traders."[70]

In addition to the broad social mobilization among the youth and urban workforce, one of the ELM's greatest strengths was its ability to take advantage of the already well-developed national identity among most Eritrean soldiers based in Sudan, who now offered their services to the new organization. In explaining the ELM's advantage in procuring soldiers' support, Nawud recalled that through their service in the Sudanese army in previous years they "were bound together by belonging to the Eritrean nation and not because of tribal or clannish affiliation. They enjoyed a high degree of consciousness and deep nationalistic spirit."[71]

Despite the initial claims of the ELM's success, the organization's insistence on secrecy, its decentralized activities, and political agenda of nonviolence failed to persuade a large segment of the diaspora activists that Eritrean "liberation" could in fact be achieved without taking up arms. Whatever its intellectual and political contributions, the ELM's short-lived prominence in the movement gave way to a more aggressive nationalist faction. The establishment and eventual dominance of the counterorganization that later became the ELF transformed the course of nationalism not simply by advocating armed struggle, but by dramatically shifting the debate about Muslim identity in the context of national liberation.

Transnational Activism and the ELF's Origins

While the ELM continued to build up its membership within Eritrea and its branches in eastern Sudan, a wider and more aggressive movement developed among the political exiles and students, principally in Cairo. The growth of the exile community in Cairo during the 1950s offers an important avenue to understand how diaspora-based mobilization contributed to the growing urgency in the nationalist movement. From a purely religious perspective, Cairo already held an important place for generations of Eritrean Islamic scholars who sought instruction at Al-Azhar University. Many of Eritrea's most prominent Islamic clerics, including Ibrahim al-Mukhtar, attended the university after engaging in preliminary study at schools in Eritrea and Sudan. Other members of Eritrea's Islamic clergy claimed to have had ancestors who attended the school as far back as the sixteenth century. Consequently, Cairo boasted a sizeable Eritrean community even before the influx of political exiles that began arriving in the mid- and late 1950s.[72] In addition, Ibrahim al-Mukhtar's earlier efforts to solidify relations between the Eritrean ulama and Al-Azhar officials had strengthened the institutional relationship by arranging for delegations of teachers and Arabic instructors to travel from Al-Azhar to assist in strengthening curricula in Eritrea's Islamic schools.[73] However, Eritrean student participation also had broader ramifications than just religious training, as many students helped chart a new course of nationalist activity throughout much of the next decade.[74]

Some observers have commented that the nationalist migration occurred mainly because by the mid-1950s, Cairo had become one of the major centers of growing Arab nationalist thought.[75] Indeed, the positioning of Eritrean students in the heart of the Arab world during the 1950s helped produce an increasingly aggressive cross section of anticolonial, anti-imperialist student activists. Wolde-Yesus Ammar also notes that Eritrean Muslim students were "among the first" to be directly exposed to the broadcasts and writings of Arab nationalist leaders. Consequently, "tuning in to Cairo became a long-lasting habit to many Eritrean nationalists with some knowledge of Arabic."[76] As early as 1950, concerned Al-Azhar students became involved in Eritrea's political debates when a group submitted their own pro-independence memorandum to delegates when the UN Commission for Eritrea stayed in Egypt on their way to Eritrea.[77]

However, the most significant aspect of student political activism developed with the formation of the Eritrean student club at Al-Azhar in January 1952.[78] Although formed after a series of prolonged discussions among a core of eighteen students, the club's activities picked up in the aftermath of the Egyptian revolution, and the organization functioned initially as a charity dedicated to assisting newly arrived Eritrean students.[79] Former club member Abdelkarim Ahmad noted that the organization also helped foster national unity by downplaying regional and cultural differences between members and thus "there was no strong ethnic differentiation among the Eritreans in Cairo at that time."[80] Although concerned primarily with student welfare, club leaders closely followed events in Eritrea, and by 1957 the club itself functioned as an important body to facilitate nationalist activity.[81] Beyond procuring scholarships for newly arrived students, the club emerged as a quasi information desk on developments in Eritrea and organized several anti-Ethiopian demonstrations during the 1950s and early 1960s.[82] The club's strategic location also allowed its members to meet with various Eritrean delegates during their international travels. While en route to New York to submit his memorandum, Muhammad Umar Kadi stayed with club members in Cairo who allegedly helped arrange a meeting between him and UN Secretary General Dag Hammarskjöld.[83]

Club members also coordinated activities aimed at promoting greater cultural and political unity among students by organizing group discussions about Eritrean history and guest lectures with professors and political activists, as well as participating in dialogues with other student groups.[84] According to cofounder and former club president Abd al-Qadir Haqus al-Jibirti, club members strongly followed political events in Egypt and consequently took in the basic tenants of Nasserism. Supposedly, Egyptian president Gamal Abdel Nasser spoke in favor of the club's objectives and on various occasions met with student representatives, whom he encouraged in private to fight for their independence.[85]

Throughout the 1950s and particularly by the end of the decade, club leaders involved themselves in the wider political movements taking place across the Islamic world. Other students participated in the growing activism among diaspora communities by taking part in meetings in Port Sudan and Kassala. In other instances, club members branched out and participated in Islamic youth conferences in Pakistan, Egypt, and elsewhere. By the end of the decade, club members

Hamid Adem and al-Jibirti also participated in the creation of the African Student League, founded in Cairo, again under Nasser's supposed encouragement.[86] In addition, club representatives developed more concrete relationships directly with the nationalist leadership in Eritrea, as delegates began making trips to Eritrean cities to gather money in secret for their activities. Consequently, many of the student representatives came into contact with prominent nationalist leaders as well as arranged meetings with Islamic leaders and Muslim League officials in Asmara, Mendefera, Keren, Agordat, and other cities.[87] As the repression of political expression increased after the 1958 general strike, the club's rhetoric took on a similar tone with the league's defense of Muslim institutional autonomy.

At a 1959 conference of African and Asian youth organizations in Cairo, a delegation from the club argued that the federation could only continue to exist if Ethiopian authorities were willing to allow local officials to retain control of Eritrea's internal affairs, including the management of taxation, transportation issues, customs, religious and educational institutions, and other areas of governance.[88] Significantly, the delegation's platform mirrored the Muslim League's basic consensus, which had long proclaimed the necessity for maintaining independent, local institutions in the political decision-making process.[89] Moreover, the tone of the nationalist language among the Eritrean students focused on dispelling the perception that Eritrea shared any cultural or political affinities with Ethiopia. In this respect, the club also reflected Eritrean independence as argued by Ibrahim Sultan and other league officials before the Four Power Commission in 1947 and the UN General Assembly two years later.[90]

Activism among Cairo students and exiles only increased after the arrival of Ibrahim Sultan and Idris Muhammad Adam, in late March 1959. According to the latter, most of the leading student representatives supported the idea of launching an armed struggle and by December 1959 they had decided to form a new organization for that explicit purpose. Nevertheless, supporters remained largely inactive in proceeding with any concrete political plans for the first half of 1960, although according to Idris 'Uthman Glawdiyos the leadership established an executive council in early February.[91] The founding of the ELF finally took place in July 1960 when eleven members came together to refute previous efforts at a peaceful resolution and establish a guerrilla-based movement for national liberation.[92] Under the primary leadership of its chairmen, Idris Muhammad Adam, the ELF (colloquially known as Jebha) quickly emerged as the dominant political entity across the diaspora in Northeast Africa and the Middle East. With the outbreak of armed resistance, and specifically the rise of the ELF, Islam and Muslim identity became increasingly tangled with more aggressive nationalist articulations that emerged as the federal system gave way to formal Ethiopian occupation.

The ELF's Role in Reshaping Eritrean Nationalism among Muslims

While the growth of the ELF signaled a dramatic turn in the course of political activism, it also had significant consequences for the role of Muslim identity as a tool for articulating a new kind of Eritrean identity. This identity was fundamentally shaped by activists across the diaspora, who functioned as the principal agents of change on the eve of Eritrea's war against Ethiopia.[93] In particular, student involvement in Cairo contributed to the success of many of the veteran Muslim nationalist politicians in building support. According to Abdelkarim Ahmad, the decision to create the ELF did not take place in July 1960, as widely claimed, but actually several months earlier, in December 1959, when a group of students and Idris Muhammad Adam went on a retreat to Jabal Muqaddam, on the outskirts of Cairo. After taking a secret oath and agreeing to launch an armed struggle, participants in the retreat elected Adam as its chairman and began the process of expanding membership. However, other accounts have downplayed student influence in actually calling for the new nationalist body. Instead, some have argued that the ELF's creation occurred after Ibrahim Sultan and Idris Muhammad Adam's 1960 diplomatic visit to Saudi Arabia, where the pair "made contacts with the Eritrean community" and later expressed their desire to "form an organization and start an armed struggle."[94]

Yet Ibrahim Sultan's recollections of this period paint a far more complex picture of the supposed unified "desire" among Eritrea's nationalist leaders. He contended that even much of the leadership suffered from ideological divisions. Sultan claimed that the most decisive issue that confronted Muslim communities in western Eritrea involved the divisions within the Beni-Amer (tigre) population, which was divided into two camps, those who identified with the traditions of the Khatmiyya *tariqa* and those who began displaying reactionary,

"Wahhabist" leanings, including allegedly Idris Muhammad Adam and his group of supporters.[95] Sultan's description of the rapport between Idris Muhammad Adam and Saudi prince Faisal (including the latter's decision to give the former funding to "form a party and destroy al-rabita") suggests that by the early 1960s there were clear ideological divisions within Eritrea's Muslim community, as some hard-line activists perceived the Muslim League as a political entity too outdated and moderate to lead an armed struggle.[96] For his part, Idris Muhammad Adam claimed that ELF members later found refuge and support among conservative Saudi elements:

> When Eritreans came illegally to Saudia and claimed to be ELF they were not touched. This came after we met with King Faysal after he became King and he gave us facilities. Eritreans in Saudia had come as skilled workers as at that time Saudia was open for workers from all sides. There was no real Eritrean association among the workers as they were lacking the leaders for it. When we visited Saudia for the first time we met with all the young Eritreans in Jeddah after speaking with King Saud.[97]

Sultan's mentioning of his alliance during this period with other former Muslim League members against Idris Muhammad Adam's group suggests that a faction within the early fluid structure of the ELF continued to embrace a more inclusive perspective even when activists' armed rebellion was the next course of action.[98] Even Ibrahim al-Mukhtar's formal "nonpolitical" role aligned with that of Ibrahim Sultan's ideological wing by his continued defense of Islamic religious institutional autonomy, even after the Ethiopian government formally annexed Eritrea, in 1962. Ibrahim al-Mukhtar's previous alleged support for the ELM is also indicative of the mufti's predilection toward supporting nationalist efforts that were led by activists who were not intent on using a strict, exclusionary interpretation of Islam as a primary mobilizing factor in rallying for independence.

By discussing his exclusion from the official founding of the ELF due to alleged pressure from the Saudi government, Sultan's testimony suggests that Adam's rise to power within the new organization marked a change in how many within the nationalist leadership perceived the significance of Islam to the struggle.[99] In discussing the drastic political divergence between the two organizations, Kibreab rightly noted that "dynamic internal debate and relative tolerance"

within the ELM gave way to a more aggressive view of the nationalist struggle inside the ELF, which had "a narrower membership base
and lacked the experience and conceptual frameworks to create an
inclusive front that could reflect the social and political diversity of
Eritrean society."[100]

While the early ELF may have lacked a "clear ideological line"
in comparison to the ELM, its leaders did emphasize the historical
oppression of Eritrean Muslims by the Ethiopian government. Consequently, the organization became the ideal incubator for the rise of
genuine "Moslem militants."[101] The ELF's call for an armed struggle
also encouraged many of the ELM's members to lose patience with
the limitations of their own efforts. Former ELM organizer 'Ali Said
Mehamed Berhatu summed up the frustration when he observed
that "following *Harakat* was like a kind of plebiscite" and that people
did not truly understand its intricacies, but that rather people were
mainly interested "in some kind of activity against Ethiopia."[102]

Less than a year after its founding, the ELF succeeded in winning
over many former ELM supporters and built on the existing diaspora
networks across Sudan. By mid-1960 even many disaffected ELM
members had established direct communication with ELF leaders in
Cairo and began laying the groundwork to arrange for arms trans-
ports. ELF leaders also overtook the ELM's influence elsewhere in
the diaspora by winning support of Eritrean workers based in Saudi
Arabia.[103] Largely due to their leadership's continued refusal to engage
in armed combat, the ELM's rank and file gradually began to abandon
the party, as the ELF increased its outreach efforts to build their cause
as a genuine "Muslim" movement against Ethiopian oppression:

> When the ELF was declared and many confrontations with
> the Ethiopian army took place, many of our friends went to
> Jebha and were no longer with us. All of those, my friends
> in the committee, with the exception of myself, they went
> to Jebha, all of them. They became the leadership of Jebha.
> And that also was because the leadership of Jebha at that time
> tried to create new propaganda against us. They said that Ha-
> rakat are communist and we [Jebha] Muslims. To be called a
> communist at that time was a very, very bad thing.[104]

By early 1961 the ELF solidified its operations in both Khartoum and Kassala and succeeded in gaining the support of most
of the ELM officials in eastern Sudan. Even ELF chairman, Idris

Muhammad Adam, traveled to Sudan on several occasions and spoke out against Haraka's leadership while seeking the allegiance of most ELM members in the crucial areas in and around Kassala.[105] In some instances, the ELF leader allegedly received correspondence directly from disaffected ELM members who expressed their desire to leave the organization.[106] Former Haraka members noted that the ELF's campaign to discredit the ELM as an alien, "Marxist" organization succeeded in winning the majority support of ELM members in some Eritrean cities in only a few weeks.[107]

Armed Struggle and Shifting Strands of Muslim Identity

Although gaining the support of most former Haraka members provided the organization with a new avenue to broaden its operations in eastern Sudan, the most important aspect of the ELF's initial success was its members gaining the allegiance of religious and community leaders on both sides of the border who could facilitate the actual logistics of building an armed struggle:

> The people who were moving to form the ELF were doing so very secretly because they were afraid of the Sudanese as well as the Ethiopian government. Because of this there were no official letters sent inside from Kassala. But people who were coming from the inside to Kassala were telling the people there that there was some movement inside concerning Eritrean freedom or independence. The same thing went the other way. People who moved from Kassala to the inside were telling them that there was some movement in Kassala. This was the linkage between Kassala and the inside in the beginning. Later, regular messages were sent. Sometimes we wrote them on the inside of the clothes of messengers.[108]

By 1961 many ELF affiliates across the region used broad ideas of a "Muslim struggle" to gain the support of prominent Muslim raiders and former shifta to help take up the struggle. ELF members were especially concerned about garnering the support of Hamid Idris Awate, one of the Western Province's most well known former shifta leaders. By all accounts, the most ardent ELF proponent to encourage Awate was Muhammad Sheikh Dawd. The grandson of a Beni-Amer Sufi leader, Dawd "was motivated by religious feelings" in his political dealings with the ELF, particularly by his deep resentment of the abolition of Arabic as a language of education by the federation government. Allegedly, he called Awate to a meeting in Agordat in early 1961, where he told the shifta leader that "he should declare a jihad" against Ethiopia because of the banning of Arabic and since the situation in Eritrea now required that "the Muslims should fight for the divine right of the Muslims and Islam" against Ethiopian aggression.[109]

Months before the start of hostilities, in September 1961, another ELF organizer, Shaykh Sayedna Mehamed 'Ali, held a meeting with Awate and supporters in the village of Mogolo. A well-known religious leader, 'Ali allegedly had a reputation as a "living saint" among the Beni-Amer community in the area. Under the guise of a Sufi festival, the meeting attracted more than two thousand people and helped raise money and arms for Awate's cause to lead the revolt.[110] While it remains doubtful that Awate and his core group of fighters actually joined the ELF in any official capacity, later accounts by ELF officials often emphasized their organization's efforts to reach out to Awate throughout mid-1961. In the wake of Awate's death, many ELF leaders also went to great efforts to connect Awate's actions as being part and parcel of the ELF operations by claiming that Awate remained in direct contact with representatives in Kassala throughout most of the year. Other accounts claim that when Awate first met with ELF representatives in Agordat in May 1961, he informed the representatives that he wished to speak directly with ELF leaders about the logistical challenges of beginning a guerrilla war.[111] Despite these overt efforts to paint Awate as working exclusively within the ELF camp and forging a "Muslim" struggle, the perception that the ELF planned to protect Muslim interests carried more weight in the wider diaspora than among the organization's rural base in western Eritrea and eastern Sudan.

One of the best illustrations of this de-emphasis of purely religious motivations across the immediate region was the relative absence of traditional Sufi authorities in even contributing to the ELF's mobilization. While the ELF received broad support from many rural clerics in the villages and towns, their participation developed without the involvement of the influential al-Mirghani family. Having been relegated to the outside of Eritrean politics since Sayyid Muhammad Abu Bakr al-Mirghani switched to the Unionist Party, in 1948, the apparent unwillingness of the al-Mirghani family in Sudan and Eritrea to assist in "the national struggle" only served to further delegitimize

Khatmiyya leaders' political credibility.[112] Consequently, even many devout ELF supporters with connections to the order looked elsewhere for religious guidance as the armed struggle progressed. The al-Mirghani family's general indifference to the political situation by 1960, in combination with the ELF leadership's rapport with more "reactionary" Muslim authorities across the Middle East, suggests that unlike the early movement for independence during the late 1940s, this new, aggressive movement for national liberation largely dismissed the Khatmiyya leadership as a nonentity in the impending struggle.

In addition to the apparent indifference of the Khatmiyya leadership, the transnational nature of the early ELF's operations demonstrated that the organization's concern for building support across the region resulted in a majority of its efforts being concentrated in areas in the Muslim world where they could expect more meaningful logistical and political support. Once again, the ELF's Cairo-based leadership and its relationship with students proved to be a major advantage in building support:

> In Cairo there was an active movement to discuss with the Arab embassies the Eritrean case. We asked for permission for Idris Muhammad Adam to visit different Arab countries. Somalia was among the first to respond very enthusiastically about the Eritrean case. Also the Saudi government gave permission. Sabbe was first in Jidda and went with him to Somalia. The Somali government agreed to allow an Eritrean office to be opened: the Eritrean-Somali Friendship Association. It was opened in November 1960 and 'Uthman Saleh Sabbe was the first representative.[113]

The ELF's connection with the Somali cause in particular became one of its most proactive international efforts. According to Shumet Sishagne, the organization not only sought support from Somali activists but received considerable aid directly from the Somali government, which provided "the earliest source of financial military support for the Eritrean insurgency. It also provided Somali passports to ELF members and its sympathizers living abroad."[114] Idris Muhammad Adam later admitted to traveling to Somalia at the beginning of the decade after receiving an invitation from Somali supporters. After establishing the Eritrean-Somali Friendship Association as an umbrella group to facilitate the creation of multiple ELF branches,

Idris Muhammad Adam returned to Cairo, while ELF official 'Uthman Saleh Sabbe remained in country for nearly a year, continuing to develop a support base.[115] Meanwhile, ELF branches also sprang up across the Red Sea in Jeddah and Riyadh as ELF representatives organized workers in the cities' exile communities.[116]

With Somali backing and the growing interest of supporters based in Saudi Arabia, Egypt, Sudan, and elsewhere in the Eritrean diaspora, the ELF moved ever closer to fully embracing the spirit of "Muslim solidarity" that many Muslim League officials and writers themselves had promoted years earlier, albeit through a much more rigid interpretation. While this shift in Islamic identity resulted in part from the organization's outreach efforts across the Muslim world to the younger generation in the diaspora, a major thrust in this transformation came through the efforts of one of the ELF's major international organizers: 'Uthman Saleh Sabbe.

'Uthman Saleh Sabbe and Widening "Muslim" Nationalist Mobilization

Born in the town of Hirgigo in 1932, Sabbe came from a respected Saho family with connections to the local ulama.[117] Sabbe had received particular support from his mentor and family associate Saleh Ahmed Kekiya. After finishing his initial Qur'anic studies, he attended the Hirgigo charity school and later traveled to Addis Ababa, where he enrolled in teacher-training courses from 1950 to 1952. After returning to Eritrea in 1953, Sabbe took a position as an instructor at the Hirgigo charity school (renamed Emperor Haile Selassie I School in 1950) and became the institution's director in September 1955. During his time in the Massawa-Hirgigo area, Sabbe immersed himself in nationalist politics and became leader of a local group of activists, helping publish a pro-independence, handwritten newsletter entitled *Al-Nahdha*. Sabbe also came into frequent conflict with Eritrea's federation government regarding the lack of funds for the promotion of Arabic-language study. During the late 1950s Sabbe also worked clandestinely with Sudan-based activists to send Eritrean student groups to Cairo. Having been arrested for subversion by federation authorities in 1958, Sabbe was later released and finally left Massawa in August 1959 and worked for a short time for a shipping company in Assab before committing full time to political activity.[118]

Almost immediately after being brought into the ELF fold through Adam's encouragement, Sabbe proved to be the organization's most astute international spokesman and fundraiser. Besides early success in Somalia and his efforts in North Yemen and Saudi Arabia, Sabbe attempted to carry the ELF's message beyond the Red Sea region, going so far as to plan a diplomatic mission to Pakistan.[119] Eventually, Sabbe, Adam, and ELF colleague Idris 'Uthman Glawdiyos appointed themselves members of the organization's Supreme Council.[120] As one of ELF's main leaders and its secretary for foreign affairs, Sabbe worked against other Eritrean activists deemed too secular or radical by the ELF hierarchy.[121]

This shift also helps explain why many later non-Muslim activists in the diaspora felt increasingly uneasy about the religious divide that developed in the early armed struggle. The predominantly Christian leaders within what eventually became the EPLF alluded to the legacy of this above-mentioned ELF faction when they claimed that the group, consisting of Idris Muhammed Adam and other "peasant chieftains and reactionary petty bourgeois intellectuals," received the backing of several Arab states and then used the armed struggle to promote personal agendas of "political opportunism and religious fanaticism."[122] Significantly, the ELF's rise also paralleled a decline among many former Muslim League leaders in working within the new organization. Adam's background as a leader with the MLWP had already been a cause of rivalry with Ibrahim Sultan and only created greater division among others in the league's hierarchy. The establishment of the ELF thus began a change in which the previous legacy of interreligious cooperation as argued by the Muslim League and later the ELM became increasingly marginalized, as more sectarian actors sought to divest Eritrean Muslims from the previous legacy of interreligious cooperation that had defined the earlier period of nationalist activity.[123]

While the ELF emerged by the early 1960s as the organization most capable of leading the armed struggle, the reluctance of some ELF members to adopt this more rigid outlook of Islamic identity may have resulted from the continued influence of Ibrahim Sultan, who, in addition to serving as an informal adviser for some ELF members in Cairo, continued to maintain strong relations with exiled Christian nationalists, particularly Woldeab Woldemariam. Ultimately, this "first major rift in the ELF" between Sultan and Adam foreshadowed the later issues that arose as a greater number of ELF supporters resented the direction that Adam and the other members of the supreme council had taken the organization by embracing a notable "anti-Christian" sentiment in its nationalist language.[124]

Reclaiming the Moral Conscience of Eritrean Muslim Nationalism

Although largely an outside observer to the ELF's rise and its later dominance in the mid-1960s, Ibrahim Sultan remained the most active Muslim nationalist leader to emphasize religious cooperation, even as sectarianism within the ELF leadership seemed to increase simultaneously with the intensity of the armed conflict. Decades after the early ELF's exclusionary view of non-Muslim Eritreans had already contributed to the political fracturing in the nationalist movement, Sultan continued to attempt to mend internal divisions among various Muslim-majority factions as well as remind activists about the "grace of brotherhood" that all Eritreans had shared in the nationalist movement.[125] As he had done throughout his tenure with the league, he reminded his fellow activists of the need to embrace all faiths as part of the struggle. Sultan's arguments expressed the spirit of the previous years of the league's nationalist message, embracing a discourse that emphasized Islam as a vital identity marker but that also held a pragmatic view that the independence movement required broad ideological acceptance and interfaith accommodation to achieve its goals.[126]

Espousing his own ideal of Islam's capacity for tolerance and cooperation, Sultan argued in one memorandum from the early 1980s that Islam could unite the fractured national movement through promoting activists' common objectives and national identity.[127] In his tract, Sultan harked back to the federation's earliest days and noted that "the only rays of light" to come out of the "dark period" were due to the efforts of league members and their associates within the Independence Bloc. Having witnessed the ELF's attempts to commandeer the armed struggle as the true representative organ for Muslim interests, Sultan provided both a defense of the league's historic importance and an argument for its resurrection in the current political climate:

> The Muslim League, as any organization in life, has had many weaknesses . . . this is life, but coming back to strength is possible. And possibilities of life are still there and Muslims all over this beloved land still have their hopes on the Muslim

League. They did not wipe their hands of it and they are still
calling it a place of authority to defend the faith, protect the
[Arabic] language and bring victory to the Eritrean people.[128]

Although Sultan's memorandum appeared long after the ELF
itself had lost its place in leading the war of independence, its wide
circulation among several Muslim-majority political factions across
the diaspora illustrated that the "major rift" in the ELF that first began
in the early 1960s had important ramifications for how nationalist
leaders continued to frame Islam as a component of national liberation for decades after the start of the war of independence.[129]

Conclusions

Between the start of pervasive civil unrest in Eritrea's major cities,
in early 1958, and continuing through much of 1961, the virtual collapse of Eritrean autonomy within the federation government had
tremendous significance for the course of Muslim political activism
and specifically on the Muslim League's legacy as the vanguard of
the independence movement. The formal banning of political activity
within Eritrea, in April 1958, signaled the end of the league's existence as a formal power, and it necessitated that activists look abroad
to engage in the growing resistance movement through the widening
diaspora. Initially, many former Muslim League members took solace
in the early success of the ELM.

In many ways, the ELM's rise defied convention, given the context of political repression within Eritrea. Yet the inability of the
ELM leadership to ultimately put forth a program of armed rebellion against Ethiopian encroachment allowed a new, more reactionary leadership from the ELF to siphon off a substantial portion of
its membership and build on its considerable diaspora networks
throughout the early 1960s. The ELF's rise represented a fundamental break in the overall political ideology among Muslims as
defined by the league. Abandoning the league's previous legacy of
interreligious cooperation and general inclusion in the independence movement, the ELF's Cairo-based leadership dramatically
shifted the debate concerning both Eritrean identity and Islam's
place in the nationalist struggle.

Part of the shift in ideology came as a result of the fact that much of
the ELF's leadership had not been affiliated with the inner workings

of the Muslim League, but actually with rival organizations including the IML and the MLWP. Moreover, the relatively youthful composition of its members in the diaspora represented a marked change for the generation of nationalist leaders that arose during the political debates of the 1940s and early 1950s. Consequently, the ELF's dismissal of the Muslim League leadership and pro-independence Christian leaders illustrated the drastic shift in their nationalist program. Seen as an outdated organization, far too moderate to take the reins of an armed struggle, the Muslim League and its former leaders watched largely from the sidelines as the ELF developed its own, much narrower ideological construct to engage in its own nationalist struggle.

While part of this came about as a result of the sincere belief of some within the ELF hierarchy, the push toward more exclusive, pro-Muslim rhetoric also reflected the practical realities of building an armed struggle across the Red Sea region in the early 1960s. In need of funding, arms, and political legitimacy, the ELF reinvented itself as a Muslim nationalist movement pitted against Ethiopian Christian domination. Throughout the Eritrean diaspora—whether in Egypt, Sudan, Saudi Arabia, or elsewhere in the Red Sea region—the nationalist impetus became increasingly tied to more aggressive articulations of Muslim identity. This newfound Muslim identity centered largely on a common feeling of representing an oppressed people denied both political power and religious freedom by Ethiopian authorities. The attacks on Islamic institutions and the Arabic language, coupled with the worsening economic situation, instilled further resentment at the fact that Ethiopian authorities had favored many Tigrinya-speaking unionists at the expense of the general Muslim population. Ironically, these reactionary attitudes developed even as ELF leaders began embracing more secular strands of Arab nationalism and especially Nasserism throughout the 1960s. Consequently, the early ELF's embrace of this new Muslim Eritrean identity contained a paradoxical and sometimes uneasy mix of self-proclaimed Muslim nationalist fighters and those who latched onto the wider secular nationalist trends from across the Arab world.

Ultimately, these new transformations of Muslim identity and the backlash against the league's leadership illustrated how the changing circumstances of Ethiopian domination fundamentally altered the dialogue that had emerged in previous years through Eritrea's vibrant but fragile nationalist contact zone. Without the input of the Muslim League's intellectual and political leaders to emphasize the nuance of national identity and Muslim-Christian cooperation as integral elements of national liberation, an important break in Eritrean Muslim political and cultural identity took place. As the ELF solidified its power during the early and mid-1960s, it weakened the previous legacy of interfaith camaraderie in the nationalist movement by falsely recasting Eritrean nationalism as an inherently sectarian struggle. The contradictions of this newfound view of Muslim identity helped sow the seeds for the later conflict that fractured the ELF during the late 1960s and led to the eventual establishment of the EPLF.

Epilogue

This book has explored an often overlooked yet critical chapter in the early period of African nationalism. It has investigated the relationship between religious identity, intellectual activism, and political mobilization in Eritrea's Muslim communities during the crucial period between the end of Italian colonial rule and the start of Eritrea's armed struggle against Ethiopia. In doing so, *Paths toward the Nation* speaks to broader regional developments as much as it does to nationalist mobilization specifically within Eritrea. Any analysis of Eritrea's independence movement between 1941 and 1961 cannot begin to understand the internal cultural and political developments without appreciating the degree to which nationalist actors engaged in and were informed by external trends across the Islamic world. While not as influential and celebrated as nationalist movements in Pakistan, Egypt, Algeria, and elsewhere that emerged during the decade after World War II, Eritrea's course toward independence nevertheless embodied one of the more complicated movements to frame national consciousness within the language of Islam. The Muslim League's promotion of its own broad understanding of Islamic modernism demonstrates the extent to which the early stages of Eritrean nationalism were very much dependent on the realities of the region's diverse ethnic and religious composition. Through an analysis of the formation, growth, and eventual disintegration of the Eritrean Muslim League, we can better understand how the earliest notions of an Eritrean national identity took shape and ultimately had major implications far beyond the country's physical boundaries.

Equally significant is that the Muslim League's experience exemplified the centrality of indigenous intellectuals in both constructing and facilitating the public discourse that established the earliest understandings of a shared "Eritreaness."[1] In this sense, *Paths toward the Nation* has examined the rise of early nationalism through two specific lenses: the framework of intellectual history and the broader analysis of grassroots Islamic community activism. In both instances, I have sought to provide a greater understanding of how and why the league represented the most integral organizational component within the nationalist cause.

The league's founding and subsequent expansion during the late 1940s touched off a brief but intense period of intellectual debate in which the organization's leading writers and affiliates internalized Eritrea's future status and its significance to Muslim security, religious institutions, educational progress, and political freedom. The main thrust of this intellectual discussion occurred within the pages of the league's official newsletter, *Sawt al-rabita al-islamiyya* and later in other Arabic-language publications such as *Wahda Iritriyya* and *Sawt al-Iritriyya*. Through written commentaries, news reports, and public declarations, the league's leading intellectuals involved themselves directly in the emerging nationalist contact zone, the broad public space of intellectual and critical discussion that allowed activists to address issues concerning the country's cultural and political development. This book thus represents the first in-depth study to critique the precise relationship between cultural and social trends among Eritrea's Muslim intellectuals and the wider political changes that took place during the period.

While throughout its relatively short history the Eritrean Muslim League faced numerous internal divisions and external pressures, it nonetheless provided the organizational apparatus needed to encourage the growth of a collective Muslim identity in the context of an emerging Eritrean state. In contrast to many of the other rival organizations with broad Muslim-based memberships that developed in the wake of the league, including the IML, MLWP, and even NEPIP, the Muslim League not only retained the support of the majority of the country's Muslim residents but also received the backing and guidance of the country's leading Islamic clerics and scholars, giving the organization added credibility through the support of its affiliated intellectuals and community leaders. As the only legitimately "Muslim" organization to consistently express support for Eritrean independence and (later) the preservation of local autonomy within the Ethiopian-Eritrean Federation, the league served as the primary ideological bridge between early nationalists of the 1940s and the armed liberation movement.

In addition to the league's considerable intellectual dominance, the organization's success owed much to the groundswell of grassroots activism that emerged in the region during the early and mid-1940s. The growth of a broad-based tigre emancipation movement across the country's Western Province as well as the increased participation of the region's urban residents in supporting the expansion of Islamic religious and educational institutions had the effect of encouraging wider community mobilization to secure Muslim interests. Consequently, Muslim activists across the country's diverse regional and ethnic boundaries began to articulate concerns about how the country's political future would impact their respective communities, especially in the wake of Ethiopian attempts to promote the cultural links between Eritrea's Tigrinya-speaking Christian communities and Ethiopia. Although many of Eritrea's nationalist activists did not, initially, view the independence issue as having any particular religious connotation, the gradual politicization of religion convinced most Muslim observers that their interests would be better served through an independent Eritrean state rather than through union with Ethiopia or by partition to Sudan.

The league's ability to tap into the growing wave of grassroots mobilization and to retain its intellectual influence became major sources of strength when the organization did eventually encounter serious obstacles. By the late 1940s the league struggled to maintain momentum as rival organizations, including the Muslim League of the Western Province and the Independent Muslim League, challenged its overall aims and the integrity of its leadership. The organization nevertheless succeeded in helping prevent complete union between Eritrea and Ethiopia. League leaders built support for their agenda by emphasizing the historical oppression of Muslims already living in Ethiopia. By arguing that Ethiopian rule represented an inherent threat to Muslim community interests, league leaders and the general membership supported the idea that religious and cultural freedom needed protection as integral components in a legitimate, independent Eritrean state. Even after the United Nations General Assembly ultimately rejected the idea of unconditional Eritrean independence and voted in favor of creating the Ethiopian-Eritrean Federation, in December 1950, the league, through its supporters within the Independence Bloc managed to create enthusiasm for the impending federation system. In their efforts, leaders promised constituents that the organization would seek assurances from federation authorities to protect key religious and political institutions. Consequently, the major cultural markers of Muslim culture, including the preservation of Arabic as an official language, the autonomy of religious institutions, and the strengthening of Muslim education were all embraced as core issues of concern by the league, even after hopes for complete independence were dashed.

Beginning in the mid-1950s and continuing through the start of the armed struggle in September 1961, the authoritarian measures of the federation government forced league members and most of its leadership into exile. Consequently, Eritrean diaspora communities in Sudan and Egypt became major centers of nationalist activity for former league members as well as the new emerging generation of activists that eventually formed the core of the Eritrean Liberation Movement and the Eritrean Liberation Front. The ELF's eventual dominance over the ELM during the early 1960s also represented a major break from the previous ways in which the league had used Islam and Muslim identity to promote the nationalist cause. Thus the ELF not only represented a new political organization, it also signaled a major shift in the ideology of Muslim nationalist leaders who expressed a far more aggressive and rigid interpretation of their collective "Muslim" identity, one that largely abandoned the league's proactive insistence on interreligious cooperation in the independence cause.

The ongoing conflict between Eritrea's present-day government and the various opposition groups across the global diaspora represents just one of the many repercussions of the ELF's decline and ultimate defeat at the hands of the largely secular Eritrean People's Liberation Front during the early 1980s. The subsequent domination of the EPLF's present-day incarnation, the People's Front for Democracy and Justice, within a sovereign Eritrean state continues to elicit widespread criticism and protest from organizations, particularly groups concerned with the issues of religious freedom and human rights abuses. Related to these criticisms has been an ongoing preoccupation with how the militaristic nature of the PFDJ government and its sanctioned national narrative has developed alongside the recent trends in much of the opposition-based scholarship. Many observers have argued that these competing narratives of nationalism have now extended to the very function and positioning of the Eritrean state itself: "The emergence of alternative narratives, however subterranean and suppressed, is thus at the heart of Eritrean

political battles fought by the regime through the state's myriad institutions, and by non-state actors through research, publication and
the internet."[2]

This book has sought to further these current discussions within
the scholarship by attempting to shed greater light on how the league's
origins, ideological foundations, and internal mechanisms ultimately
demonstrate the continuity between the organization's original agenda
and many of the current concerns found within the political debates
taking place across the diaspora.

By looking at this particular chapter of Eritrean history with an
emphasis on the Muslim League and its lasting influence, we are able
to critique the current rivalry between the PFDJ-sanctioned narrative and the broader revisionist scholarship that only recently has
emerged. In doing so, we can begin to address what historian Jacques
Depelchin has referred to as the danger of producing "conceptual"
silences that often result in the suppression of true counterhegemonic
narratives in African history.[3] Given the current political climate
both in Eritrea and the increasing concerns about the country's deteriorating human rights record under the PFDJ's one-party state,
understanding the significance of such narratives that explore the
relationship between nationalism, religious-based discourse and political freedom remains a highly relevant issue both within Eritrea
and across the global diaspora.

Notes

Abbreviations in Notes

FCB	Fabian Colonial Bureau
FO	Foreign Office
GAOR	[UN] General Assembly Official Records
NARA	National Archives and Records Administration
RDC	Research and Documentation Center, Asmara

Introduction

1. "Speech of the President of the Muslim League in Asmara," *Sawt al-rabita al-islamiyya*, June 24, 1947, 1.

2. Here the Arabic word *mejlis* is best translated as "committee."

3. Elizabeth Schmidt, "Top Down or Bottom Up? Nationalist Mobilization Reconsidered, with Special Reference to Guinea (French West Africa)," *American Historical Review* 110, no. 4 (October 2005): 1014.

4. Martin Riesebrodt, *Pious Passion: The Emergence of Modern Fundamentalism in the United States and Iran* (Berkeley: University of California Press, 1993), 16.

5. Ibid., 10–20.

6. Kwame Anthony Appiah, *In My Father's House: Africa in the Philosophy of Culture* (New York: Oxford University Press, 1992), 4.

7. Albert Hourani, *Arabic Thought in the Liberal Age, 1798–1939* (Oxford: Oxford University Press, 1962), 345.

8. Schmidt, "Top Down," 976.

9. Victoria Bernal, "Islam, Transnational Culture, and Modernity in Rural Sudan," in *Gendered Encounters: Challenging Cultural Boundaries and Social Hierarchies in Africa*, ed. M. Grosz-Ngaté and O. Kokole (New York: Routledge, 1997), 148.

10. *Tewahedo*, derived from the ancient Ge'ez language and meaning "unified" or "being made one," is the term given to followers of the Oriental Orthodox Christian Church in Ethiopia and Eritrea. As one of the oldest Christian sects in the world, followers in the Tewahedo community adhere to the Monophysite tradition in regard to the singular nature of Christ. They form the largest Christian denomination in both Ethiopia and Eritrea.

11. The official designation of these nine groups has not been without controversy. The current government, under the control of the People's Front for Democracy and Justice, has promoted an official policy of recognizing these specific cultural groups only since the period of Eritrea's armed struggle against Ethiopia (1961–91). Historically, even establishing "ethnic" distinctions for some of these particular groups has been problematic. For example, several of the subgroups in the country's Tigre-speaking communities consider themselves to be separate ethnicities. See S. F. Nadel, "Notes on Beni Amer Society," *Sudan Notes and Records* 26, no. 1 (1951): 51–94; Abba Isaak Ghebre Iyesus, *Arguments for Shedding Some Light on the Tigré Phenomenon* (Asmara: MBY Press, 1996).

12. Arabic serves as the primary language of communication between most of the region's Muslim-majority ethnicities, as well as the first language among the Rashaida.

13. Tekeste Negash, *Eritrea and Ethiopia: The Federal Experience* (New Brunswick, NJ: Transaction Publishers, 1997), 13.

14. Ibid., 15.

15. Jonathan Miran, "A Historical Overview of Islam in Eritrea," *Die Welt des Islams* 45, no. 2 (2005): 195.

16. Jonathan Miran, "Between Control, Co-option and Accommodation: Italian Colonialism and Islam in Eritrea (1885–1941)," unpublished paper delivered at the Institute of Advanced Studies, University of Bologna, March 15, 2011, 11.

17. Between 1881 and 1898 much of the territory in the modern Republic of Sudan came under the rule of the Mahdiyah, or the Mahdist state. It began initially as a broad-based religious movement under the Islamic mystic Muhammad Ahmad. In June 1881 he proclaimed himself as the *Mahdi* (anointed one) in fulfillment of supposed religious prophecy. Upon defeating local Sudanese rivals as well as British forces, his followers later established an independent state that posed a serious threat to several European powers in the region, including Italy, France, and especially Great Britain. See P. M. Holt, *The Mahdist State in Sudan* (Oxford: Clarendon Press, 1970); Robert S. Kramer, *Holy City on the Nile: Omdurman during the Mahdiyya, 1885–1898* (Princeton: Markus Wiener, 2010).

18. See Silvia Bruzzi, "Italian Colonialism and Muslim Woman Leadership: The Case of Sharīfa 'Alawiyya in Eritrea," paper presented at the

conference "Negotiating the Sacred: Politics, Practice, and Perceptions of Religion in Africa," Stanford University, October 25, 2009, 4.

19. G. K. N. Trevaskis, *Eritrea: A Colony in Transition, 1941–52* (London: Oxford University Press, 1960), 22.

20. See Amare Tekle, "The Creation of the Ethio-Eritrean Federation: A Case Study in Post-war International Relations, 1945–50" (PhD diss., University of Denver, 1964), 71.

21. See Trevaskis, *Eritrea;* Lloyd Ellingson, "The Emergence of Political Parties in Eritrea, 1941–1950," *Journal of African History* 18, no. 2 (1977): 261–81.

22. See Shumet Sishagne, *Unionists and Separatists: The Vagaries of Ethio-Eritrean Relation 1941–1991* (Hollywood, CA: Tsehai Publishers, 2007), 22–29. For further information on the Greater Tigray movement, see Alemseged Abbay, "The Trans-Mareb Past in the Present," *Journal of Modern African Studies* 35, no. 2 (1997): 321–34.

23. Alemseged Tesfai, *Aynfelale: 1941–1950* (Asmara: Hdri Publishers, 2002), 79–102.

24. James McDougall, *History and the Culture of Nationalism in Algeria* (Cambridge: Cambridge University Press, 2006), 9. Emphasis in original.

25. Ibid., 6.

26. Ibid., 7.

27. Ibid., 8.

28. Uoldelul Chelati Dirar, "Colonialism and the Construction of National Identities: The Case of Eritrea," *Journal of Eastern African Studies* 1, no. 2 (2007): 269.

29. Ibid., 268. See also Dirar, "From Warriors to Urban Dwellers: Ascari and the Military Factor in the Urban Development of Colonial Eritrea," *Cahiers d'études africaines* 44, no. 3, cah. 175 (2004): 533–74.

30. Frederick Cooper, "Possibility and Constraint: African Independence in Historical Perspective," *Journal of African History* 49, no. 2 (2008): 173.

31. Louis Brenner, "Muslim Representations of Unity and Difference in the African Discourse," in *Muslim Identity and Social Change in Sub-Saharan Africa*, ed. Louis Brenner (Bloomington: Indiana University Press), 4.

32. Frantz Fanon, *The Wretched of the Earth* (New York: Grove Press, 1963), 172.

33. Mejlis Ibrahim Mukhtar, "The Eritrean Covenant: Towards Sustainable Justice and Peace," http://awate.com/the-eritrean-covenant-towards-sustainable-justice-and-peace/ (accessed April 15, 2010).

34. Alemseged Tesfai alluded to this dilemma when he noted that much of the historiography has failed to explore the complexities of the "Eritrean social fabric" in relation to nationalist development. Tesfai, interview, March 21, 2010, Athens, Ohio.

35. See Tricia Hepner, "Collective Memories and Embodied Events: Eritrean 'Nation-History,'" *Journal of Imperial and Postcolonial Historical Studies* 1, no. 1 (2000): 41–69. These misconceptions of Eritrean independence also echo Basil Davidson's broader observation that rather than idealistically embracing the nation-state for its own supposed merit, many nationalists understood that the nation-state framework represented merely the most effective means to "strike away the chains of foreign rule." See Basil Davidson, *The Black Man's Burden: Africa and the Curse of the Nation-State* (New York: Random House, 1993), 164. Just as Tekle Woldemikael argued that the present-day Eritrean government has merged the one-party state's political ideology with the commemoration of independence, the scholarship has also fallen victim to the militarization of Eritrean nationalism. See Woldemikael, "Pitfalls of Nationalism in Eritrea," in *Biopolitics, Militarism and Development: Eritrea in the Twenty-First Century,* ed. David O'Kane and Tricia Redeker Hepner (New York: Berghahn Books, 2009), 1–16; Hepner, "Collective Memories," 67; Richard J. Reid, "The Challenge of the Past: The Quest for Historical Legitimacy in Independent Eritrea," *History of Africa* 28 (2001): 239–72.

36. See Richard Sherman, *Eritrea: The Unfinished Revolution* (New York: Praeger, 1980); David Pool, *Eritrea: Africa's Longest War* (London: Anti-Slavery Society, 1982); Haggai Erlich, *The Struggle over Eritrea, 1962–1978: War and Revolution in the Horn of Africa* (Stanford: Hoover Institution Press, 1983); Permanent Peoples' Tribunal, *The Eritrean Case: Proceedings of the Permanent Peoples' Tribunal of the International League for the Rights and Liberation of Peoples: Session on Eritrea* (Milan: Research and Information Center on Eritrea, 1982).

37. Hepner, "Collective Memories," 50.

38. Eritreans for Liberation in North America, "Our Struggle and Its Goals," *Harnet* 2, no. 3 (1973): 3.

39. Hepner, "Collective Memories," 59. See James Firebrace and Stuart Holland, *Never Kneel Down: Drought, Development and Liberation in Eritrea* (Trenton: Red Sea Press, 1985); Robert Machida, *Eritrea: The Struggle for Independence* (Trenton: Red Sea Press, 1987). In the past few years this view has continued to some extent with more recent publications that have centered on various aspects of the armed struggle. See David Pool, *From Guerillas to Government: The Eritrean People's Liberation Front* (Athens: Ohio University Press, 2001); Michela Wrong, *I Didn't Do It for You: How the World Used and Abused a Small African Nation* (London: Fourth Estate, 2005). In contrast, Tekeste Negash has argued that much of the scholarship produced by "nationalist historians" throughout the 1980s and 1990s amid the war of independence selectively used "the

nationalist discourse of the 1940s" to offset the supposed dearth of evidence concerning the actual legitimacy of nationalism during the period in question. See Negash, "Italy and its Relations with Eritrean Political Parties, 1948–1950," *Africa* (Rome) 59, nos. 3–4 (2004): 420.

40. See Woldemikael, "Pitfalls of Nationalism," 1–16.

41. See Tricia Redeker Hepner, *Soldiers, Martyrs, Traitors, and Exiles: Political Conflict in Eritrea and the Diaspora* (Philadelphia: University of Pennsylvania Press, 2009).

42. Richard J. Reid, *Frontiers of Violence in North-East Africa: Genealogies of Conflict since c. 1800* (Oxford: Oxford University Press, 2011), 20.

43. Ibid., 21.

44. For additional information on "nation-language" as a component of religious institutions, see Eddie S. Glaude Jr., *Exodus! Religion, Race, and Nation in Early Nineteenth-Century Black America* (Chicago: University of Chicago Press, 2000).

45. Ruth Iyob, *The Eritrean Struggle for Independence: Domination, Resistance, Nationalism, 1941–1993* (Cambridge: Cambridge University Press, 1995), 4. Although Iyob's book was one of the few studies to address the growth of nationalism *both* before and after the start of armed hostilities, *The Eritrean Struggle* took only a generalized view of how "religious camaraderie" became one of the hallmarks of the early nationalist period.

46. John Markakis, *National and Class Conflict in the Horn of Africa* (Cambridge: Cambridge University Press, 1987), 61. Arguing that "religious enmity" was a well-established tradition between Muslim and Christian leaders by the late 1940s, Markakis proposes that religious identity was relevant in early nationalist politics even though there were clear "material interests" among those involved in both the independence and the unionist cause. Unlike all other studies produced during this period, Markakis illustrated how the religious rivalries of the 1940s and early 1950s were connected to the later conflict that engulfed members of the ELF leadership, who saw themselves as waging a Muslim movement. According to Markakis, ELF leaders "could not resist the flattery of seeing Eritrea portrayed as part of the Arab world." Markakis, "The National Revolution in Eritrea," *Journal of Modern African Studies* 26, no. 1 (1988): 57. For more information on Italian colonial education in Eritrea, see R. R. De Marco, *The Italianization of African Natives: Government Native Education in the Italian Colonies, 1890–1937* (New York: Teachers College, Columbia University Publication, 1943); Berhane Teklehaimanot, "Education in Eritrea during the European Colonial Period," *Eritrean Studies Review* 1, no. 1 (1996): 1–22; FO 371/27583, "Future of Government Schools in Eritrea and Somalia."

47. Gaim Kibreab, *Critical Reflections on the Eritrean War of Independence: Social Capital, Associational Life, Religion, Ethnicity and Sowing Seeds of Dictatorship* (Trenton: Red Sea Press, 2008), 88.

48. Miran, "Islam in Eritrea," 205.

49. Ghirmai Negash, *A History of Tigrinya Literature in Eritrea: The Oral and the Written, 1890–1991* (Leiden: Research School of Asian, African and Amerindian Studies, 1999), 55.

50. Fanon, *Wretched of the Earth*, 148. See Ghirmai Negash, "Native Intellectuals in the Contact Zone: African Responses to Italian Colonialism in Tigrinya Literature," *Biography* 32, no. 1 (2009): 73–87.

51. Redie Bereketeab notes that the founders of the Eritrean Muslim League sought to create their organization in the same vein as Pakistan's Muslim League. Bereketeab, *Eritrea: The Making of a Nation, 1890–1991* (Trenton: Red Sea Press, 2007), 270.

52. See Giulia Barrera, "Mussolini's Colonial Race Laws and State-Settler Relations in Africa Orientale Italiana (1935–41)," *Journal of Modern Italian Studies* 8, no. 3 (2003): 425–43.

53. Mary Louise Pratt, "Arts of the Contact Zone," *Profession* 91 (1991): 33.

54. G. Negash, "Native Intellectuals," 75.

55. Alemseged Tesfai, interview.

56. Reid, *Frontiers of Violence*, 23.

57. Astier M. Almedom, "Re-reading the Short and Long-Rigged History of Eritrea 1941–1952: Back to the Future?," *Nordic Journal of African Studies* 15, no. 2 (2006): 116.

58. Dirar, "Colonialism and Construction," 268.

59. The early coalescence of this intellectual and political activity under British authority is a running theme in the early chapters of Tesfai's study. Tesfai, *Aynfelale*, 1–48.

60. For a broader discussion on the role of African languages and knowledge production, see Ngugi wa Thiong'o, *Decolonizing the Mind: The Politics of Language in African Literature* (New York: Heinemann, 1986).

Chapter 1: Early Rumblings

1. Jonathan Miran, *Red Sea Citizens: Cosmopolitan Society and Cultural Change in Massawa* (Bloomington: Indiana University Press, 2009), 169.

2. Ibid., 30.

3. Ibid., 170.

4. Jonathan Miran, "A Historical Overview of Islam in Eritrea," *Die Welt des Islams* 45, no. 2 (2005): 192.

5. Miran, *Red Sea Citizens*, 172.

6. From the Arabic *na'ib*, or "deputy," Na'ib refers to the historical group of Beja-descended Balaw authorities that developed widespread influence over Muslim authorities and extended their power in the area between Eritrea's Red Sea coast and the highland plateau until the mid-nineteenth century. See Jonathan Miran, "Power without Pashas: The Anatomy of *Na'ib* Autonomy in Ottoman Eritrea (17th-19th C.)," *Eritrean Studies Review* 5, no.1 (2007): 33–88; Miran and Emeri van Donzel, "Na'ib," in *Encyclopaedia Aethiopica*, ed. Siegbert Uhlig (Wiesbaden: Harrassowitz, 2007), 3:1116–18.

7. Miran, *Red Sea Citizens*, 178. Miran argues that in addition to the Khatmiyya and the 'Ad Shaykh, other "Tigre holy families and clans," including the 'Ad Darqi and 'Ad Mu'allim transmitted their own forms of "Islamic education and religious expertise within essentially recently-converted Tigre-speaking societies." Miran, "Constructing and Deconstructing the Tigre Frontier Space in the Long Nineteenth Century," in *History and Language of the Tigre-Speaking Peoples*, ed. Gianfrancesco Lusini (Naples: Università degli Studi di Napoli "L'orientale," 2010), 44. See also John O. Voll, "A History of the Khatmiyyah Tariqah in the Sudan" (PhD diss., Harvard University, 1969).

8. Miran, *Red Sea Citizens*, 30.

9. Miran, "Constructing and Deconstructing," 43. See also Abba Isaak Ghebre Iyesus, *Arguments for Shedding Some Light on the Tîgré Phenomenon* (Asmara: MBY Press, 1996).

10. Richard J. Reid, *Frontiers of Violence in North-East Africa: Genealogies of Conflict since c. 1800* (Oxford: Oxford University Press, 2011), 22.

11. "The Tigre-Speaking Peoples," Papers of Sir Kennedy Trevaskis, MSS Brit Emp S. 367, box 1(B), 126 (henceforth cited as Trevaskis Papers).

12. For information about the origins of *tigre* as a marker for vassal status, see Ghebre Iyesus, *Tîgré Phenomenon*, 30–37; Alberto Pollera, *Le popolazioni indigene dell 'Eritrea* (Bologna: L. Cappelli 1935), 196–17, 226–27; Carlo Conti Rossini, *Principi di diritto consuetudinario dell 'Eritrea* (Rome: Tipografia dell'Unione Editrice, 1916), 541–721.

13. At the height of tigre discontent, representatives claimed that more than one hundred subgroups existed across the territory. "Letter of Tigré Representatives," Trevaskis Papers, box 2(A), *Four Power Commission of Investigation for the Former Italian Colonies*, Report on Eritrea, app. 18, 3 (henceforth cited as *Four Power Commission*).

14. Alemseged Tesfai, *Aynfelale: 1941–1950* (Asmara: Hdri Publishers, 2002), 69.

15. "The Tigre-Speaking Peoples," Trevaskis Papers, box 1(B), 128.

16. Ibid., 137.

17. See Tesfai, *Aynfelale*, 69–74.

18. Kennedy Trevaskis, "Dispute between the Shumagulle and Tigre of the Ad Takles," 1, BMA/DIS 260/kel 10957/62, Research and Documentation Center, Asmara. Henceforth cited as RDC.

19. Major Lea, "Major Lea to the Military Administrator, OETA, Eritrea," 4, BMA/DIS 260/kel 10957/1, RDC.

20. Ibid., 1

21. Trevaskis, "Dispute between the Shumagulle and Tigre," 1.

22. Ibid.

23. Stephen Longrigg, "Dispute between Shumagulle and Tigre," 7, BMA/DIS 260/kel 109577, RDC.

24. "Tigre-Shumagalle Dispute," 1, BMA/DIS 260/kel 10957/68, RDC.

25. "Land Disputes (Shumagulle v. Tigre: Ad Takles)," 1, BMA/DIS 260/kel 10957/15, RDC. Tahgé is also listed in BMA records as Hamed Humid Tahge and Hamid Humed Tei.

26. In later years, Tahgé continued his political efforts and became a leading representative of the Eritrean Muslim League's Keren branch.

27. "Memo from Major Lea to Military Administrator, OETA, Eritrea," 4, BMA/DIS 260/kel 10957/1, RDC.

28. "Ad Takles Exiles," 1, BMA/DIS 260/kel 10957/113, RDC.

29. John Markakis, *National and Class Conflict in the Horn of Africa* (Cambridge: Cambridge University Press, 1987), 59.

30. While Shentu was imprisoned and sentenced to pay compensation for his act, Ibrahim Sultan allegedly came to his aid and launched a public campaign in his defense. See Tesfai, *Aynfelale*, 73–74.

31. Major R. Signals, "Mohammed Nur Mohammed Abdulla, Mohammed Suleiman Idris Nur, Ismael Sicap, Mohammed Adam Abdulla, Hamid Said Osman," 1, BMA/DIS 260/kel 10957/32, RDC. Historically, tigre efforts to create new independent "tribes" among the different Tigre-speaking groups occasionally surfaced. Miran claims that during the nineteenth century the 'Ad Shaykh attracted "entire families of tigre vassals to join their ranks by undermining the master/serf structure of the Tigre-speaking pastoralist and agro-pastoralist societies." Miran, "Islam in Eritrea," 186.

32. Signals, "Mohammed Nur Mohammed Abdulla," 1. The author of the report, Major R. Signals, recommended that the five accused activists be sent into exile in Assab.

33. Reid, *Frontiers of Violence*, 23.

34. Miran, "Islam in Eritrea," 195.

35. Ibid., 196.

36. Ibid., 203.

37. Miran, "Constructing and Deconstructing," 47.

38. Ibid., 44.

39. "The Tigre-Speaking Peoples," Trevaskis Papers, box 1(B), 107.

40. Many shumagulle also served in influential positions within the order throughout much of northern and western Eritrea. Aberra Osman Aberra, telephone interview, Columbus, Ohio, July 23, 2010.

41. "Ad Takles Exiles, Assab ex. Keren," 1, BMA/DIS 260/kel 10957/66, RDC.

42. Despite his prestigious position within the order, Sayyid Muhammad Abu Bakr al-Mirghani often received criticism for his apparent disinterest and idleness in local affairs. Major R. Signals noted in his communication that only after he gave Sayyid Abu Bakr "a sound lecture" and had officials in Agordat speak directly with his father did he finally commit to speaking with the Tigre communities. Major R. Signals, "Ad Tecles Tigre Dispute," 1, BMA/DIS 260/kel 10957/59, RDC.

43. Major R. Signals, "Ad Tecles Disobedience," 1, BMA/DIS 260/kel 10957/42, RDC.

44. BMA/DIS 260/kel 10957/92, 6.

45. See "Letter of Tigré Representatives," Trevaskis Papers, box 2(A), app. 18, 3–4. Trevaskis also discussed this religious dynamic among the Bet Asghede. With the coming of Shaykh al-Amin b. Hamid b. Naf'utay of the 'Ad Shaykh holy family during the early nineteenth century, most shumagulle converted to Islam even though "many of their serfs and more especially the subject Almada [*sic*] peoples were Moslems either by long tradition or later conversion." "The Tigre-Speaking Peoples," Trevaskis Papers, box 1(B), 19. Tigre representatives' claims were, however, complicated by the fact that the Khatmiyya-sponsored "revival" during the nineteenth century among the 'Ad Shaykh, the 'Ad Mu'allim had essentially reconverted even these already Islamicized tigre. See Miran, "Constructing and Deconstructing," 44.

46. "To H. E. Brigadier C. D'arcy Mc.Carthy OBE, Chief Administrator-Eritrea-Asmara," BMA/DIS 260/kel 10957/89, 9. The Four Power Commission's 1947 report also took note of this distinction. Members observed, "It is strange how these Christian Abyssinian populations, instead of attracting the inhabitants of the territories occupied by them, were themselves attracted by the subjected populations whose language and religion they absorbed." See also "The Question of the Tigré," Trevaskis Papers, box 2(A), *Four Power Commission*, app. 17, 2.

47. "To H. E. Brigadier C. D'arcy Mc.Carthy," 7.

48. BMA/DIS 260/kel 10957/92, 6.

49. See "To H. E. Brigadier C. D'arcy Mc.Carthy," 15–20.

50. "Letter of Tigré Representatives," Trevaskis Papers, box 2(A), 2.

51. "The Tigre Speaking Population," Trevaskis Papers, box 1(B), 116. In the midst of his political involvement, Sultan himself owned and

operated a cheese-processing plant in Tessenei from 1943 through 1945. See Woldeyesus Ammar, "Ibrahim Sultan Ali: A Liberator Who Passed Away 20 Years ago Today," Eritrean Human Rights Electronic Archive, http://www.ehrea.org/Ibrahim0Sulta20Ali.pdf (accessed July 12, 2010).

52. "Letter of Tigré Representatives," Trevaskis Papers, box 2(A), 5.

53. Markakis, *National and Class Conflict*, 59.

54. Ibrahim Sultan, interview by Ahmed Haji Ali, Cairo, March 20–25, 1982. See also Senior Civil Affairs Officer to BMA Headquarters, "Ad Takles Tribe-Tigre/Shumagalle Dispute," 2, BMA/DIS 260/kel 10957/93, RDC.

55. Arefayne Bairu, "A Short History of Shaykh Ibrahim Sultan," RDC, January 10, 1990, 2–3.

56. Ibid., 3. See S. F. Nadel, "Notes on Beni Amer Society," *Sudan Notes and Records* 26, no. 1 (1951): 57.

57. Ibrahim Sultan, interview.

58. Ibrahim Sultan, taped interview, Sudan, n.d., RDC, Audio-Visual Collection.

59. Idris Shubek, taped interview, Agordat, 1988, RDC, Audio-Visual Collection. Shubek claimed to be a nephew of Tahgé.

60. "Letter of Tigré Representatives," Trevaskis Papers, box 2(A), app. 18, 8.

61. Ibid.

62. Ibid., 1.

63. Ranajit Guha, *Elementary Aspects of Peasant Insurgency in Colonial India* (Delhi: Oxford University Press, 1983), 18.

64. Ismael al-Mukhtar, interview.

65. The most vocal supporter for his appointment came from Degiat Hassan 'Ali, a colonial civil servant and diplomat who also served as one of Asmara's ward chiefs.

66. According to Salim al-Mukhtar, Italian authorities had employed only three handpicked qadis to serve in local positions before the mufti's arrival. Salim al-Mukhtar, "Shaykh Ibrahim al-Mukhtar Ahmed Umar," *Al-Ittihadi al-dawlia*, March 8, 1997. In theory, Ibrahim al-Mukhtar's appointment as mufti placed him in charge of thirty-nine separate Islamic courts, including those in Ethiopia under Italian authority during World War II. Salim al-Mukhtar, "Shaykh Ibrahim al-Mukhtar Ahmed Umar: His Return to Eritrea, 1940–1952," *Al-Ittihadi al-dawlia*, May 10, 1997.

67. Jonathan Miran, "Grand mufti, érudit et nationaliste érythréen: Note sur la vie et l'oeuvre de cheikh Ibrâhîm al-Mukhtâr (1909–1969)," *Chroniques yéménites* 10 (2002): 40. Allegedly the Italian administration, in

its efforts to appease Muslims, first suggested bringing an Islamic cleric from Libya to take charge of Islamic religious affairs. Local leaders rejected this effort and instead petitioned for Ibrahim al-Mukhtar. Ismael al-Mukhtar, electronic interview, Athens, Ohio, October 14, 2009.

68. Al-Mukhtar, "Shaykh Ibrahim al-Mukhtar Ahmed Umar: His Return to Eritrea, 1940–1952," *Al-Ittihadi al-dawlia*, 1997, pt. 4.

69. Ibrahim al-Mukhtar, "The Mufti Describes the Conditions of Muslims until His Arrival and His Reform Efforts," Ismael al-Mukhtar, http:// www.mukhtar.ca/contentN.php?type=viewarticle&id=70&category=ma wakef_mukhtar (accessed June 10, 2010); Ismael al-Mukhtar, interview.

70. Ismael al-Mukhtar, interview.

71. Ibid. His father was also an adherent of the Khatmiyya and according to Salim al-Mukhtar, Ibrahim al-Mukhtar became an initiated member during his brief stay in Kassala.

72. Ibid.

73. Aberra Osman Aberra, interview.

74. Ibrahim al-Mukhtar, "The Position of the Mufti on Tribal and Religious Differences," Ismael al-Mukhtar, http://www.mukhtar.ca/contentN .php?type=viewarticle&id=139&category=mawakef_mukhtar (accessed June 10, 2010).

75. See Salim al-Mukhtar, "Shaykh Ibrahim al-Mukhtar Ahmed Umar: His Return to Eritrea, 1940–1952," *Al-Ittihadi al-dawlia*, May 17, 1997.

76. Ibid. By 1945 the mufti had succeeded in making sure that all the courts coordinated the fast for 'Eid al-Fitr on the same day throughout Eritrea.

77. Ibrahim al-Mukhtar, "The Position of the Mufti on Tribal and Religious Differences," Ismael al-Mukhtar, http://www.mukhtar.ca/contentN .php?type=viewarticle&id=139&category=mawakef_mukhtar (accessed June 10, 2010).

78. Ibid., 40; Yassin M. Aberra, "Muslim Institutions in Ethiopia: The Asmara Awqaf," *Journal of the Institute of Muslim Minority Affairs* 5, no. 1 (1984): 207.

79. Aberra, "Muslim Institutions," 207.

80. Ibrahim al-Mukhtar, "Mufti Describes the Conditions of Muslims."

81. See Miran, "Grand mufti," 41–42.

82. "An Amazingly Good Exemplar," *Nay Ertra semunawi gazzetta*, March 13, 1944, 1.

83. "Great Celebration for the Opening of Hirgigo School," *Nay Ertra semunawi gazzetta*, March 20, 1944, 1. For his part, the mufti noted that he had initially tried to persuade Kekiya to build the school in Massawa or Asmara because of the cities' more strategic locations. See Ibrahim al-Mukhtar, "Mufti Describes the Conditions of Muslims."

84. Miran, "Islam in Eritrea," 196. See Aberra, "Muslim Institutions," 203–7.

85. Nebil Ahmed, interview, Athens, Ohio, November 23, 2009.

86. Ibid.

87. Although instructors and Arabic teachers arrived from Al-Azhar periodically during the early and mid-1940s, the first official delegation of scholars from Cairo came in 1948 under the direction of Shaykh 'Ali Mustafa Alughabi al-Shafi.

88. Aberra Osman Aberra, interview. See also Abd al-Qadir Haqus al-Jibirti, *Abushehada Abdelkadir Kebire* (Cairo: Al-Nasri Dehebi, 1998), 40.

89. Jamil Aman Mohammed, interview, Ottawa, July 18, 2010.

90. Ismael al-Mukhtar, interview.

91. Of these institutions, twenty-two were reserved for Arabic instruction, thirty-one for Tigrinya, and one for Kunama. Major H. F. Kynaston-Snell to Dr. Rita Hinden, April 19, 1946, Fabian Colonial Bureau, MSS Brit EMP S. 365 180/3/50 (henceforth cited as FCB).

92. Ibid. To illustrate how understaffed the BMA were in their efforts, Kynaston-Snell mentioned in his correspondence that he had served simultaneously as the director of eleven separate educational facilities, the colony's director of education, head of the Italian schools, and an advisor to several private "community schools" in the major cities. See FCB 180/3/51.

93. "Eritrean Education," Trevaskis Papers, box 2(A), 69–71.

94. "God Is the All-Seeing—It Is Written in the Qur'an," *Nay Ertra semunawi gazzetta*, February 28, 1944, 1.

95. "Education in Mother Tongue in the Native Schools," *Nay Ertra semunawi gazzetta*, April 24, 1944, 1.

96. Gebremeskel Woldu and Abdelkadir Kebire served as president and vice president, respectively. See al-Jibirti, *Abushehada Abdelkadir Kebire*, 31.

97. On the day of the demonstrations, delegates from the MFH met with the first governor of BMA-occupied Eritrea, Brigadier Brian Kennedy-Cooke, and presented their grievances. Abdelkadir Kebire acted as the main representative to Kennedy-Cooke, who, by all accounts, received Kebire's concerns with indifference. After their meeting, BMA authorities notified the demonstrators that their gathering violated the ongoing curfew on public gatherings and they soon dispersed the crowds. See Tesfai, *Aynfelale*, 33–36; Warka Solomon, "The Life and Political Career of Abdul Kadir Kebire," in *Proceedings of a Workshop on Aspects of Eritrean History*, ed. Tekeste Melake (Asmara: Hdri Publishers, 2007), 194–207.

98. The hotel, constructed and opened in 1935 on Via Cagliari, was allegedly the first hotel built, owned, and operated by native-born Eritreans

in Asmara. The hotel also served as the setting where MFH members elected their twelve official delegates of the organization's executive council. Aberra Osman Aberra, interview. See Woldeab Woldemariam, "Do You Remember?," *Sagam* 1 (1987); Asanadai Tekwabo Arasai, *Merusat 'Anqasat Ato Woldeab: 1941–1991* (Asmara: Hdri Publishers, 1995), 318–21.

99. Ruth Iyob, *The Eritrean Struggle for Independence: Domination, Resistance, Nationalism, 1941–1993* (Cambridge: Cambridge University Press, 1995), 65.

100. Jordan Gebre-Medhin, *Peasants and Nationalism in Eritrea: A Critique of Ethiopian Studies* (Trenton: Red Sea Press, 1989), 81. Some recent studies continue to frame the MFH as an overwhelmingly unionist organization. Shumet Sishagne has argued that the organization "adopted the prevailing demand for union with Ethiopia as its primary objective and built its membership around this idea." Shumet Sishagne, *Unionists and Separatists: The Vagaries of Ethio-Eritrean Relation, 1941–1991* (Hollywood, CA: Tsehai Publishers, 2007), 24; Ruth Belay, "The Political Biography of Ibrahim Sultan" (BA thesis, University of Asmara, 2000), 13–16.

101. Tekeste Negash, *Eritrea and Ethiopia: The Federal Experience* (New Brunswick, NJ: Transaction Publishers, 1997), 26.

102. See Sishagne, *Unionists and Separatists*.

103. Literally meaning "oneness" in Tigrinya, *hadinet* came to embody the philosophy of those who supported the creation of a single government between Eritrea and Ethiopia.

104. Woldemariam, "Do You Remember?"

105. Iyob, *Eritrean Struggle*, 69.

106. The evening before the conference, pro-unionist officials demoted Gebremeskel Woldu from his post as president of the MFH in favor of Bairu. See Iyob, *Eritrean Struggle*, 69; Gebre-Medhin, *Peasants and Nationalism*, 93–95.

107. Tesfai, *Aynfelale*, 185.

108. Ibid., 186.

109. Ibrahim Sultan, interview.

110. Bairu, "Shaykh Ibrahim Sultan," 6.

111. Gaim Kibreab, *Critical Reflections on the Eritrean War of Independence: Social Capital, Associational Life, Religion, Ethnicity and Sowing Seeds of Dictatorship* (Trenton: Red Sea Press, 2008), 106.

Chapter 2: Founding Success

1. Alemseged Tesfai, *Aynfelale: 1941–1950* (Asmara: Hdri Publishers, 2002), 193.

2. Ibrahim Sultan, interview.

3. Nebil Ahmed, "A History of al-Rabita al-Islamiya al-Eritrea (1946–50)," in *Proceedings of a Workshop on Aspects of Eritrean History*, ed. Tekeste Melake (Asmara: Hdri Publishers, 2007), 135.

4. The duties of the league's secretary general, as defined by the organization's statutes, included the "preservation of the documents of the League; fixing dates of meetings of the Superior Council; addressing invitations to the Provincial Committees; preparing documents and arguments subject to discussion; registration of statements of decisions; and despatching of copies of decisions to Provincial Committee etc." "Memorandum on Aims and Program," *Four Power Commission*, app. 106, 4.

5. Nebil Ahmed, interview. One of the more prominent league supporters was Osman al-Mirghani, Sayyid Muhammad Abu Bakr's younger brother and a close confident of Ibrahim Sultan. See FO 742/23, 32.

6. See *Sawt al-rabita al-islamiyya*, April 17, 1947, 1.

7. Ahmed, "Al-Rabita al-Islamiya al-Eritrea," 134; "This Is the Muslim League," *Sawt al-rabita al-islamiyya*, February 25, 1947, 2.

8. Ahmed, "Al-Rabita al-Islamiya al-Eritrea," 136; Nebil Ahmed, interview. Among the initial members of the executive council were Ibrahim Sultan, Abdelkader Kebire, Hajj Suleiman Ahmed Umar, Degiat Hassan 'Ali, Adem Muhammad Kusmallah, Hajj Imam Musa Abdu, Muhammad 'Uthman Hayuti, Berhanu Ahmedin, and Yasin Mahmud Ba Tuq. Hajj Zeinu Adem Kusmallah, interview by Nebil Ahmed, Asmara, January 2, 2003.

9. Ismael al-Mukhtar, "Founding Conference at Keren, First and Second Years," http://www.mukhtar.ca/contentN.php?type=viewarticle&id=43&category=hawadith_mukhtar (accessed July 12, 2010).

10. Ismael al-Mukhtar, interview.

11. Al-Mukhtar, "Founding Conference at Keren."

12. Ismael al-Mukhtar, interview.

13. Jamil Aman Mohammed, interview.

14. Eritrean Peoples Liberation Front, Central Administration of Eritrean Liberation, "A Questionnaire Regarding the Political Parties of the 1940s and 1950s," March 1, 1991, RDC/01714 (henceforth cited as RDC/01714). 'Ali Se'id Bekhit Umar, interview.

15. RDC/01714; Hajj Abdel Hadi Hajji Beshir Se'id, interview.

16. RDC/01714; Umardin Abdelkadir Mahmud Muhammad, interview.

17. Scholars continue to debate whether or not some league officials intentionally presented the league as a purely religious organization as a means of garnering the widest possible support from their respective constituencies.

18. Ismael al-Mukhtar, "Qadi 'Ali Umar 'Uthman, Senior Scholar and Leader of Eritrea," http://www.mukhtar.ca/contentN.php?type=viewarticle&id=7&category=bios_mukhtar (accessed July 6, 2010).

19. RDC/01714; Mehmedin Ahmed Se'id, interview.

20. RDC/01714; 'Ali Se'id Bekhit Umar, interview; Mehmedin Ahmed Se'id, interview.

21. The NEPIP was formed in late September 1947 as an amalgamation of the Eritrean War Veterans Association and the Italo-Eritrean Association. The latter group was composed of "mixed" residents with Italian and indigenous-Eritrean heritage.

22. *Four Power Commission*, app. 143, 1–2. The Four Power Commission of Inquiry included representatives from Britain, France, the Soviet Union, and the United States. Representatives were charged in Eritrea and elsewhere in the postwar period to develop a consensus on the future of Italy's former colonies.

23. Ibid. In their testimony to the Four Power Commission in December 1947, NEPIP representatives also claimed that this pressure justified the low turnout of its members at the commission's official hearings.

24. Ahmed, "Al-Rabita al-Islamiya al-Eritrea," 137. See "Moslem League—File SB/A/6," FO 742/23; "Memorandum on Aims and Programme," *Four Power Commission*, app. 106, 3.

25. Ironically, some former league members noted that from the League's very beginning "mosques were not good contributors because of the lack of revenues and sources of income they encountered." Ahmed, "Al-Rabita al-Islamiya al-Eritrea," 137; RDC/01714; Hajj Abdel Hadi Hajji Beshir Se'id, interview.

26. RDC/01714; Mehmedin Ahmed Se'id, Umardin Abdelkadir Mahmud Muhammad, Idris Ibrahim Hussein, interview. Once the organization firmly established itself, voluntary contributions were augmented by monthly and annual fees for league members. See *Four Power Commission*, app. 106, "Memorandum on Aims and Programme," 4.

27. "CFM/D/L/47/ICCOM Sixth Hearing," *Four Power Commission*, app. 124, 5.

28. "This Is the Muslim League," *Sawt al-rabita al-islamiyya*, February 25, 1947, 2. See *Nay Ertra semunawi gazzetta*, March 5, 1947, 1; Tesfai, *Aynfelale*, 199; Ahmed, "Al-Rabita al-Islamiya al-Eritrea," 135.

29. "Memorandum on Aims and Programme," *Four Power Commission*, app. 106, 3.

30. Henceforth cited in text as *Sawt al-rabita*.

31. Ismael al-Mukhtar, "Professor Yasin Mahmud Ba Tuq: Writer, Thinker and Political Leader," http://www.mukhtar.ca/contentN.php?type =viewarticle&id=88&category=bios_mukhtar (accessed July 9, 2010). Born in Massawa in 1914, Yasin Mahmud Ba Tuq came from a prominent merchant family and received his initial education from local Islamic and Italian-sponsored schools. During the early 1940s, he studied under

the mufti and became a steadfast supporter of his reform efforts. During this period, he also served on Massawa's school advisory board and eventually became the chairman of the schools' committee in 1942; he later became a member of the waqf committee in Massawa. After attending the league's founding, in December 1946, he served simultaneously on the executive council and as secretary of Massawa's league branch.

32. See FO 742/23, 30.

33. "This Is the Muslim League," *Sawt al-rabita al-islamiyya*, February 25, 1947, 2.

34. Yasin Ba Tuk, "We and Independence," *Sawt al-rabita al-islamiyya*, March 4, 1947,1. See *Nay Ertra semunawi gazzetta*, March 18, 1947, 1–2.

35. Muhammad 'Uthman Hayuti, "Our Duties toward Independence," *Sawt al-rabita al-islamiyya*, March 4, 1947, 1.

36. Muhammad Said Abu, "Let Us Leave Ignorance and Move toward Knowledge and Work," *Sawt al-rabita al-islamiyya*, April 17, 1947, 2.

37. Yasin Ba Tuq, "Which Are the Best Means to Create Reform?," *Sawt al-rabita al-islamiyya*, April 17, 1947, 1.

38. Abdel Nebi Muhammad Ibra Haqus, "Toward the Duty," *Sawt al-rabita al-islamiyya*, June 17, 1947, 2.

39. Mahmud Nurhussein Berhanu, "On Two Articles," *Sawt al-rabita al-islamiyya*, March 11, 1947, 2.

40. Yasin Ba Tuq, "Best Means to Create Reform?"

41. Mahmud Nurhussein Berhanu, "Our Ministers Are Writing with Scissors," *Sawt al-rabita al-islamiyya*, June 3, 1947, 4.

42. 'Ali Muhammad Hassan, "No Muslim Wants to Unite with Ethiopia," *Sawt al-rabita al-islamiyya*, November 11, 1947, 2.

43. Ibid.

44. "Speeches on the June Demonstration," *Sawt al-rabita al-islamiyya*, July 8, 1947, 2.

45. "Memorandum from the Eritrean Muslem League," FO 743/23, emphasis in original.

46. Saleh A. A. Younis, "Abdulkadir Kebire," Dehai-Eritrea Online, http://www.ephrem.org/dehai_archive/1997/feb/0171.html (accessed July 29, 2010); Tesfai, *Aynfelale*, 197.

47. Hassan, "No Muslim Wants to Unite."

48. "The Consensus of Muslims by the Principals of the Islamic League," *Sawt al-rabita al-islamiyya*, December 9, 1947, 2.

49. See Yusef Sadeq, "The Arabic Language in Pakistan," *Sawt al-rabita al-islamiyya*, December 9, 1949, 2.

50. Much of the coverage included excerpts from speeches and articles from other international Arabic publications, particularly from presses based in Cairo. See Joseph L. Venosa, "'Because God Has Given Us the Power of

Reasoning': Intellectuals, the Eritrean Muslim League and Nationalist Activism, 1946–1950," *Northeast African Studies* 12, no. 2 (2012): 38–40.

51. Yasin Ba Tuq, "The Eritrean Sea and Ports," *Sawt al-rabita al-islamiyya*, December 7, 1950, 1.

52. Warka Solomon, "The Life and Political Career of Adbulkader Kebire," in *Proceedings of a Workshop on Aspects of Eritrean History*, ed. Tekeste Melake (Asmara: Hdri Publishers, 2007), 197.

53. "The Society for Cultural Cooperation," *Sawt al-rabita al-islamiyya*, June 3, 1947, 2. Several prominent Muslim League members held positions in the organization, including Shaykh Idris Hussein Suleiman, Shaykh Ahmed Suri, and Hajj Sulieman Musa, himself a close associate of Ibrahim al-Mukhtar.

54. See Sadeq, "Arabic Language in Pakistan."

55. Tesfai, *Aynfelale*, 401.

56. Aberra Osman Aberra, interview.

57. Ibid. See also FO 742/23, 33; Tesfai, *Aynfelale*, 402. The transliteration *Shuban al-rabita* is based on Nebil Ahmed's model. Henceforth cited as the "Youth Association."

58. Aberra Osman Aberra, interview.

59. Ahmed, "Al-Rabita al-Islamiya al-Eritrea," 138. See Tesfai, *Aynfelale*, 402–5.

60. Nebil Ahmed, interview.

61. During the spring and summer of 1947, many of the league's top officials were also targets of assassination attempts. Degiat Hassan 'Ali claimed that pro-union activists made three attempts on his life, including several instances in which individuals threw live grenades into his residence. See *Four Power Commission*, app. 124, "CFM/D/L/47/ICCOM Sixth Hearing," 3. Trevaskis noted that before the demonstrations unionists threw a bomb into the league's office in Asmara. On evenings after the protests, he also recorded that "four more bombs were pitched into the houses of Asmara Muslims & two were thrown at the house of a prominent Liberal." See Gerald Kennedy Trevaskis to Dr. Rita Hinden, January 4, 1947, FCB/180/3, 9 (henceforth cited as Trevaskis to Hinden); "Bomb Incidents in Asmara," *Eritrean Daily News*, June 12, 1947, 3; "Another Asmara Bomb Attack," *Eritrean Daily News*, July 4, 1947, 3.

62. See FO 742/23.

63. By all accounts, the group's self-designated term Muslim Brotherhood did not have any relation to the more notable Muslim Brotherhood based in Egypt. See FO 742/23, 33.

64. *Four Power Commission*, app. 156, 2.

65. Ibrahim Sultan, interview.

66. RDC/01714, Mehmedin Ahmed Se'id, Umardin Abdelkadir Mahmud Muhammad, and Idris Ibrahim Hussein, interview.

67. "CFM/D/L/47/ICCOM Sixth Hearing," *Four Power Commission*, app. 124, 6.

68. RDC/01714, Hajj Ibrahim Otban Ahmed, interview.

69. In later years, calls by some proactive Muslim women only increased. Some of the most outspoken activists even began contributing written commentaries to *Sawt al-rabita* by 1949.

70. Despite providing generally detailed accounts of the June protests and an estimated number of each city's protesters, Trevaskis could not confirm the participation of women and children, unlike the previous month's pro-Unionist demonstrations. See Trevaskis to Hinden, January 4, 1947, FCB/180/3, 8.

71. Woldeab Woldemariam, "Eritrea for Whom?," *Nay Ertra semunawi gazzetta*, May 5, 1947, 1.

72. Yasin Ba Tuq, "We and Independence," *Sawt al-rabita al-islamiyya*, March 4, 1947 1; Tesfai, *Aynfelale*, 199.

73. Redie Bereketeab, *Eritrea: The Making of a Nation, 1890–1991* (Trenton: Red Sea Press, 2007), 147. As Semitic languages, both Tigrinya and Arabic were spoken across Eritrea by Muslim and Christian communities alike. In particular, many Muslim residents living in the major urban centers such as Asmara, Keren, and Massawa were often exposed to Tigrinya and had some command of the language.

74. Trevaskis to Hinden, January 4, 1947, FCB/180/3, 3.

75. Ruth Iyob, *The Eritrean Struggle for Independence: Domination, Resistance, Nationalism, 1941–1993* (Cambridge: Cambridge University Press, 1995), 66. For additional information on the "Greater Tigray" concept and its development, see Alemseged Abbay, "The Trans-Mareb Past in the Present," *Journal of Modern African Studies* 35, no. 2 (1997): 321–34; Abbay, *Identity Jilted, or, Re-imagining Identity? The Divergent Paths of the Eritrean and Tigrayan Nationalist Struggles* (Lawrenceville, NJ: Red Sea Press, 1998).

76. "The Party of the Free Eritrean," *Sawt al-rabita al-islamiyya*, March 11, 1947, 1.

77. Ahmed, "Al-Rabita al-Islamiya al-Eritrea," 138. The term "half-caste" referred to those residents who were the product of mixed Eritrean and Italian backgrounds. They were also often categorized as "Italo-Eritreans."

78. "There Is No Oppression against Any Person in the Islamic Tradition," *Sawt al-rabita al-islamiyya*, March 11, 1949, 2.

79. Iyob, *Eritrean Struggle*, 70.

80. Ibid.

81. Ibid., 71.

82. See FCB/180/3.

83. Younis, "Abdulkadir Kebire"; Tesfai, *Aynfelale*, 196.

84. See Masoud Kamali, *Multiple Modernities, Civil Society and Islam: The Case of Iran and Turkey* (Liverpool: Liverpool University Press, 2006), 244. These developments within the regional Sufi institutions support Kamali's argument that Islamic civil society, at its heart, is based on understandings of and reverence for diversity, and "pluralism in terms of religion and lifestyles." See Ismael al-Mukhtar, "The Plight of the Family of Ras Tessema Asberhom during the Federal Period," http://www.mukhtar.ca/contentN.php?type=viewarticle&id=169&category=hawadith_mukhtar (accessed July 27, 2010).

85. "CFM/D/L/47/ICCOM Sixth Hearing," *Four Power Commission*, app. 124, 5–6.

86. RDC/01714, Mehmedin Ahmed Se'id, Umardin Abdelkadir Mahmud Muhammad, Idris Ibrahim Hussein, interview.

87. Gaim Kibreab, *Critical Reflections on the Eritrean War of Independence: Social Capital, Associational Life, Religion, Ethnicity and Sowing Seeds of Dictatorship* (Trenton: Red Sea Press, 2008), 105.

88. RDC/01714, Hajj Ibrahim Otban Ahmed, interview.

89. "A Major Demonstration in All the Cities of Eritrea," *Sawt al-rabita al-islamiyya*, June 17, 1947, 1.

90. See Trevaskis to Hinden, January 4, 1947, FCB/180/3, 8.

91. Al-Jibirti, *Abushehada Abdelkadir Kebire*, 58.

92. "Speech of the President of the Muslim League in Asmara," *Sawt al-rabita al-islamiyya*, June 24, 1947, 1.

93. "Speeches on the June Demonstration," *Sawt al-rabita al-islamiyya*, July 8, 1947, 2.

94. Trevaskis to Hinden, July 24, 1947, FCB/180/3, 9.

95. Ibid., 2. This estimate placed the LPP's membership at around seventy thousand.

96. RDC/01714, 'Ali Se'id Bekhit Umar, interview.

97. Gebre-Medhin, *Peasants and Nationalism*, 152.

98. Trevaskis to Hinden, July 24, 1947, FCB/180/3, 3–4. See Venosa, "'Power of Reasoning,'" 41–44.

99. "A Report on Tribal Reorganization in the Western Province," FO 1015/138, 1–34. See Jan-Bart Gewald, "Making Tribes: Social Engineering in the Western Province of British-Administered Eritrea, 1941–1952," *Journal of Colonialism and Colonial History* 1, no. 2 (Winter 2000).

100. Kibreab, *Eritrean War*, 88.

101. G. K. N. Trevaskis, "Report on Serfdom," June 5, 1948, FO 230/255; Ibrahim Sultan, interview.

102. The towns selected for the commission's official tour included Geshnashim, Decamere, Adi Caiee, Senafe, Teramni, Adi Quala, Arresa,

Keren, Agordat, Barentu, and Massawa. Their spelling is based on the commission's original version. See FO 742/19.

103. *Diglal* is the traditional title of the supreme chief among the Beni Amir.

104. Ahmed Muhammad Ibrahim al-Tigrawi, "Feudal System," *Sawt al-rabita al-islamiyya*, December 9, 1949, 1. See "Council of Foreign Ministers (Deputies): Two Chiefs of the Western Province," *Four Power Commission*, app. 128.

105. "Letter of Tigré Representatives," *Four Power Commission*, app. 18, 16.

106. Ibid., 1.

107. Ibid.

108. Trevaskis to Hinden, July 24, 1947, FCB180/3, 4.

109. Ibid., 3.

110. "Council of Foreign Ministers (Deputies)," *Four Power Commission*, app. 128, 2. The term *kantebay* (also written as *kantibai*) developed as a title designating the status of the ruling clan or district chief within several Tigre-speaking groups, including the Habab and 'Ad Takles, across the region. See Anthony D'Avray, with Richard Pankhurst, *The Nakfa Documents: The Despatches, Memoranda, Reports, and Correspondence Describing and Explaining the Stories of the Feudal Societies of the Red Sea Littoral from the Christian-Muslim Wars of the Sixteenth Century to the Establishment 1885–1901 of the Italian Colony of Eritrea* (Wiesbaden: Harrassowitz, 2000), 2.

111. "Council of Foreign Ministers (Deputies)," *Four Power Commission*, app. 128, 2.

112. Trevaskis to Hinden, January 4, 1947, FCB/180/3, 3.

113. Ibid. The issue of "tribal" restructuring remained an ongoing problem for BMA authorities despite the relative success of activists in ending the payment of the customary dues. See Trevaskis to Hinden, October 1947, FCB/180/3, 1.

114. "Moslem League, Eritrea," *Four Power Commission*, app. 107, 3.

115. "Summary of Views of Representatives at Hearing at Massawa I (Samhar Area)," *Four Power Commission*, app. 171, 4.

116. "CFM/D/L/47/ICCOM Sixth Hearing," ibid., app. 124, 5. Despite some notable defections of these community elites, both the league's leadership and BMA officials noted that "with few exceptions the Moslem League has succeeded in gaining the support of any Moslem of consequence in the territory." Trevaskis to Hinden, January 4, 1947, FCB/180/3, 3.

117. "Summary of Views of Representatives at Hearing at Agordat (Agordat District)," *Four Power Commission*, app. 169, 2.

118. "CFM/D/L/47/ICCOM Sixth Hearing," *Four Power Commission*, app. 124, 5.

119. "Moslem League, Eritrea," ibid., app. 107, 1.

120. "Memorandum from the Eritrean Moslem League," ibid., app. 103, 4–5, emphasis in original.

121. FO 742/23, 34.

122. "To: The Hon. International Commission of Investigation," *Four Power Commission*, app. 105, 3.

123. Ibid.

124. "Moslem League, Eritrea," *Four Power Commission*, app. 107, 1.

125. Ibid., 4.

126. Ibid.

127. "Summary of Views of Representatives at Hearing at Geshnashim (North Hamasien)," *Four Power Commission*, app. 160, 3. See also "Summary of Views of Representatives at Hearing at Barentu (Barentu and Tessenni District)," *Four Power Commission*, app. 170, 2. Summarizing this general trend among representatives, Lloyd Ellingson notes that many delegates to the commission seemed to have had no idea "just whom or what they were supposed to be representing." He added that "some of their responses to the commission were parrot-like, especially among those who favored the Unionist cause, as if they had been carefully memorized." Lloyd Ellingson, "The Emergence of Political Parties in Eritrea, 1941–1950," *Journal of African History* 18, no. 2 (1977): 265.

128. "Moslem League, Eritrea," *Four Power Commission*, app. 107, 6.

129. RDC/01714, Hajj Ibrahim Otban Ahmed, interview.

130. "Moslem League, Eritrea," *Four Power Commission*, app. 107, 6. For their part, the leaders of the NPM claimed that they in fact represented the "great majority" of the Muslim population in Eritrea and expressed their desire to remain under British governance for at least fifteen years based on the British success at presenting "new and excellent institutions" for the local population. See FO 1015/4, 18 C. According to Ellingson, the party claimed a membership of more than fifty-six thousand, including a large number of the Afar-speaking clans in northern Dankalia. Ellingson, "Political Parties in Eritrea," 273; *Four Power Commission*, app. 134, 1. The alleged support among local Afar-speaking communities for the NPM was somewhat undermined by the league's claims regarding its own membership in the region. See "Representatives from Massawa Confirm League Demands," *Sawt al-rabita al-islamiyya*, December 23, 1949, 1.

131. "Men Are Known by Their Deeds," FO 742/23, 28.

132. See "Moslem League, Eritrea," *Four Power Commission*, app. 107, 2.

133. Aberra Osman Aberra, interview; Jamil Aman Mohammed, interview. Despite allegations that they faced serious opposition from some

of the Massawa-based merchants, Muslim League supporters sponsored fairly large demonstrations during the commission's stay in Massawa and fielded more than three hundred representatives from the area and Northern Dankalia to appear before the commission. See "Representatives from Massawa Confirm League Demands," *Sawt al-rabita al-islamiyya*, December 23, 1949, 1.

134. The representatives included Abdelkadir Kebire, Sayyid Muhammad 'Uthman Hayuti, Qadi Musa Adam, Ibrahim Sultan, Hajj Sulieman Ahmed Umar, and Degiat Hassan 'Ali. "CFM/D/L/47/ICCOM Sixth Hearing," *Four Power Commission*, app. 124, 1.

135. Ibid., 3.

136. "Clarification for Four Power Commission Concerning the Memorandum Submitted by the Moslem League on the 10th November, 1947," *Four Power Commission*, app. 96, 5.

137. Ibid., 11.

138. Ibid., 5.

139. "CFM/D/L/47/ICCOM Sixth Hearing," ibid., app. 124, 6.

140. "Emergency," FO 371/63222, 38762/OET.

141. See "Eritrean Police Force, Asmara," *Four Power Commission*, annex to app. 153, 1.

142. "Summary of Views of Representatives at Hearing at Geshnashim (North Hamasien)," ibid., app. 160, 3.

143. Ibid., 5.

144. "There Is Nothing More Preferable to the Muslim than Dying for the Truth," *Sawt al-rabita al-islamiyya*, December 23, 1947, 1.

145. Ghirmai Negash, "Native Intellectuals in the Contact Zone: African Responses to Italian Colonialism in Tigrinya Literature," *Biography* 32, no. 1 (2009): 75.

Chapter 3: Navigating Rough Seas

1. Before joining the Unionist Party, Sayyid Ahmed Hayuti served as a founding member of the National Party of Massawa, which had petitioned the BMA with a separate independence platform. See FO 1015/4.

2. FO 742/23, 26. See *Ethiopia*, January 4, 1948, 1.

3. FO 742/23, 28. The personal nature of the character attacks strongly suggested that Kebire and Hayuti's feud went well beyond their nationalist-unionist political rivalry.

4. Ibid.

5. Ibid.

6. See Trevaskis to Hinden, January 4, 1948, FCB/180/3; March 29, 1948.

7. N'Bisrat Debessai, "The Shifta Movement in Eritrea: The Case of Mosazgi's Sons," in *Proceedings of a Workshop on Aspects of Eritrean History*, ed. Tekeste Melake (Asmara: Hdri Publishers, 2007), 110–12.

8. Ibid.

9. Fekadu Ogbasellassie, "Shifta Problems in the Kebesa Regions of Eritrea (1947–1952)," in *Proceedings of a Workshop on Aspects of Eritrean History*, ed. Tekeste Melake (Asmara: Hdri Publishers, 2007), 55.

10. Ibid.

11. FO 1015/146, J2621/1543/66, May 4, 1948.

12. Richard J. Reid, *Frontiers of Violence in North-East Africa: Genealogies of Conflict since c. 1800* (Oxford: Oxford University Press, 2011), 124.

13. Ibid., 126

14. "Note on Shifta Activities in Eritrea," FO 1015/146, 27(B).

15. Jordan Gebre-Medhin, *Peasants and Nationalism in Eritrea: A Critique of Ethiopian Studies* (Trenton: Red Sea Press, 1989), 120.

16. "Shifta Incidents," FO 1015/146, 27(B).

17. Ibid., 20(A).

18. Alemseged Tesfai, *Aynfelale: 1941–1950* (Asmara: Hdri Publishers, 2002), 402.

19. Ogbasellassie, "Shifta Problems," 56; "Monthly political report-Akeleguzai," April 4, 1948, RDC, box/294, 13471.

20. "No. 30 Monthly Political Report, Eritrea—June 1948," FO 1015/146, 50(A).

21. Activities also included an increase in "nonpolitical" raids by shifta leaders, including prominent Muslim raiders such as Hamid Idris Awate. See "Extract from Eritrea Monthly Political Report, No. 31, dated July, 48," FO 1015/146, 57(A).

22. See FO 742/23.

23. "22 Zulhigga 1367 (25/10/48)," FO 742/23, 33.

24. Ibid.

25. Report no. 6610/61928, FO 742/23.

26. Report no. 6610/61930, FO 742/23.

27. Aberra Osman Aberra, interview; Joseph L. Venosa, "Adapting to the New Path: Khatmiyya Sufi Authority, the al-Mirghani Family, and Eritrean Nationalism during British Occupation, 1941–1949," *Journal of Eastern African Studies* 7, no. 3 (2013): 413–31.

28. "The Case of Morgani and Its Possible Development," FO 742/23. A founding member of the MFH, Kadi was also one of the major behind-the-scenes organizers at the Bet Giyorgis conference.

29. Ibid.

30. Ibid.

31. Ibid.

32. See *Sawt al-rabita al-islamiyya*, December 23, 1947, 3; Venosa, "Adapting to the New Path," 422–24.

33. "Eritrea: Monthly Political Summer No. 1," FO 403, no. 48, 105.

34. "The Case of Morgani and its Possible Development," FO 742/23. One of the more controversial aspects of al-Mirghani's activities involved his alleged exploits with several of his female "servants." In particular, BMA reports noted authorities caught one domestic worker, a thirty-year-old woman from Agordat named Ama Tasein Kidanei, as she tried to deliver information about the league's political affairs to unionist supporters. Although al-Mirghani later fired her, his compromised position further weakened his reputation and ability to gain control of the league's political operations. See "Said Moh'd Osman Morgani, Resident of Agordat, Head of Moslem League," FO 742/23.

35. FO 1015/138, 2(A).

36. Ibid., 10.

37. Ibid.

38. Ibid., 17.

39. Ibid., 35–36.

40. The BMA noted that tigre clan reorganization in the Keren District proved more difficult than in the Agordat and Nakfa Districts because of the political objectives linked with the new structures. Ibid., 17–19.

41. Ibid., 13.

42. For his part, Ibrahim Sultan became chief of one subtribe (badanna) of the Rugbat clan, heading a group of more than thirteen thousand residents. See "New Tribal Organization of the Nacfa District," FO 1015/138, app. B, 35–37.

43. Ibid., 23.

44. Ibid., 26.

45. This base of support was particularly crucial to the league's campaign to discredit splinter organizations that later emerged, particularly the MLWP in early 1950.

46. "J. M. Benoy, January 24, 1949," FO 1015/138, app. B, 2(A).

47. Saleh A. A. Younis, "Abdulkadir Kebire," http://www.ephrem.org/dehai_archive/1997/feb/0171.html (accessed July 29, 2010).

48. See "No. 39 Monthly Political Report, Eritrea—March 1949," FO 1015/187, 1.

49. Aberra Osman Aberra, interview.

50. Warka Solomon, "The Life and Political Career of Abdulkader Kebire," in *Proceedings of a Workshop on Aspects of Eritrean History*, ed. Tekeste Melake (Asmara: Hdri Publishers, 2007), 203.

51. "News about the Mourning of Kebire's Death," *Sawt al-rabita al-islamiyya*, May 19, 1949: 1.

52. "No. 39 Monthly Political Report—Eritrea—March 1949," FO 1015/187, 1, emphasis in original.

53. See *Sawt al-rabita al-islamiyya*, April 28, 1949, 4. In this issue, the editors took the time to explain the publication difficulties and to thank their members' contributions in helping finance the paper's continued printing and circulation.

54. Ja'far al-Sharif 'Umar al-Suri, "The Freedom Martyr," *Sawt al-rabita al-islamiyya*, May 9, 1949, 1.

55. "Eritrean Muslims' Delegation to the UN and Their Efforts for Their Nation's Independence Demands," *Sawt al-rabita al-islamiyya*, April 28, 1949, 3–4.

56. Ibid., 4.

57. "Egypt and Arabic Countries Support Eritrean Independence," *Sawt al-rabita al-islamiyya*, June 11, 1950, 1.

58. "Eritrea's Future," *Sawt al-rabita al-islamiyya*, August 4, 1950, 3.

59. "Pakistan," *Sawt al-rabita al-islamiyya*, September 6, 1950, 1.

60. See "A Summary of the Life of Muhammad 'Ali Jinnah, the Great Leader and Founder of Pakistan," *Wahda Iritriyya*, November 8, 1950, 3.

61. "Pakistan Representative and the Eritrean Issue," *Wahda Iritriyya*, June 28, 1950, 1.

62. Okbazghi Yohannes, *Eritrea: A Pawn in World Politics* (Gainesville: University of Florida Press, 1991), 124. See [UN] General Assembly Official Records, Fifth Session, Ad Hoc Political Committee, Summary Records of Meetings, September 30–December 14, 1950, 332–37 (henceforth cited as GAOR).

63. Yohannes, *Eritrea*, 126. See GAOR, 332–34.

64. Yohannes, *Eritrea*, 113.

65. See Hassan Mahmud Abu Bakr, "Rescue Eritrea from the Consequences of Division," *Sawt al-rabita al-islamiyya*, May 26, 1949, 1.

66. Yasin Ba Tuq, "Solidarity Is Strength," *Sawt al-rabita al-islamiyya*, May 26, 1949, 1.

67. Ibid.

68. "No. 41 Monthly Political Report, Eritrea—May 1949," FO 1015/187, 1.

69. See "Delegation of the Eritrean Muslims to the United Nations and Their Efforts in the Independence Demands," *Sawt al-rabita al-islamiyya*, April 28, 1949, 2.

70. Yasin Ba Tuq, "A Victory on the Horizon," *Sawt al-rabita al-islamiyya*, June 30 1949, 1. Other groups included the LPP, the Independent Eritrean Party, the NEPIP, the National Muslim Party of Massawa, the Eritrean War Veterans Association, and the Intellectual Association. See Ruth Iyob, *The Eritrean Struggle for Independence: Domination, Resistance,*

Nationalism, 1941–1993 (Cambridge: Cambridge University Press, 1995), 75–76; Tekeste Negash, "Italy and Its Relations with Eritrean Political Parties, 1948–1950," *Africa* (Rome) 59, nos. 3–4 (2004): 439.

71. Yasin Ba Tuq, "A Victory on the Horizon," *Sawt al-rabita al-islamiyya*, June 30, 1949, 1.

72. "No. 42 Monthly Political Report, Eritrea—June 1949," FO 1015/187, 3.

73. Ibid.

74. "No. 44 Monthly Political Report, August 1949," FO 1015/187, 1–2.

75. Ibid.

76. Ibid.

77. Yasin Ba Tuq, "Nationalist Political Party Conference Decides to Accept Italo-Eritreans in the Independence Bloc," *Sawt al-rabita al-islamiyya*, July 7, 1949, 1.

78. T. Negash, "Italy and Its Relations," 425. Negash's comment about Italian contributions to *Sawt al-rabita* is also important to note. In light of the organization's well-documented financial troubles, the £300 monthly stipend that the league allegedly received from the CAE to continue the paper's circulation is more than plausible. Nevertheless, it seems to have had little if any effect on the actual content of what *Sawt al-rabita*'s editors published, as anti-Italian commentaries and accusations of unwanted Italo-Eritrean political influence were featured regularly. If the CAE indeed represented a major source of revenue, Negash's argument also fails to explain why *Sawt al-rabita* nevertheless faced major financial troubles and even ceased publication for more than fourteen months, beginning in January 1948. See ibid., 439.

79. See "No. 44 Monthly Political Report, August-1949," FO 1015/187; "From Asmara to Foreign Office," September 19, 1949, FO 371/73847.

80. "No. 44 Monthly Political Report, August 1949," FO 1015/187, 1.

81. Muhammad 'Uthman Hayuti, "Three Years Later: This Is the Muslim League," *Sawt al-rabita al-islamiyya*, September 22, 1949, 3.

82. "No. 44 Monthly Political Report, August 1949," FO 1015/187, 1.

83. Ibid., emphasis in original.

84. "Memorandum of the Muslim League," FO 371–69365, app. 103.

Chapter 4: Maintaining Momentum

1. "Complaint Filed by the Muslim League," *Sawt al-rabita al-islamiyya*, September 8, 1949, 1.

2. Lloyd Ellingson, "Eritrea: Separatism and Irredentism, 1941–1985" (PhD diss., Michigan State University, 1986), 78.

3. "No. 45 Monthly Political Report September—1949," FO 1015/187, 2.

4. "May God Bless the People of Massawa," *Sawt al-rabita al-islamiyya*, September 22, 1949, 1.

5. Ibid.

6. FO 371/ 73847, J 7730, September 30, 1949. See *Report of the United Nations Commission for Eritrea*, GAOR, 5th sess., supp. no. 8 (A/1285): 119–27 (henceforth cited as *Report of the United Nations Commission*).

7. Muhammad Se'id Umar, "Declaration and Warning," *Sawt al-rabita al-islamiyya*, July 17, 1949, 2.

8. "Dangerous Announcement," *Wahda Iritriyya*, February 18, 1950, 1.

9. "Countryside News: Shifta in Hirgigo," *Sawt al-rabita al-islamiyya*, July 14, 1949, 4.

10. "No. 47. Monthly Political Report, November 1949," FO 1015/187, 1.

11. Ellingson, "Separatism and Irredentism," 79.

12. See Alemseged Tesfai, *Aynfelale: 1941–1950* (Asmara: Hdri Publishers, 2002), 583.

13. Ellingson, "Separatism and Irredentism," 106.

14. Ahmed Kusmallah, interview.

15. Tesfai, *Aynfelale*, 430.

16. Ibid, 433. Nashif claimed that the meeting could have been called by Trevaskis rather than Stafford but that, regardless, Stafford was the "primary" official responsible for executing such policies.

17. Ahmed Kusmallah, interview.

18. Ibid.

19. Tesfai, *Aynfelale*, 435.

20. *Report of the United Nations Commission*, 20. Ironically, U.S. officials estimated that the MLWP had attracted a total membership of 275,000 people. Ellingson, "Separatism and Irredentism," 80; U.S. Department of State, 777.008/1850.

21. *Report of the United Nations Commission*, app. 17, 119–27.

22. Ellingson, "Separatism and Irredentism," 80.

23. Woldeab Woldemariam, "Hanti Ertra," *Hanti Ertra*, January 22, 1950, 1.

24. "Relief to the Members of the Independence Bloc from Injuries from the Shifta," *Hanti Ertra*, February 18, 1950, 3.

25. See "Educators in the Hands of Shifta," *Wahda Iritriyya*, July 12, 1950, 3; "Operations of Shifta in Keren," *Wahda Iritriyya*, October 4, 1950, 3; "Is There Any End to These Attacks?," *Sawt al-rabita al-islamiyya*, May 11, 1950, 3.

26. Richard J. Reid, *Frontiers of Violence in North-East Africa: Genealogies of Conflict since c. 1800* (Oxford: Oxford University Press, 2011), 122.

27. Young Soul, "People of Intellect Will Be in Comfort," *Wahda Iritriyya,* July 26, 1950, 3.

28. Ibid.

29. Ibid.

30. F. M., "The Eritrean Muslim Female," *Wahda Iritriyya,* September 6, 1950, 3.

31. Ibid.

32. Ibid.

33. Ibid.

34. Ibid.

35. M. S. A., "Muslim Education," *Sawt al-rabita al-islamiyya,* September 14, 1950, 1.

36. Ibid.

37. Aqbdobay, "Women and Education," *Wahda Iritriyya,* November 15, 1950, 3.

38. Hamid al-Emin al-Harathi, "Alert and Warning," *Wahda Iritriyya,* June 21, 1950, 3.

39. Amru, "From Amru," *Sawt al-rabita al-islamiyya,* May 5, 1949, 1.

40. Ibid.

41. Ahmed Hassan al-Ziyad, "Islam Is Strength," *Sawt al-rabita al-islamiyya,* May 5, 1949, 1.

42. See "The Arabic Language," *Sawt al-rabita al-islamiyya,* June 2, 1949, 1.

43. Yasin Ba Tuq, "Muslims in Danger!" *Sawt al-rabita al-islamiyya,* May 5, 1949, 1.

44. Ibid.

45. See "Muslim Ethiopia," *Sawt al-rabita al-islamiyya,* May 12, 1949, 2.

46. "No. 44 Monthly Political Report, August 1949," FO 1015/187, 1. Officials later noted that "his [Sultan's] signing of this document has not precluded his acceptance of Italian money to pay for passages for himself and others to New York." "From Asmara to Foreign Office," September 19, 1949, FO 371/73847.

47. "No. 45 Monthly Political Report, September 1949," FO 1015/187, 3.

48. For their part, British officials appeared especially worried about the implications of the impending political unity between the groups represented by the delegates. See "From Asmara to Foreign Office," September 19, 1949, FO 371/73847.

49. See Okbazghi Yohannes, *Eritrea: A Pawn in World Politics* (Gainesville: University of Florida Press, 1991), 133–36.

50. *Report of the United Nations Commission,* 30.

51. In the commission's report, delegates noted that Mohamed Hamid Tahgé, the former tigre activist from the 'Ad Takles, served as an ML representative to the commission during its inquiry in the

village of Kemchewa, in the Western Province, in mid-March 1950. Ibid., 125.

52. See "Egypt Agrees for Muslim Eritrea to Join Christian Ethiopia!" *Sawt al-rabita al-islamiyya*, October 5, 1950, 2.

53. Ibrahim Sultan, "Call to the Eritrean People," *Wahda Iritriyya*, November 8, 1950, 1.

54. High Council of the Muslim League, "The League Celebration of Five Years," *Sawt al-rabita al-islamiyya*, December 21, 1950, 1.

55. "This Is True Nationalism," *Sawt al-rabita al-islamiyya*, December 28, 1950, 4.

56. "The Speech of the Muslim League and Independence Bloc Secretary," *Sawt al-rabita al-islamiyya*, December 21, 1950, 1.

57. "Eritrea Was Ruled by Nine Nations in Thirteen Centuries," *Sawt al-rabita al-islamiyya*, December 23, 1950, 2–3.

Chapter 5: Holding the Line

1. "Statement by the Chairman of the delegation of the Moslem League of Eritrea made at the 55th meeting of the Ad Hoc Political Committee on 24 November 1950 in reply to questions which had been asked by members of the Committee," RDC/006872, 7.

2. "Victory for the Eritrean People," *Hanti Ertra*, December 5, 1950, 1. See also Alemseged Tesfai, *Federation Ertra ms Etyopiya: Kab Matienzo ksab Tedla, 1951–1955* (Asmara: Hdri Publishers, 2005), 28–29.

3. Degiat Sebhatu Yohannes, "The Voice of Eritrean Independence Is Filled with Joy," *Hanti Ertra*, January 17, 1951, 4.

4. Tesfai, *Federation Ertra*, 29.

5. "Statement by the Chairman of the delegation of the Moslem League of Eritrea," 9.

6. Ibid.

7. "The Day of Peace," *Sawt al-rabita al-islamiyya*, January 4, 1951, 1.

8. Ibid.

9. Ibid. Following the passage of Resolution 390-A, the BMA was partially reorganized in late 1950 and early 1951 in anticipation of the impending transfer of power. It was rebranded as a largely civilian organization known simply as the British Administration (BA).

10. "Speech of the Independence Bloc," *Sawt al-rabita al-islamiyya*, January 11, 1951, 2.

11. "Statement by the Chairman of the delegation of the Moslem League of Eritrea," 7.

12. "Transcript of the Speech that Hussein 'Ali Nehari gave in Massawa on the Celebration of the Fifth Anniversary of the Establishment of the Muslim League," *Sawt al-rabita al-islamiyya*, January 4, 1951, 2.

13. J. E. Eccles, "Subject: Degiac Abraha Tesemma," January 8, 1951, FO 742/25.

14. "About the League's Political Activities," *Sawt al-rabita al-islamiyya*, March 22, 1951, 1.

15. Ibid.

16. Tesfai, *Federation Ertra*, 62.

17. Ibrahim Sultan, "A Word of Greeting to the Muslim People of Eritrea," *Hanti Ertra*, October 3, 1951, 4.

18. "We and the Arabic Language," *Sawt al-rabita al-islamiyya*, April 5, 1951, 1.

19. Ahmed Muhammad Haji Ferraj, "What Is the Arabic Language?," *Sawt al-rabita al-islamiyya*, August 20, 1951, 4.

20. "We and the Arabic Language," *Sawt al-rabita al-islamiyya*, April 5, 1951, 1.

21. Jonathan Miran and R. S. O'Fahey, "The Islamic and Related Writings of Eritrea," in *Arabic Literature of Africa*, ed. O'Fahey and J. O. Hunwick, Volume 13, 3, *Fascicle A. The Writings of the Muslim Peoples of Northeastern Africa* (Leiden: E. J. Brill, 2003), 4.

22. Ibrahim al-Mukhtar, "Part 3: Detraction of the Traitors Concerning the Arabic Language in Eritrea and Habesha," *Sawt al-rabita al-islamiyya*, August 13, 1951, 3.

23. Ironically, the perception that Muslims had by and large been overlooked by colonial authorities ran counter to the historical record on Italian colonial policy. Jonathan Miran notes that Italian authorities in Eritrea, as elsewhere in Africa, expressed an "inherently contradictory discourse depicting Italy as a colonial power 'protecting' Islam and Muslims" and consequently gave significant authority and funding to religious authorities to gain the support of its colonial Muslim subjects. This process continued and reached a high point during the 1920s and 1930s, when Italy's Fascist government "deployed explicit pro-Muslim propaganda" to achieve its political objectives, including the building and renovation of mosques and schools throughout Eritrea. Miran, "Islam in Eritrea," 201-202.

24. Ibrahim al-Mukhtar, "Part 3," 3.

25. Ibid.

26. Ibrahim al-Mukhtar, "The Mufti's Speech to the United Nations Representative in Eritrea about the Arabic Language," http://mukhtar .ca/contentN.php?type=viewarticle&id=58&category=letters_mukhtar (accessed December 20, 2008).

27. Ibid. See Tesfai, *Federation Ertra*, 66–70; Jonathan Miran, "Endowing Property and Edifying Power in a Red Sea Port: Waqf, Arab Migrant

Entrepreneurs, and Urban Authority in Massawa, 1860s—1880s," *International Journal of African Historical Studies* 42, no. 2 (2009): 151–78.

28. Ibrahim al-Mukhtar, "Establishment of the Eritrean Ulama Front," http://mukhtar.ca/contentN.php?type=viewarticle&id=187&category =hawadith_mukhtar (accessed March 3, 2010).

29. Ibid. During the previous August, Muslim leaders received news that 'Ali Mustafa al-Gharabi, the head of the Al-Azhar mission in Eritrea, had been called back to Cairo. Having taught students at the King Farouk Institute in Asmara and been praised for his promotion of "Islamic culture" and substantial charity work, al-Gharabi's departure worried many within the league, who believed that his return to Egypt represented "an awful shock to the hopes of the Muslims of this nation." See "Al-Azhar Council Calls back the Head of Al-Azhar Mission in Eritrea," *Sawt al-rabita al-islamiyya*, September 3, 1951, 1.

30. Ismael al-Mukhtar, "Establishment of the Eritrean Ulama Front." See "Programma del Consiglio Islamico Superiore per l'istruzione," FO 742/23. Several internal memos between staffers in the BMA suggest that both before and after creation of the federation, British officials were concerned about the local influence of the visiting Egyptian scholars, particularly those associated with Egypt's Muslim Brotherhood.

31. Adem Musa Berhanu, "About the Arabic Language," *Sawt al-rabita al-islamiyya*, August 30, 1951, 2.

32. "And I Say You Work," *Sawt al-rabita al-islamiyya*, November 18, 1951, 1.

33. Ibid.

34. Hamid Mahmud Ibrahim, "The Arabic Language," *Sawt al-rabita al-islamiyya*, November 18, 1951, 1.

35. See "Question: Presented to the Author of the Open Letter Published in the Last Issue of the Arabic Daily Newspaper," *Sawt al-rabita al-islamiyya*, May 10, 1951, 3–4.

36. "Governor General Meets with Eritrean Political Party Leaders," *Sawt al-rabita al-islamiyya*, January 15, 1951, 1.

37. "A Letter from the Muslims of Akkele Guzay to the UN," *Sawt al-rabita al-islamiyya*, September 3, 1951, 3.

38. "Representatives of the Hal-Hal Tribes Present Their Views in Front of the UN Envoy," *Sawt al-rabita al-islamiyya*, October 1, 1951, 1. Curiously, several representatives also stated that they were open to the idea of allowing both Arabic and Amharic to serve as the federation's official languages, rather than Arabic and Tigrinya.

39. Tesfai, *Federation Ertra*, 169. For his part, Jabarti leader and league activist Berhanu Ahmedin purportedly claimed that only Arabic be

considered as Eritrea's official language. Even several of the conference's unionist attendees expressed an openness to allow Arabic as an official language, at least temporarily.

40. Ibid., 170.

41. Ibid.

42. See High Council of the Moslem League of Eritrea, *Memorandum of the Moslem League in Eritrea to Commissioner of United Nations for Eritrea H. E. Eduardo Anze Matienzo* (Asmara, 1951), 1–2.

43. Ibid., 12.

44. Ibid.

45. Mulcahy to State Department, "Ibrahim Sultan's Current Line of Thought," 777.00/12–651, December 6, 1951. See also Tekie Fessehatzion, *Eritrea: From Federation to Annexation, 1952–1962* (Washington, DC: Eritreans for Peace and Democracy, 1990), 18–20.

46. High Council of the Moslem League of Eritrea, *Memorandum of the Moslem League*, 4–5.

47. Ibid., 5.

48. Ibid.

49. Ibid., 13.

50. Lloyd Ellingson, "Separatism and Irredentism" (PhD diss., Michigan State University, 1986), 142. Haile Selassie validated the league's fears when his government announced in September 1952 that it intended "to send a large number of Amharas to Eritrea to assume jobs in the federal services, ignoring Eritreans who were qualified to fill these posts."

51. Ibid., 121.

52. Ibid., 122. *Report of the Government of the United Kingdom of Great Britain and Northern Ireland to the General Assembly Concerning the Administration of Eritrea, 1952,* no. 52, UNGA, A/2233. Trevaskis provided slightly different statistics for this shift, claiming "at the time of the transfer of power only 348 foreigners remained in the employment of the Administration, as against 2,217 who had been serving it a year earlier." G. K. N. Trevaskis, *Eritrea: A Colony in Transition, 1941–1952* (London: Oxford University Press, 1960), 125.

53. "The Organization of an Eritrean Administration and the Induction of Eritreans into the Administration," Trevaskis Papers, box 2(B), sec. 4(d), 25.

54. Ellingson, "Separatism and Irredentism," 121; UNGA, A/2233, 68. The league also made a point of drawing attention to Muslim citizens' "successes" by publishing the results of entrance exams for the civil service. See "About the Employment of Eritreans in Administrative Jobs," *Sawt al-rabita al-islamiyya*, January 20, 1952, 4.

55. Yasin Ba Tuq, "The Heads of the Instigation," *Sawt al-rabita al-islamiyya,* June 4, 1951, 1.
56. M. A., "The Heads of the Instigation, Part 3," *Sawt al-rabita al-islamiyya,* June 28, 1951, 4.
57. Ibid.
58. "Memorandum of the Independent Islamic League to the UN Committee," RDC/01850, 6.
59. See Muhammad Umar Kadi, "Open Letter to Ato Gebreyohannes Tesfamariam," *Hanti Ertra,* August 5, 1951, 3.
60. "Consultations with the Inhabitants of Eritrea," Trevaskis Papers, sec. 4(d), 46.
61. Ibid.
62. Trevaskis, *Colony in Transition,* 130.
63. Tesfai, *Federation Ertra,* 116.
64. Ibid., 119. Tesfai notes that activists' attempts to win the support of Asmara's "Arab" merchants were limited because they had believed falsely that the majority Yemani/Hadrami merchants could intervene in the political affairs in Saudi Arabia. See Jonathan Miran, "Red Sea Trans-locals: Hadrami Migration, Entrepreneurship, and Strategies of Integration in Eritrea, 1840s–1970s," *Northeast African Studies* 12, no. 1 (2012): 129–68.
65. Tsegaye Kahsay, Kefila Beraki, and Zerai Cristos, "Conditions That People Should Pay Attention to Regarding Employment," *Hanti Ertra,* November 7, 1951, 1; Tesfai, *Federation Ertra,* 119. The reference to the Arabs' "denial" of Christian Eritrean workers reflected the widely held belief that the Saudi government directly interfered and prevented laborers from being allowed into the country to work.
66. Delegates of the Eritrean Workers, "Audacious Locust Stays Out on the Door Even after Eating All Your Crops," *Hanti Ertra,* November 28, 1951, 4.
67. "Regarding Eritrean Workers and Saudi Arabia," *Hanti Ertra,* November 14, 1951, 1. See also "Notice about Eritrean Workers and the Arab Association," *Hanti Ertra,* December 5, 1951, 4.
68. Tsegaye Kahsay, interview by Günter Schröder, Rome, May 1988.
69. "Eritrean Workers Association Is Needed," *Hanti Ertra,* October 31, 1951, 1.
70. Ibrahim Sultan, "Word of Greeting to the Muslim People of Eritrea," 4.
71. "Advice on Unity of Eritrean Workers Association [Regarding Lack of Employment]," *Hanti Ertra,* December 26, 1951, 1.
72. Aberra Osman Aberra, interview.
73. Ibid.

74. Tom Killion, "Eritrean Workers' Organization and Early Nationalist Mobilization: 1948–1958," *Eritrean Studies Review* 2, no. 1 (1997): 17. See also General Union of Eritrean Workers, "Constitution of the General Union of Eritrean Workers," RDC/04607.

75. Tsegaye Kahsay, interview.

76. Killion, "Eritrean Workers' Organization," 18. Abdu also served as syndicate president after Woldeab Woldemariam fled Eritrea in 1953.

77. Ibid., 17.

78. Ellingson, "Separatism and Irredentism," 124.

79. See Fessehatzion, *Eritrea*, 21.

80. Trevaskis Papers, box 2(B), "Section 4 (d) Consultations with the Inhabitants of Eritrea," 54.

81. "Leading Personalities in Eritrea," FO 403/473–18351, 106. Allegedly, Alama's tensions with the mufti resulted in his resigning as qadi of Massawa. He was allegedly transferred to Agordat at the mufti's request. Ibid.

82. Tesfai, *Federation Ertra*, 140. See also Mulcahy to State Department, April 29, 1952, 777.00/4f/4–2952. During this period Stafford worked as a special adviser to the chief administrator.

83. Ellingson, "Separatism and Irredentism," 127.

84. Mulcahy to State Department, April 17, 1952, 777.00/4–1752. See also Tesfai, *Federation Ertra*, 141.

85. Fessehatzion, *Eritrea*, 22. See Mulcahy to State Department, "Instances of Moslem Discontent in Current Eritrean Politics," April 29 1952, 777.000/4–2952.

86. Ellingson, "Separatism and Irredentism," 124.

87. Woldeab Woldemariam acknowledged that the EDF's real decline was due to internal divisions. He also downplayed the importance of the alleged underhanded ways of the BA, arguing that they went about the wider electoral process in a "commendable way." See Tesfai, *Federation Ertra*, 140–42.

88. Muhammad Umar Kadi, "Call to All Muslims," *Sawt al-rabita al-islamiyya*, April 27, 1952, 1.

89. See *Sawt al-rabita al-islamiyya*, May 11, 1952.

90. "The Assembly in a Week," *Sawt al-rabita al-islamiyya*, June 22, 1952, 4.

91. Ellingson, "Separatism and Irredentism," 127. See Mulcahy to State Department, April 29 1952, 777.00/4–2952.

92. "The Assembly in a Week," *Sawt al-rabita al-islamiyya*, June 15, 1952, 1.

93. Ibid.

94. 'Ali Berhanu, "Who Are the Extremists?," *Sawt al-rabita al-islamiyya*, June 8, 1952, 1.

95. Iman Musa, "Truppe Etiopiche in Eritrea?," *Sawt al-rabita al-islamiyya*, August 24, 1952, 3.

96. Ruth Iyob, *The Eritrean Struggle for Independence: Domination, Resistance, Nationalism, 1941–1993* (Cambridge: Cambridge University Press, 1995), 88.

97. See *Sawt al-rabita al-islamiyya*, June–September 1952; Mulcahy to State Department, September 5, 1952, 777.00/9-552.

98. Tekeste Negash, *Eritrea and Ethiopia: The Federal Experience* (New Brunswick, NJ: Transaction Publishers, 1997), 93.

99. Trevaskis, *Eritrea*, 130.

Chapter 6: Struggling for Muslim Autonomy

1. Gaim Kibreab, *Critical Reflections on the Eritrean War of Independence: Social Capital, Associational Life, Religion, Ethnicity and Sowing Seeds of Dictatorship* (Trenton: Red Sea Press, 2008), 130. Unless otherwise noted, all references to the Muslim League refer to the Eritrean Muslim League and not the Independent Muslim League.

2. Tekeste Negash, *Eritrea and Ethiopia: The Federal Experience* (New Brunswick, NJ: Transaction Publishers, 1997), 112.

3. Ibid., 78.

4. Alemseged Tesfai, *Federation Ertra ms Etyopiya: Kab Matienzo ksab Tedla, 1951–1955* (Asmara: Hdri Publishers, 2005), 309.

5. Tom Killion, "Eritrean Workers' Organization and Early Nationalist Mobilization: 1948–1958," *Eritrean Studies Review* 2, no. 1 (1997): 18. See also Kibreab, *Eritrean War*, 131.

6. Killion, "Eritrean Workers' Organization," 18–19; Tesfai, *Federation Ertra*, 309–19.

7. Killion, "Eritrean Workers' Organization," 18.

8. "Celebration of the Seventh of the Anniversary of the Muslim League," *Sawt al-Iritriyya*, December 18, 1952, 3.

9. Muhammad Saleh Mahmud, "The Economic Reality," *Sawt al-Iritriyya*, November 8, 1952, 3.

10. British Consul, Asmara, to British Embassy, Addis Ababa, September 12, 1953, FO 371/102633. See also T. Negash, *Eritrea and Ethiopia*, 86. Although Negash argues that the memorandum included signatures from several nationalist groups besides the league, including the IML and the NPM, much of the document's grievances echoed objections that the league's leaders had articulated for more than a year before the federation's establishment.

11. British Consul, Asmara, to Foreign Office, December 24, 1953, FO 371/108196. Federal authorities ultimately responded to the public

complaints from the Muslim political leadership by sentencing Sultan, Muhammad Umar Kadi, and National Party secretary general Ahmed Abdelkadir Beshir to short-term prison sentences for their alleged transgression of subverting federal authority. Edward Clark to Secretary of State, February 3, 1956, 775A.00/2–356.

12. For information on Eritrea's "deindustrialization," see Sylvia Pankhurst, *Eritrea on the Eve: The Past and Future of Italy's "First-Born" Colony, Ethiopia's Ancient Sea Province* (Woodford Green, Essex: "New Times and Ethiopia News" Books, 1952). Tekeste Negash summarizes the league's complaints as an attempt to present a counterhistory of the federation's beginnings and inherent failures. He also alleges that during this period, Ibrahim Sultan was "virtually excluded" from the rest of the ML leadership because of his supposed connections with Unionist leader Keshi Dimetros. T. Negash, *Eritrea and Ethiopia*, 94–95.

13. Many of the commentaries that appeared, even those authored by league members, were less concerned with articulating what made Eritrea a truly different entity from Ethiopia than they were worried about the continued deterioration of Muslim political freedom and cultural expression within the federation. See Hajj Ibrahim Muhammad, "How Is It Going to Be with Our Rights in the Federation?," *Sawt al-Iritriyya*, January 17, 1953, 2; Saleh Karrar, "Freedom of Opinion and Press, as Inspired by Independence," *Sawt al-Iritriyya*, March 6, 1954, 4; 'Uthman Asholani, "Apply the Constitution, Parliament Members!" *Sawt al-Iritriyya*, March 26, 1954, 2; "Self Determination—How Do Eritrean Muslims Benefit from It?," *Sawt al-Iritriyya*, May 4, 1954, 4; Ibrahim Sultan, "People of Eritrea Rejoice and Gird Your Loins," *Dehay Ertra*, May 22, 1954, 1; Muslims and Self-Rule," *Sawt al-Iritriyya*, July 3, 1954, 3.

14. Karrar, "Freedom of Opinion and Press," 4.

15. Lloyd Ellingson, "Eritrea: Separatism and Irredentism, 1941–1985" (PhD diss., Michigan State University, 1986), 245.

16. Salim al-Mukhtar, *Shaykh Ibrahim al-Mukhtar ab giziye ewan nay federation* (Asmara: Research and Documentation Center), 1–2. Much of this interpretation was based on Article 28 of the Eritrean constitution, which recognized religious bodies as persons before the law and allowed such entities to "establish and maintain institutions for religious, educational and charitable purposes." See Habtu Ghebre-Ab, *Ethiopia and Eritrea: A Documentary Study* (Trenton: Red Sea Press, 1993), 201–32.

17. Ibrahim al-Mukhtar, "The Mufti's Speech in Protest of the Inspector's Inference in the affairs of the Waqf," Ismael al-Mukhtar, http://www.mukhtar.ca/contentN.php?type=viewarticle&id=176&category =letters_mukhtar (accessed December 12, 2008).

18. Jonathan Miran, "A Historical Overview of Islam in Eritrea," *Die Welt des Islams* 45, no. 2 (2005): 195.

19. Ibrahim al-Mukhtar, "The Mufti's Letter to the Prime Minister of Egypt on the Scientific Missions of Al-Azhar," Ismael al-Mukhtar, http://www.mukhtar.ca/contentN.php?type=viewarticle&id=60&category =letters_mukhtar (accessed December 3, 2008).

20. Ibid.

21. "Important, Dangerous Declarations—The Eritrean Treasurer Who Prevents Muslims from Going on Hajj," *Sawt al-Iritriyya*, June 4, 1954, 2. See "Moslem League to HIM the Emperor of Ethiopia, memo, Asmara," January 3, 1956, FO 371/118744.

22. Muhammad Umar Kadi, "Tarikh hagerkha meflat," unpublished manuscript, Asmara, 1951, 44.

23. Ibid.

24. Ellingson, "Separatism and Irredentism," 170.

25. T. Negash, *Ethiopia and Eritrea*, 112.

26. For more information on Asfaha Woldemikael's service to the Ethiopian government before the federation, see FO 742/26.

27. Report, "Eritrean Political Developments," Asmara Consul to State Department, December 14, 1956. National Archives and Records Administration (henceforth cited as NARA), RG 84, box 3, Addis Ababa, Classified General Records, 1950–58.

28. For a deeper analysis of the effects of economic marginalization against urban workers, see Killion, "Eritrean Workers' Organization"; T. Negash, *Eritrea and Ethiopia*, 125; Semere Haile, "Historical Background to the Ethiopian-Eritrean Conflict," in *The Long Struggle of Eritrea for Independence and Constructive Peace*, ed. Basil Davidson and Lionel Cliffe (Trenton: Red Sea Press, 1988); Semere Haile, "The Root of the Ethiopian-Eritrean Conflict: The Erosion of the Federal Act," *Journal of Eritrean Studies* 1, no. 1 (1986): 9.

29. Moslem Mosques Committee of Asmara, *Memorandum Submitted by the Moslem Mosques Committee of Asmara to the Office of the Chief Executive* (Asmara, 1956).

30. Ibid.

31. Salim al-Mukhtar, *Shaykh Ibrahim al-Mukhtar*, 1–2. See T. Negash, *Eritrea and Ethiopia*, 126–32; "Copy. Telegram. Asmara 5.3.1958 (Memorandum Submitted by the Muslim League and Federalist Youth Party of Eritrea)," March 5, 1958, FO 371/131245.

32. Redie Bereketeab, *Eritrea: The Making of a Nation: 1890–1991* (Trenton: Red Sea Press, 2007), 167.

33. Earle J. Richey to State Department, August 15, 1956, NARA, RG 84, 3/350.

34. "Eritrea Annual Review for 1955," FO 371/118738.

35. Eritrean Muslim League Conference Memorandum, RDC/001007, 2.

36. Ibid.

37. Ibid.

38. See also British Consul, Asmara, to British Embassy, Addis Ababa, July 12, 1954, FO 371/108197.

39. Eritrean Islamic League Management Council/Planning Committee, "Memorandum," February, 1956, RDC/001010, 2.

40. Ibid.

41. Ibid.

42. Ibid., 3

43. Ibid., 5.

44. T. Negash, *Eritrea and Ethiopia*, 78. See Tekie Fessehatzion, *Eritrea: From Federation to Annexation, 1952–1962* (Washington, DC: Eritreans for Peace and Democracy, 1990), 28. This "Christianization" was, however, also tied to the larger concern that Eritreans as a whole were being excluded from the legislative mechanisms of the Federation government; see Eritrean Liberation Front, *The Federal Case of Eritrea with Ethiopia* (Damascus: Eritrean Liberation Front Office, 1965), 53–57.

45. Ibrahim Sultan, interview.

46. See T. Negash, *Eritrea and Ethiopia*, 111–47; Bereket Habte Selassie, "From British Rule to Federation and Annexation," in *Behind the War in Eritrea*, ed. Basil Davidson, Lionel Cliffe and Habte Selassie (Nottingham: Spokesman, 1988), 32–47. John Sorenson notes that Christianity was simply "one aspect of the civilizing mission which the Amhara saw as their imperial duty." See John Sorenson, *Imagining Ethiopia: Struggles for History and Identity in the Horn of Africa* (New Brunswick, NJ: Rutgers University Press, 1993), 13.

47. Miran, "Islam in Eritrea," 209.

48. See British Consul, Asmara, to British Embassy, Addis Ababa, October 26, 1955, FO 371/113520.

49. Fessehatzion, *Eritrea*, 37.

50. Ibid.

51. "Eritrean Political Developments," Earle J. Richey to State Department, December 14, 1956, NARA, RG 84, 3/350.

52. The Muslim Youth League should not be confused with the league's previous youth organization, Shuban al-rabita.

53. Earle J. Richey to State Department, June 14, 1956, 775A.00/6–1456. See also Ellingson, "Separatism and Irredentism," 250.

54. Earle J. Richey to State Department, November 7, 1957, 775A.00/11-757.

55. "SENT DEPT 294 RPTD Info Addis Ababa from Jidda," November 24, 1956, 360.012, NARA, RG 84, 3/350.

56. Ellingson, "Separatism and Irredentism," 216.

57. "Shades of Pravda," Earle J. Richey to State Department, June 21, 1957, NARA, RG 84, 3/350.

58. "Political Developments," Earle J. Richey to State Department, June 13, 1957, NARA, RG 84, 3/350.

59. Ibid.

60. Ibid.

Chapter 7: New Beginnings at the Federation's End

1. Tom Killion, "Eritrean Workers' Organization and Early Nationalist Mobilization: 1948–1958," *Eritrean Studies Review* 2, no. 1 (1997): 26.

2. The league's support for Kadi's actions did not imply, at least among the executive council, that he had now joined the league's leadership. Kadi himself did not acknowledge his official position, although Tekeste Negash has claimed that Kadi effectively became "one of the self-appointed leaders of the Moslem League." See Tekeste Negash, *Eritrea and Ethiopia: The Federal Experience* (New Brunswick, NJ: Transaction Publishers, 1997), 126. See also FO 371/131245.

3. "Complaint on Present Status of Eritrea," George LaMont to American Embassy, Addis Ababa, November 23, 1957, NARA, RG 84, 3/350.

4. Muhammad Umar Kadi, "The Complaint of the Eritrean People against the Ethiopian Government," 1956.

5. "Complaint on Present Status of Eritrea," NARA, RG 84, 3/350.

6. "Memorandum of Conversation," George C. Moore to American Embassy, Addis Ababa, February 24, 1958, NARA, RG 84, 3/350.

7. See "Complaint on Present Status of Eritrea," NARA, RG 84, 3/350.

8. Although tried initially for leaving Eritrea without a proper exit visa, Kadi was ultimately convicted on the sole count of sedition.

9. See T. Negash, *Eritrea and Ethiopia*, 130–31. This is an issue that most scholars have not adequately addressed in the context of nationalist development, although several sources have noted the sizable protests and demonstrations that took place within Muslim communities in Keren, Agordat, and Massawa in response to Kadi's sentencing. See FO 371/131245, March 12, 1958; Eritrean Liberation Front, *The Federal Case of Eritrea with Ethiopia* (Damascus: Eritrean Liberation Front Office, 1965), 15.

10. "Muslim Trials in Asmara," George C. Moore to American Embassy, Addis Ababa, June 20, 1958, NARA, RG 84, 3/350.

11. Ibid.

12. George C. Moore to American Embassy, Addis Ababa, June 2, 1958, NARA, RG 84, 3/350.

13. "Muslim Trials in Asmara," George C. Moore to American Embassy, Addis Ababa, June 20, 1958, NARA, RG 84, 3/350.

14. "Summary of Petition from Residents of Keren and Sahel, January 28, 1958," Earle J. Richey to American Embassy, March 10, 1958, NARA, RG 84, 3/350.

15. "Summary of the Telegram to HIM and Chief Executive, allegedly sent February 14th from the Asmara group," Earle J. Richey to American Embassy, Addis Ababa, March 10, 1958, NARA, RG 84, 3/350.

16. FO 371/1311245, Asmara, March 5, 1958. See "Comments of Moslem League Secretary General Concerning Political Demonstrations in Eritrea," George C. Moore to American Embassy, Addis Ababa, March 24, 1958, NARA, RG 84, 3/350; T. Negash, *Eritrea and Ethiopia*, 130.

17. Eritrean Liberation Front, *Federal Case of Eritrea*, 20.

18. "Summary of Telegram from Keren Members of Moslem League of Eritrea to HIM, January 31, 1958," Earle J. Richey to American Embassy, Addis Ababa, March 10, 1958, NARA, RG 84, 3/350.

19. The most prominent of these figures tried included Shaykh Muhammad Seraj Abdu, who had served previously as the vice president of the Syndicate of Eritrean Workers under Woldeab Woldemariam. See Killion, "Eritrean Workers' Organization," 20–21.

20. Ibid.

21. "Comments of Moslem League Secretary General Concerning Political Demonstrations in Eritrea," NARA, RG 84, 3/350. In private testimony, Sultan noted that the unrest in Asmara had followed the mass Muslim disobedience centered in Keren and Agordat that arose in the previous months after more than one hundred league officials had sent a telegram to the UN complaining of rampant abuse by Eritrean police, wholesale arrests of citizens, and other "anti-constitutional activities" embraced by the unionists in the Eritrean Assembly.

22. Eritrean Liberation Front, *Federal Case of Eritrea*, 24.

23. "Memorandum of Conversation," Earle J. Hickey to American Embassy, Addis Ababa, March 20, 1958, NARA, RG 84, 3/350.

24. Ibid. In a conversation between Sultan and American consuls George C. Moore and Earle J. Richey, the league leader compared the unrest in Asmara with the previous uprising that had erupted in Budapest in 1956.

25. "Muslim Trials in Asmara," George C. Moore to American Embassy, Addis Ababa, June 20, 1958, NARA, RG 84, 3/350.

26. George C. Moore to Secretary of State, April 8, 1958, NARA, RG 84, 3/350. See also Killion, "Eritrean Workers' Organization," 52.

27. "Eritrean Riots," W. Astill to American Embassy, Addis Ababa, March 13, 1958, NARA, RG 84, 3/350.

28. Gaim Kibreab, *Critical Reflections on the Eritrean War of Independence: Social Capital, Associational Life, Religion, Ethnicity and Sowing Seeds of Dictatorship* (Trenton: Red Sea Press, 2008), 135.

29. Ibid.

30. "Memorandum of Conversation," George C. Moore to American Embassy, Addis Ababa, March 21, 1958, NARA, RG 84, 3/350. Despite the growing discontent within the Muslim community, federation officials continued with previous efforts to win Muslim support by proclaiming the Ethiopian government's religious objectivity. In a speech given by Asfaha Woldemikael on the celebration of the Prophet's birthday in late September 1958, the chief executive stressed to the public that "for the population of Ethiopia, religion is nothing other than the means by which each can communicate with his God and through which he has the power to distinguish right from wrong." In his appeal to Asmara's Muslim residents, Woldemikael reassured the public of both the Ethiopian and federal government's intentions to protect Muslim religious equality despite no formal legal guarantees. He claimed that "freedom of religion, which others have found necessary to put into their constitutions, is for us no novelty, rather something which has been with us through countless epochs." See "Speech Given on the Prophet's Birthday by Asfaha Woldemikael," Earle J. Richey to State Department, October 3, 1958, NARA, RG 84, 3/350.

31. Killion, "Eritrean Workers' Organization," 33.

32. Tekie Fessehatzion, *Eritrea: From Federation to Annexation, 1952–1962* (Washington, DC: Eritreans for Peace and Democracy, 1990), 3; FO 371/131245, December 5, 1958. See Zewde Retta, *Ye Eritrea Guday: 1941–1963* (Addis Ababa: Central Publishing, 1998).

33. "Official-Informal Secret," George C. Moore to American Embassy, Athens, July 1, 1959, NARA, RG 84, 3/350.

34. Ibrahim Sultan, interview.

35. Mehamed Umar Abdala, "Abu Tiyara," interview by Günter Schröder, Kassala, Sudan, March 23, 1989, trans. Gebrai Weldeselassie and Mahmud Mai Betot Amar.

36. Ibrahim Sultan, interview. Sultan claimed that federation authorities imprisoned his wife for nearly two years and subjected her to electric-shock torture before she was finally released and fled to Kassala.

37. Ibrahim Sultan to Edward Mulcahy, July 24, 1959, NARA, RG 84, 3/350.

38. Tricia Redeker Hepner, *Soldiers, Martyrs, Traitors, and Exiles: Political Conflict in Eritrea and the Diaspora* (Philadelphia: University of Pennsylvania Press, 2009), 21.

39. Ibrahim Sultan to Edward Mulcahy, July 24, 1959, NARA, RG 84, 3/350.

40. Ahmed Suri, interview by Günter Schröder, Kassala, Sudan, January 26, 1991, translated by Wodi Qeshi.

41. Ibid. According to Suri, the committee also ran into problems when some members voiced concern about their political involvement and suggested that members "restrict the committee exclusively to social matters."

42. Saleh Heduq, interview by Günter Schröder, Khartoum, March 14, 1989, translated by Abdurrahman Tahanna.

43. Ibid.

44. Adem Mehamed Hamid "Gendifel," interview by Günter Schröder, Kassala, Sudan, February 9, 1991, translated by Mehari Testaledet (henceforth cited as Adem Gendifel).

45. Ibid.

46. Saleh Heduq, interview.

47. Ibid.

48. Saleh Ahmed Eyay, interview by Günter Schröder, Kassala, Sudan, January 10, 1988.

49. Muhammad Se'id Nawud, *Harakat Tahrir Iritriyya: Al-haqiqa wa'l-ta'rikh*, 17–18.

50. Mehamed Said Nawd, interview by Günter Schröder, Khartoum, July 11, 1988. Spelling is based on Schröder's model.

51. Muhammadberhan Hassan, *Menqesqas Harnet Ertra: Ma'arfo kab ma'arfotat gu'azo hagerawi qalsna* (Asmara, 2001), 21.

52. See Nawud, *Harakat Tahrir Iritriyya*, 9.

53. Ahmed Suri, interview.

54. Nawud, *Harakat Tahrir Iritriyya*, 24.

55. Ibid., 27.

56. Ibid., 10.

57. See Hassan, *Menqesqas Harnet Ertra*.

58. Nawud, *Harakat Tahrir Iritriyya*, 14.

59. Ahmed Suri, interview.

60. Nawud, *Harakat Tahrir Iritriyya*, 27.

61. Mehamed Said Nawd, interview by Günter Schröder, Khartoum, December 19, 1987. Spelling is based on Günter Schröder's model.

62. Nawud, *Harakat Tahrir Iritriyya*, 81–82.

63. Muhammad Said Nawd, interview, December 19, 1987.

64. Saleh Ahmed Eyay, interview, January 10, 1988.

65. Saleh Ahmed Eyay, interview by Günter Schröder, Khartoum, July 13, 1988.

66. Ruth Iyob, *The Eritrean Struggle for Independence: Domination, Resistance, Nationalism, 1941–1993* (Cambridge: Cambridge University Press, 1995), 100.

67. Ibid.

68. Hassan, *Menqesqas Harnet Ertra*, 50.
69. Ibid., 49. See Tsegaye Kahsay, interview.
70. Iyob, *Eritrean Struggle*, 99.
71. Nawud, *Harakat Tahrir Iritriyya*, 19.
72. Jonathan Miran argues that this proximity came about largely as a result of Italian colonial policy and its effect on Muslim learning, under which "Eritrean Muslims were able to travel more freely for religious education in the Middle East, especially to Egypt and the Hijaz," resulting in the emergence of "a more conscious Muslim urban intelligentsia." Miran, "A Historical Overview of Islam in Eritrea," *Die Welt des Islams* 45, no. 2 (2005): 202.
73. See Jonathan Miran, "Grand mufti, érudit et nationaliste érythréen: Note sur la vie et l'oeuvre de cheikh Ibrâhîm al-Mukhtâr (1909–1969)," *Chroniques yéménites* 10 (2002): 35–47. Before the establishment of the federation, Muslim League members worked with British officials in guaranteeing entry for Al-Azhar representatives. See FO 742/23.
74. Curiously, Abd al-Qadir Haqus al-Jibirti claimed that the Eritrean Student Club did not espouse any particular religious program or agenda and that the mufti was not in direct contact with the organization during the period in question. Abd al-Qadir Haqus al-Jibirti, telephone interview, January 5, 2010.
75. See John Markakis, *National and Class Conflict in the Horn of Africa* (Cambridge: Cambridge University Press, 1987).
76. Woldeyesus Ammar, "The Role of Asmara Students in the Eritrean Nationalist Movement, 1958–1968," *Eritrean Studies Review* 2, no. 1 (1997): 64.
77. Abd al-Qadir Haqus al-Jibirti, *Thikryati an Dewr al-Haraka al-Talabiya Labina Iritriyya fi Misr* (Cairo, 1994), 35.
78. Ibid., 2.
79. Ibid., 6.
80. Abdelkarim Ahmad, interview by Günter Schröder, Kassala, Sudan, January 7, 1988, translated by Dr. Mehamed Said Beshir. Abdelkarim Ahmad also noted that "whenever a student came to Cairo and the club, he received from the club two suits, one for summer and one for winter, and he was fed and given a place to sleep till he got a scholarship."
81. Woldeab Woldemariam became one of the first of the old-guard nationalist leaders to work with the club. Members also facilitated his resettlement from Asmara to Cairo, who procured him a job as a Tigrinya instructor. Students in turn worked with Woldemariam in letter-writing campaigns and organizing other political activities. Al-Jibirti, *Thikryati an Dewr*, 35. Later, Woldemariam began broadcasting a nationalist radio program from Cairo.

82. Ibid., 65.

83. Abd al-Qadir Haqus al-Jibirti, interview.

84. Preparatory Committee for Golden Jubilee of Eritrean Students Club, *Resalah al-jial* (Cairo: Eritrean Students Club, 2002), 1–12. I am grateful to Jonathan Miran for bringing the two previously cited texts to my attention and granting me access.

85. Abd al-Qadir Haqus al-Jibirti, interview.

86. Al-Jibirti, *Thikryati an Dewr*, 32–33.

87. Ibid., 4.

88. See Eritrean Students Club, *Resalah al-jial*, 52–61.

89. Ibid.

90. See Four Power Commission of Investigation for the Former Italian Colonies, "Report on Eritrea," CFM/D/L/47/ICCOM Sixth Hearing, GAOR, 1st committee, 3rd sess., pt. 2, April 5–May 13, 1949.

91. Idris Usman Glawdiyos, interview by Günter Schröder, Khartoum, January 1, 1988. Spelling is based on Schröder's model.

92. The eleven members included Idris Glawdiyos, Idris Muhammad Adam, Muhammad Saleh Humed, Said Ahmed Hashim, Adem Akte, Ibrahim Idris Bileni, Said Hussein, and Abdelqader Ibrahim. Taha Muhammad Nur, interview by Günter Schröder, Rome, May 28–29, 1988.

93. See Iyob, *Eritrean Struggle*, 109; 'Uthman Salih Sabbe, *Jughrafiyya Iritriyya* (Beirut: Dar al-Kunuz al-Abadiyya, 1983); Woldeyesus Ammar, *Eritrea: Root Causes of War and Refugees* (Baghdad: Sindbad Publishing, 1992), 139–49. At times, even Eritrean activists living in Cairo suffered the wrath of the Ethiopian government. In November 1961 several members of the Eritrean Students Club were injured during a protest in front of the Ethiopian embassy when Ethiopian soldiers allegedly opened fire on the group of sixty students as they waved the Eritrean flag. Ironically, some of the students were later arrested by Cairo police for causing a public disturbance. Abd al-Qadir Haqus al-Jibirti, interview.

94. Permanent Peoples' Tribunal, *The Eritrean Case: Proceedings of the Permanent Peoples' Tribunal of the International League for the Rights and Liberation of Peoples: Session on Eritrea* (Milan: Research and Information Center on Eritrea, 1982), 151. Sabbe allegedly helped finance and arrange their visit to Saudi Arabia.

95. Ibrahim Sultan, interview. Ibrahim Sultan's account contrasts widely with Sabbe's recollections in *Jughrafiyya Iritriyya* on the nature and degree of factionalism in the establishment of the ELF. See Eritrean Liberation Front, *The Ethiopian Unilateral Abrogation of the UN Federal Resolution* (Damascus: Eritrean Liberation Front Office, 1967).

96. Ibrahim Sultan, interview. Ibrahim Sultan's comments about Faisal's role and the Khatmiyya-Wahhabi rivalry are particularly revealing.

Faisal, according to Haggai Erlich, represented the "embodiment of the Saudi-Wahhabi historical alliance," who throughout the period attempted to "further legitimize the regime at home and to stem revolutionary and socialist nationalism in the region." This included his sponsoring of the Islamic International Conference in Mecca in May 1962, which led to the creation of the conservative World Muslim League. See Erlich, *Saudi Arabia and Ethiopia: Islam, Christianity, and Politics Entwined* (Boulder: Lynne Rienner, 2007), 104–6.

97. Idris Muhammad Adem, interview by Günter Schröder, Khartoum, March 17, 1989, translated by Abdurrahman Tahanna. Spelling is based on Schröder's model.

98. By the late 1950s, with most of the organization's former leadership in exile or imprisoned, the Muslim League ceased to exist as a formal political party. Abd al-Qadir Haqus al-Jibirti recalled that throughout the late 1950s and 60s, several former league members living in Cairo worked with the Eritrean Students Club; many came as guest speakers on political issues and others worked with members to sponsor events and address the situation in Eritrea. Al-Jibirti, interview.

99. Ibrahim Sultan, interview.

100. Kibreab, *Eritrean War*, 152.

101. Iyob, *Eritrean Struggle*, 108.

102. 'Ali Said Mehamed Berhatu, interview by Günter Schröder, Khartoum, January 25, 1988.

103. Idris Usman Glawdiyos, interview.

104. Saleh Ahmed Eyay, interview.

105. Several of Adam's visits also involved overseeing and transporting arms to western Eritrea.

106. Ibid. In response to the ELF's apparent success in winning over large segments of the ELM's membership, the leadership in Port Sudan eventually came out against the ELF and the veteran politicians behind its activities. According to Mahmud Mehamed Saleh, a former member of the ELM's Central Regional Committee in western Eritrea, ELM leaders dispatched a pamphlet to its cells across the region stating that because Idris Muhammad Adam, Ibrahim Sultan, and other "old politicians" had refused to work with their organization's objectives, all Haraka members should "stop any relation with them from inside the country." Saleh, interview by Günter Schröder, Khartoum, April 1, 1989.

107. Adem Gendifel, interview by Günter Schröder, Kassala, Sudan, January 7, 1988. Gendifel noted that the exception was in Keren, where the ELM had strong ties to the organization's leaders in Port Sudan despite the growing pressures. Some accounts have downplayed the

supposed influence of the ELM in the diaspora. Sabbe claimed that he did not know of Haraka's existence until he arrived in Jeddah in early 1960. See 'Uthman Saleh Sabbe, interview by Günter Schröder, Khartoum, December 12, 1980.

108. Ibid.

109. Umer Damer, interview by Günter Schröder, Kassala, March 24, 1989, translated by Gebrai Weldeselasie. Also present were Abu Tiyara and Mahmud Mai Betot.

110. 'Uthman Saleh Sabbe, interview by Günter Schröder, Khartoum, April 4, 1983.

111. Despite calls by some ELF representatives in contact with Awate to support a vague "Muslim" struggle against Ethiopia, Awate's principal focus in dealing with the ELF remained largely the same as his concerns when he was first approached by the ELM: the need to receive additional arms and supplies from Sudan, building up a larger fighting force, and finding experienced fighters to coordinate guerrilla actions across other regions of Eritrea. See Mahmud Mehamed Saleh, interview.

112. Adem Gendifel, interview.

113. Idris Usman Glawdiyos, interview.

114. Shumet Sishagne, *Unionists and Separatists: The Vagaries of Ethio-Eritrean Relation, 1941–1991* (Hollywood, CA: Tsehai Publishers, 2007), 131. Sishagne even argues that the Somali government acted as the primary force behind the establishment of the Eritrean-Somali Friendship Association, which coordinated "support for the Eritrean cause."

115. Idris Mehamed Adem, interview.

116. Ibid.

117. See Günter Schröder, "'Utmān Sālih Sabī," in *Encyclopaedia Aethiopica*, 1049–50.

118. E. Correnti, "Osman Saleh Sabbe (OSS) The Unknown," May 27, 2002, http://www.awate.com/portal/content/view/606/13/ (accessed June 20, 2009).

119. Although his trip to Pakistan never materialized, Adem claimed that Sabbe did manage to speak with the Pakistani ambassador in Saudi Arabia to discuss the movement. Idris Mehamed Adem, interview.

120. Markakis, *National and Class Conflict*, 110.

121. Iyob, *Eritrean Struggle*, 105. Sabbe was particularly instrumental in thwarting the activities of Muhammad Se'id Nawud's ELM in 1964–65.

122. Eritreans for Liberation in North America, "Our Struggle and Its Goals," *Harnet* 2, no. 3 (March 1973): 3.

123. See Alemseged Tesfai, *Aynfelale: 1941–1950* (Asmara: Hdri Publishers, 2002).

124. Sishagne, *Unionists and Separatists*, 138.

125. Ibrahim Sultan, "Subject: Call for Unification of All Nine Factions of the Eritrean Revolution and Request to Form a National Council of Each Faction That Consists of Nine Members Instead of a National Council for Each Faction," n.d., RDC/01661.

126. Ibid., 1.

127. Ibid., 2.

128. Ibid.

129. Sishagne, *Unionists and Separatists*, 135. According to Sishagne, Sultan's exclusion from the ELF did not end the hostility, as "both men revived their old rivalries of the 1940s and mobilized their personal and clan followers in the struggle to gain the upper hand in the ELF and to control the exile community in the Middle East."

Epilogue

1. See Uoldelul Chelati Dirar, "Colonialism and the Construction of National Identities: The Case of Eritrea," *Journal of Eastern African Studies* 1, no. 2 (2007): 256–76.

2. Sara Rich Dorman, "Narratives of Nationalism in Eritrea: Research and Revisionism," *Nations and Nationalism* 11, no. 2 (2005): 218.

3. Jacques Depelchin, *Silences in African History: Between the Syndromes of Discovery and Abolition* (Dar es Salaam: Mkuki na Nyota Publishers, 2004), 17. For an in-depth analysis of the extent to which the PFDJ's ideological influence has dominated Eritrean civil society, see Tricia Redeker Hepner, *Soldiers, Martyrs, Traitors, and Exiles: Political Conflict in Eritrea and the Diaspora* (Philadelphia: University of Pennsylvania Press, 2009), 183–219.

Glossary

Abune   Literally meaning "our father" in Amharic and
                   Tigrinya, it refers to any bishop within the
                   Eritrean or Ethiopian Orthodox Church.

askari   A term used to describe African soldiers that
                   served in the various European armies during
                   the colonial period. Italian colonial officials relied
                   heavily on Askaris throughout Eritrea during the
                   early twentieth century.

awqāf   See *waqf.*

Degiat   An honorific military title (roughly, "Commander"
                   or "General of the Gate"); from the Amharic term
                   dejazmach.

hadith   Often translated as "tradition," it refers to
                   any saying or action attributed to the prophet
                   Muhammad or by one of his companions. The
                   broader collection of sayings or actions represents
                   one of the main foundations of Islamic law.

Hajj   An honorific title reserved for individuals within
                   the Islamic religion who have completed the Hajj.

Haraka   Another name for the Eritrean Liberation
                   Movement; from Arabic *haraka*, movement.

Jabarti   Tigrinya-speaking Muslims residing mainly in the
                   Eritrean highlands.

Jebha   A colloquial name for the Eritrean Liberation
                   Front.

khalifa   A representative, or "deputy," within a Sufi order.

khalwa — Translated as "solitude," it refers to the Sufi Islamic practice of engaging in a solitary spiritual retreat. It also is used as a term for religious schools throughout Sufi communities across the Horn of Africa.

Khatmiyya — The largest and most politically influential Sufi order across western and northern Eritrea.

Nazir — A term used across Islamic communities in Eritrea that refers to a noble in a position of authority within a clan, tribe, or specific geographic area.

Qadi — An Islamic judge.

Ras — Translated literally from Amharic as "head," it represents a title within Ethiopian society given a noble at the functional level of a prince or a duke.

Sayyid — An honorific title, reserved for males regarded as descendants of the Prophet Muhammad.

Shaykh — An honorific title (lit., elder) used as a mark of authority for a clan leader or Islamic scholar.

shifta — A bandit or raider.

shiftanet — A Tigrinya term that refers broadly to any form of *shifta* activity.

shumagulle — Members of the landowning class and political elite across much of the Tigre-speaking territories in western and northern Eritrea.

Sufism — Broadly defined as the mystical, internalized branch of Islam as practiced within many different Muslim societies.

sunnah — Generally speaking, it is defined as the normative way of life for all Muslims based on both the practices and the teachings of the Prophet Muhammad. The sunnah represents the second most authoritative source of Islamic law, after the Qur'an.

tariqa   Meaning "way" or "path." A term used to refer to most Sufi Islamic orders.

tigre   Tigre-speaking residents in western and northern Eritrea of "serf" origins.

Wahhabism   A conservative branch of Sunni Islam originally founded by Muhammad ibn Abd al-Wahhab in eighteenth-century Arabia.

waqf (pl., *awqāf*)   Generally defined within Islamic law as a religious endowment. It usually corresponds to a donation made in the form of a specific building, house, or property to be used for religious or charitable purposes (or both).

ulama   Refers broadly to members of the educated class of Islamic scholars and jurists.

Selected Bibliography

The following bibliography includes selections of all major and relevant sources within the text. It does not include citations for particular sources, including online documents, oral interviews, and individual archival documents.

Periodicals

Dehay Ertra (Tigrinya), May 1952–August 1954
Eritrean Daily News (English), May–August 1947
Hanti Ertra (Tigrinya), June 1949–January 1951
Al-Ittihadi al-dawlia (Arabic), March 1997–May 1997
Nay Ertra semunawi gazzetta (Tigrinya), June 1942–September 1953
Sawt al-Iritriyya (Arabic), May 1952–August 1954
Sawt al-rabita al-islamiyya (Arabic), November 1947–September 1952
Wahda Iritriyya (Arabic), June 1949–December 1950

Archives

Center for Research Libraries, Chicago
Fabian Colonial Bureau, Bodleian Library, Oxford University
Foreign Office, Kew Gardens, UK
National Archives and Records Administration, College Park, Maryland
Papers of Sir Kennedy Trevaskis, Bodleian Library, Oxford University
Research and Documentation Center, Asmara
United Nations Archives, New York

Books and Articles

Abbay, Alemseged. *Identity Jilted, or, Re-imagining Identity? The Divergent Paths of the Eritrean and Tigrayan Nationalist Struggles.* Lawrenceville, NJ: Red Sea Press, 1998.

————. "The Trans-Mareb Past in the Present." *Journal of Modern African Studies* 35, no. 2 (1997): 321–34.

Aberra, Yassin M. "Muslim Institutions in Ethiopia: The Asmara Awqaf." *Journal of the Institute of Muslim Minority Affairs* 5, no.1 (1984): 203–23.

Abu Bakr, Muhammad 'Uthman. *'Uthman Salih Sabbe wa-l-Thawra al-Iritriyya*. Cairo: Al-Maktab al-Misri li-Tawzi' al-Matbu'at, 1998.

Ahmed, Nebil. "A History of al-Rabita al-Islamiya al-Eritrea (1946–50)." In *Proceedings of a Workshop on Aspects of Eritrean History*, edited by Tekeste Melake, 129–48. Asmara: Hdri Publishers, 2007.

Almedom, Astier M. "Re-reading the Short- and Long-Rigged History of Eritrea, 1941–1952: Back to the Future?" *Nordic Journal of African Studies* 15, no. 2 (2006): 103–42.

Ammar, Woldeyesus. *Eritrea: Root Causes of War and Refugees*. Baghdad: Sinbad Publishing, 1992.

————. "The Role of Asmara Students in the Eritrean Nationalism Movement: 1958–1968." *Eritrean Studies Review* 2, no. 1 (1997): 59–84.

Appiah, Kwame Anthony. *In My Father's House: Africa in the Philosophy of Culture*. New York: Oxford University Press, 1992.

Arasai, Tekwabo Asanadai. *Merusat 'Anqasat Ato-Woldeab: 1941–1991*. Asmara: Hdri Publishers, 1995.

Barrera, Giulia. "Mussolini's Colonial Race Laws and State-Settler Relations in Africa Orientale Italiana (1935–41)." *Journal of Modern Italian Studies* 8, no. 3 (2003): 425–43.

Belay, Ruth. "The Political Biography of Ibrahim Sultan." BA thesis, University of Asmara, 2000.

Bereketeab, Redie. *Eritrea: The Making of a Nation, 1890–1991*. Trenton: Red Sea Press, 2007.

Bernal, Victoria. "Islam, Transnational Culture, and Modernity in Rural Sudan." In *Gendered Encounters: Challenging Cultural Boundaries and Social Hierarchies in Africa*, edited by M. Grosz-Ngaté and O. Kokole, 131–51. New York: Routledge, 1997.

Brenner, Louis. "Muslim Representations of Unity and Difference in the African Discourse." In *Muslim Identity and Social Change in Sub-Saharan Africa*, edited by Louis Brenner, 1–20. Bloomington: Indiana University Press, 1993.

Bruzzi, Silvia. "Il colonialismo italiano e la Hatmiya in Eritrea (1890–1941): Sayyid Gaafar al-Mirghani e Sharia Alawiyya nelle fonti coloniali italiene." *Africa* (Rome) 61, nos. 3–4 (2006): 435–53.

————. "Italian Colonialism and Muslim Woman Leadership: The Case of Sharifa 'Alawiyya in Eritrea." Paper presented at the conference Negotiating the Sacred: Politics, Practice, and Perceptions of Religion in Africa, Stanford University, October 25, 2009.

Cooper, Frederick. *Colonialism in Question: Theory, Knowledge, History.* Berkeley: University of California Press, 2005.

———. "Possibility and Constraint: African Independence in Historical Perspective." *Journal of African History* 49, no. 2 (2008): 167–96.

Correnti, E. "Osman Saleh Sabbe (OSS) The Unknown." http://www .awate.com/portal/content/view/606/13/ (accessed June 20, 2009).

Davidson, Basil. *The Black Man's Burden: Africa and the Curse of the Nation-State.* New York: Random House, 1993.

D'Avray, Anthony, with Richard Pankhurst. *The Nakfa Documents: The Despatches, Memoranda, Reports, and Correspondence Describing and Explaining the Stories of the Feudal Societies of the Red Sea Littoral from the Christian-Muslim Wars of the Sixteenth Century to the Establishment 1885–1901 of the Italian Colony of Eritrea.* Wiesbaden: Harrassowitz, 2000.

Debessai, N'Bisrat. "The Shifta Movement in Eritrea: The Case of Mosazgi's Sons." In *Proceedings of a Workshop on Aspects of Eritrean History,* edited by Tekeste Melake, 108–28. Asmara: Hdri Publishers, 2007.

De Marco, R. R. *The Italianization of African Natives: Government Native Education in the Italian Colonies, 1890–1937.* New York: Teachers College, Columbia University Publication, 1943.

Depelchin, Jacques. *Silences in African History: Between the Syndromes of Discovery and Abolition.* Dar es Salaam: Mkuki na Nyota Publishers, 2004.

Dirar, Uoldelul Chelati. "Colonialism and the Construction of National Identities: The Case of Eritrea." *Journal of Eastern African Studies* 1, no. 2 (2007): 256–76.

———. "From Warriors to Urban Dwellers: Ascari and the Military Factor in the Urban Development of Colonial Eritrea." *Cahiers d'études africaines,* 44, no. 3, cah. 175 (2004): 533–74.

Ellingson, Lloyd. "The Emergence of Political Parties in Eritrea, 1941–1950." *Journal of African History* 18, no. 2 (1977): 261–81.

———. "Eritrea: Separatism and Irredentism, 1941–1985." PhD dissertation, Michigan State University, 1986.

Eritrean Liberation Front. *The Federal Case of Eritrea with Ethiopia.* Damascus: Eritrean Liberation Front Office, 1965.

Eritrean Peoples Liberation Front. Central Administration of Eritrean Liberation. "A Questionnaire Regarding the Political Parties of the 1940s and 1950s." Unpublished document. Asmara: Research and Documentation Center, March 1, 1991.

Eritreans for Liberation in North America. "Our Struggle and Its Goals." *Harnet* 2, no. 3 (March 1973): 1–23.

Erlich, Haggai. *Saudi Arabia and Ethiopia: Islam, Christianity, and Politics Entwined.* Boulder: Lynne Rienner, 2007.

————. *The Struggle over Eritrea, 1962–1978: War and Revolution in the Horn of Africa*. Stanford: Hoover Institution Press, 1983.

Fanon, Frantz. *The Wretched of the Earth*. New York: Grove Press, 1963.

Fessehatzion, Tekie. *Eritrea: From Federation to Annexation, 1952–1962*. Washington, DC: Eritreans for Peace and Democracy, 1990.

Gebre-Medhin, Jordan. *Peasants and Nationalism in Eritrea: A Critique of Ethiopian Studies*. Trenton, NJ: Red Sea Press, 1989.

Gewald, Jan-Bart. "Making Tribes: Social Engineering in the Western Province of British-Administered Eritrea, 1941–1952." *Journal of Colonialism and Colonial History* 1, no. 2 (Winter 2000).

Ghebre-Ab, Habtu. *Ethiopia and Eritrea: A Documentary Study*. Trenton, NJ: Red Sea Press, 1993.

Ghebre Iyesus, Abba Isaak. *Arguments for Shedding Some Light on the Tigré Phenomenon*. Asmara: MBY Press, 1996.

Glaude, Eddie S. *Exodus! Religion, Race, and Nation in Early Nineteenth-Century Black America*. Chicago: University of Chicago Press, 2000.

Guha, Ranajit. *Elementary Aspects of Peasant Insurgency in Colonial India*. Delhi: Oxford University Press, 1983.

Habte Selassie, Bereket. *Eritrea and the United Nations*. Trenton: Red Sea Press, 1989.

————. "From British Rule to Federation and Annexation." In *Behind the War in Eritrea*, edited by Basil Davidson, Lionel Cliffe, and Bereket Habte Selassie, 32–47. Nottingham: Spokesman, 1988.

Haile, Semere. "Historical Background to the Ethiopian-Eritrean Conflict." In *The Long Struggle of Eritrea for Independence and Constructive Peace*, edited by Basil Davidson and Lionel Cliffe, 11–31. Trenton: Red Sea Press, 1988.

Hassan, Muhammadberhan. *Menqesqas Harnet Ertra: Ma'arfo kab ma'arfotat gu'azo hagerawi qalsna*. Asmara, 2001.

Hepner, Tricia. "Collective Memories and Embodied Events: Eritrean 'Nation-History.'" *Journal of Imperial and Postcolonial Historical Studies* 1, no. 1 (2000): 41–69.

Holt, P. M. *The Mahdist State in Sudan*. Oxford: Clarendon Press, 1970.

Hourani, Albert. *Arabic Thought in the Liberal Age, 1798–1939*. Oxford: Oxford University Press, 1962.

Iyob, Ruth. *The Eritrean Struggle for Independence: Domination, Resistance, Nationalism, 1941–1993*. Cambridge: Cambridge University Press, 1995.

Jibirti, Abd al-Qadir Haqus al-. *Abushehada Abdelkadir Kebire*. Cairo: Al-Nasri Dehebi, 1998.

————. *Thikryati an dewr al-haraka al-talabiya labina Iritriyya fi Misr*. Cairo, 1994.

Kadi, Muhammad Umar. "Tarikh Hagerkha Meflat." Unpublished paper, Asmara: Research and Documentation Center, 1951.

Kamali, Masoud. *Multiple Modernities, Civil Society and Islam: The Case of Iran and Turkey.* Liverpool: Liverpool University Press, 2006.

Kibreab, Gaim. *Critical Reflections on the Eritrean War of Independence: Social Capital, Associational Life, Religion, Ethnicity and Sowing Seeds of Dictatorship.* Trenton: Red Sea Press, 2008.

Killion, Tom. "Eritrean Workers' Organization and Early Nationalist Mobilization: 1948–1958." *Eritrean Studies Review* 2, no. 1 (1997): 1–58.

Kramer, Robert S. *Holy City on the Nile: Omdurman during the Mahdiyya, 1885–1898.* Princeton: Markus Wiener, 2010.

Markakis, John. *National and Class Conflict in the Horn of Africa.* Cambridge: Cambridge University Press, 1987.

———. "The National Revolution in Eritrea." *Journal of Modern African Studies* 26, no. 1 (1988): 51–70.

Mbembe, Achille. *On the Postcolony.* Berkeley: University of California Press, 2001.

McDougall, James. *History and the Culture of Nationalism in Algeria.* Cambridge: Cambridge University Press, 2006.

Miran, Jonathan. "Constructing and Deconstructing the Tigre Frontier Space in the Long Nineteenth Century." In *History and Language of the Tigre-Speaking Peoples,* edited by Gianfrancesco Lusini, 33–50. Naples: Università degli Studi di Napoli "L'Orientale," 2010.

———. "Endowing Property and Edifying Power in a Red Sea Port: Waqf, Arab Migrant Entrepreneurs, and Urban Authority in Massawa, 1860s–1880s." *International Journal of African Historical Studies* 42, no. 2 (2009): 151–78.

———. "Grand mufti, érudit et nationaliste érythréen: Note sur la vie et l'oeuvre de cheikh Ibrâhîm al-Mukhtâr (1909–1969)." *Chroniques yéménites* 10 (2002): 35–47.

———. "A Historical Overview of Islam in Eritrea." *Die Welt des Islams* 45, no. 2 (2005): 178–215.

———. "Power without Pashas: The Anatomy of Na'ib Autonomy in Ottoman Eritrea (17th–19th C.)." *Eritrean Studies Review* 5, no. 1 (2007): 33–88.

———. *Red Sea Citizens: Cosmopolitan Society and Cultural Change in Massawa.* Bloomington: Indiana University Press, 2009.

———. "Red Sea Translocals: Hadrami Migration, Entrepreneurship, and Strategies of Integration in Eritrea, 1840s–1970s." *Northeast African Studies* 12, no. 1 (2012): 129–68.

Morley, John A. E. *Colonial Postscript: Diary of a District Officer, 1935–56.* London: Radcliffe Press, 1992.

Muhammad, Ahmad al-'Awad. *Sudan Defense Force: Origin and Role, 1925–1955.* Khartoum: Khartoum University Press, 1983.

Mukhtar, Salim al-. *Shaykh Ibrahim al-Mukhtar ab giziye ewan nay federation.* Asmara: Research and Documentation Center, n.d.

Nadel, S. F. "Notes on Beni Amer Society." *Sudan Notes and Records* 26, no. 1 (1951): 51–94.

Nawud, Muhammad Se'id. *Harakat Tahrir Iritriyya: Al-haqiqa wa'l-ta'rikh.* Jidda, Saudi Arabia, n.d.

Negash, Ghirmai. *A History of Tigrinya Literature in Eritrea: The Oral and the Written, 1890–1991.* Leiden: Research School of Asian, African and Amerindian Studies, 1999.

———. "Native Intellectuals in the Contact Zone: African Responses to Italian Colonialism in Tigrinya Literature." *Biography* 32, no. 1 (2009): 73–87.

Negash, Tekeste. *Eritrea and Ethiopia: The Federal Experience.* New Brunswick, NJ: Transaction Publishers, 1997.

———. "Italy and Its Relations with Eritrean Political Parties, 1948–1950." *Africa* (Rome) 59, nos. 3–4 (2004): 417–52.

O'Fahey, R. S., and Jonathan Miran. "The Islamic and Related Writings of Eritrea." In *Arabic Literature of Africa*, edited by O'Fahey and J. O. Hunwick. 4 vols., 3:1–17. Leiden: E. J. Brill, 2003.

Ogbasellassie, Fekadu. "Shifta Problems in the Kebesa Regions of Eritrea (1947–1952)." *In Proceedings of a Workshop on Aspects of Eritrean History*, edited by Tekeste Melake, 51–63. Asmara: Hdri Publishers, 2007.

Pankhurst, Sylvia. *Eritrea on the Eve: The Past and Future of Italy's "First-Born" Colony, Ethiopia's Ancient Sea Province.* Woodford Green, Essex: "New Times and Ethiopia News" Books, 1952.

Permanent Peoples' Tribunal. *The Eritrean Case: Proceedings of the Permanent Peoples' Tribunal of the International League for the Rights and Liberation of Peoples: Session on Eritrea.* Milan: Research and Information Center on Eritrea, 1982.

Pollera, Alberto. *Le popolazioni indigene dell'Eritrea.* Bologna: L. Cappelli, 1935.

Pool, David. *From Guerillas to Government: The Eritrean People's Liberation Front.* Athens: Ohio University Press, 2001.

Pratt, Mary Louise. "Arts of the Contact Zone." *Profession* 91 (1991): 33–40.

Preparatory Committee for Golden Jubilee of Eritrean Students Club. *Resalah al-Jial.* Cairo: Eritrean Students Club, 2002.

Redeker Hepner, Tricia. *Soldiers, Martyrs, Traitors, and Exiles: Political Conflict in Eritrea and the Diaspora.* Philadelphia: University of Pennsylvania Press, 2009.

Reid, Richard J. "The Challenge of the Past: The Quest for Historical Legitimacy in Independent Eritrea." *History of Africa* 28 (2001): 239–72.

―――――. *Frontiers of Violence in North-East Africa: Genealogies of Conflict since c. 1800.* Oxford: Oxford University Press, 2011.

Rich Dorman, Sara. "Narratives of Nationalism in Eritrea: Research and Revisionism." *Nations and Nationalism* 11, no. 2 (2005): 203–22.

Riesebrodt, Martin. *Pious Passion: The Emergence of Modern Fundamentalism in the United States and Iran.* Berkeley: University of California Press, 1993.

Rossini, Carlo Conti. *Principi di diritto consuetudinario dell'Eritrea.* Rome: Tipografia dell'Unione Editrice, 1916.

Sabbe, 'Uthman Salih. *Jughrafiyya Iritriyya.* Beirut: Dar al Kunuz al-Abadiyya, 1983.

Schmidt, Elizabeth. "Top Down or Bottom Up? Nationalist Mobilization Reconsidered, with Special Reference to Guinea (French West Africa)." *American Historical Review* 110, no. 4 (October 2005): 975–1014.

Sherman, Richard. *Eritrea: The Unfinished Revolution.* New York: Praeger, 1980.

Sishagne, Shumet. *Unionists and Separatists: The Vagaries of Ethio-Eritrean Relation, 1941–1991.* Hollywood, CA: Tsehai Publishers, 2007.

Solomon, Warka. "The Life and Political Career of Abdelqadir Kebire." BA thesis, University of Asmara, 2002.

―――――. "The Life and Political Career of Abdulkader Kebire." In *Proceedings of a Workshop on Aspects of Eritrean History*, edited by Tekeste Melake, 194–214. Asmara: Hdri Publishers, 2007.

Stafford, Frank E. "The Ex-Italian Colonies." *International Affairs* 25, no. 1 (1949): 47–55.

Tafla, Bairu. "Eritrea: Remote Past and Present." *Eritrean Studies Review* 3, no. 1 (2004): 85–95.

Tekle, Amare. "The Creation of the Ethio-Eritrean Federation: A Case Study in Post-war International Relations, 1945–50." PhD dissertation, University of Denver, 1964.

Teklehaimanot, Berhane. "Education in Eritrea during the European Colonial Period." *Eritrean Studies Review* 1, no. 1 (1996): 1–22.

Tesfagiorgis, Mussie. *Eritrea (Africa in Focus).* Santa Barbara: ABC-CLIO, 2010.

Tesfai, Alemseged. *Aynfelale: 1941–1950.* Asmara: Hdri Publishers, 2002.

―――――. *Federation Ertra ms Etyopiya: Kab Matienzo ksab Tedla, 1951–1955.* Asmara: Hdri Publishers, 2005.

Tesfamariam, Tesfagaber. "Christian-Moslem Conflict in Asmara in the 1940s." BA thesis, University of Asmara, 2000.

Trevaskis, G. K. N. *Eritrea: A Colony in Transition, 1941–1952*. London: Oxford University Press, 1960.

Trimingham, J. Spencer. *Islam in Ethiopia*. Oxford: Oxford University Press, 1952.

Venosa, Joseph L. "Adapting to the New Path: Khatmiyya Sufi Authority, the al-Mirghani Family, and Eritrean Nationalism during British Occupation, 1941–1949." *Journal of Eastern African Studies* 7, no. 3 (2013): 413–31.

———. "'Because God Has Given Us the Power of Reasoning': Intellectuals, the Eritrean Muslim League, and Nationalist Activism, 1946–1950." *Northeast African Studies* 12, no. 2 (2012): 29–62.

Voll, John O. "A History of the Khatmiyyah Tariqah in the Sudan." PhD dissertation, Harvard University, 1969.

Woldemikael, Tekle M. "Pitfalls of Nationalism in Eritrea." In *Biopolitics, Militarism and Development: Eritrea in the Twenty-First Century*, edited by David O'Kane and Tricia Redeker Hepner, 1–16. New York: Berghahn Books, 2009.

Yohannes, Okbazghi. *Eritrea: A Pawn in World Politics*. Gainesville: University of Florida Press, 1991.

Index